Smaller Cities in a World of Competitiveness

T0359068

Much recent research in Urban Studies has concentrated on the notion of the "global city" but discussion has also covered a larger set of mega-cities, with populations in excess of 10 million. This analysis has raised the question of the optimal size for a city – is larger always better?

Smaller Cities explores the advantages and disadvantages of larger and smaller cities, trying to determine their place in the global economy and hierarchy. How can smaller cities gain or retain their competitiveness in a world of large cities? In a globalized world, the nation has perhaps been diminished as an economic actor, with fiscal shortcomings and political gridlock leaving cities more or less on their own in the task of enhancing their competitiveness and improving the economic lives of their residents. This book argues that smaller cities of varying population can be important actors in competitiveness, and aims to bring attention to an area often overlooked by researchers. In short, are Pittsburgh, San Diego, and Austin less competitive than London and Mumbai?

This volume will be of interest to students, researchers, and city professionals who work in urban economy and urban geography.

Peter Karl Kresl was Professor of Economics at Bucknell University in the US for almost 40 years. He co-founded the Global Urban Competitiveness Project fifteen years ago, and remains its President today.

Daniele Ietri is Associate Professor of Geography at the eCampus University, Italy, where he is responsible for the Geography courses at the Faculty of Education and the Faculty of Literature.

Regions and Cities

Series Editor in Chief
Susan M. Christopherson
Cornell University, USA

Editors
Maryann Feldman, *University of Georgia, USA*
Gernot Grabher, *HafenCity University Hamburg, Germany*
Ron Martin, *University of Cambridge, UK*
Martin Perry, *Massey University, New Zealand*
Kieran P. Donaghy, *Cornell University, USA*

In today's globalized, knowledge-driven, and networked world, regions and cities have assumed heightened significance as the interconnected nodes of economic, social, and cultural production, and as sites of new modes of economic and territorial governance and policy experimentation. This book series brings together incisive and critically engaged international and interdisciplinary research on this resurgence of regions and cities, and should be of interest to geographers, economists, sociologists, political scientists, and cultural scholars, as well as to policy-makers involved in regional and urban development.

For more information on the Regional Studies Association visit www.regional studies.org/.

There is a **30 percent discount** available to RSA members on books in the *Regions and Cities* series, and other subject related Taylor and Francis books and e-books including Routledge titles. To order just e-mail alex.robinson @tandf.co.uk, or phone on +44 (0) 20 7017 6924 and declare your RSA membership. You can also visit www.routledge.com and use the discount code: **RSA0901.**

Smaller Cities in a World of Competitiveness

Peter Karl Kresl and Daniele Ietri

LONDON AND NEW YORK

First published 2016
by Routledge

2 Park Square, Milton Park, Abingdon, Oxfordshire OX14 4RN
52 Vanderbilt Avenue, New York, NY 10017

Routledge is an imprint of the Taylor & Francis Group, an informa business

First issued in paperback 2019

British Library Cataloguing in Publication Data
A catalogue record for this book is available from the British Library

Library of Congress Cataloging in Publication Data
A catalog record for this book has been requested

ISBN: 978-1-138-84657-9 (hbk)
ISBN: 978-0-367-87204-5 (pbk)

Typeset in Times New Roman
by Wearset Ltd, Boldon, Tyne and Wear

Contents

Illustrations

Figure

Tables

1 Introduction to small cities

How to describe/define them?

The emergence of the city, or urban economy, as an economic actor has been chronicled often, but most compellingly by Peter Hall (Hall 2001) and Paul Bairoch (Bairoch 1988). From small settlements in Mesopotamia to the 20 million inhabitant cities of today, the city has been the central actor in economic development, with occasional intrusions by a superior level of government such as the empire or the nation state. One of the most persistent aspects of this history has been the increase in the size of human settlements. Economists have studied agglomeration economies and geographers have developed notions of central place and location theory to understand how they function (Balchin *et al.* 2000, chapters 2 and 5). This is a story that is quite familiar to students of urban economics, so we will not dwell long on it here.

Along with the recognition of growing city size has come, for many, a presumption that large size confers insurmountable advantages on the large city. Saskia Sassen and Peter Taylor wrote of global cities and world cities, respectively. But size was not the crucial factor for them; Sassen was concerned with New York, London, and Tokyo as centers of finance and decision-making and Taylor focused on the position of world cities and their position in the hierarchy of global urban networks (Sassen 1991, Taylor 2013). Peter Hall foresaw that the global economy would be dominated by mega urban regions (Hall 2009). These regions would be composed of up to 50 cities – networked, clustered around one or two world cities and benefiting from a new functional division of labor. A. J. Scott has written of metro city regions as being the structure which cities must seek to create (Scott 2012, pp. 165–168). While all of these writers see benefits from large size, they are also aware of their negative aspects in terms of income inequality and social exclusion, marked by the proliferation of gated communities. Other scholars, such as Joel Kotkin (Kotkin 2014) have contested this, arguing that smaller cities have certain advantages over larger cities in this competitive struggle. His alternative categories of midopolis, similar to Joel Garreau's edge cities (Garreau 1992), nerdistan, and small cities and towns give a range of classifications that include, respectively, (1) suburban Boston, Silicon Valley, and northern New Jersey, (2) Austin, Salt Lake City, and Raleigh–Durham, and (3) hundreds of cities and towns of fewer than 500,000 residents. We will discuss the attractions of each of these three sets of cities in the next chapter, but Kotkin saw smaller cities as being able to avoid some of the negative aspects of larger cities.

It is clear that smaller cities and larger cities have different characteristics, and advantages and disadvantages. Some categories of city size will be attractive to firms in certain specific economic activities, but it is unlikely that any one will be attractive to all of them. Financial markets, automobile assembly, research, product design, data analysis, graphic design, aircraft maintenance, to name just a few, all have specific requirements for inputs and urban assets that make cities of certain sizes attractive or unattractive to them. Firms in these sectors may need an airport hub, or high-speed connectivity, or a set of research universities and institutions, or cultural and recreational assets, or firms in other supporting sectors. Large and smaller cities will sort themselves out according to the attributes they possess. The task of the leaders of smaller cities is that of ascertaining what inputs and assets they have that are attractive to which specific economic activities and firms, as well as being attractive to the skilled labor that will be required by these firms. As we will demonstrate later, there is no correlation between city size and urban competitiveness – some cities may simply be too large to be competitive (Kresl and Singh 2012, The Economist Intelligence Unit 2013, Ni *et al.* 2014).

The concept of size

The definition of small cities, or simply of a small city, is not a straightforward task. The first, and most obvious, approach would be that of simple population size. Mega-cities have captured the imagination of much of the public but also of much of the research community. The simple facts of a large population and the complexities that arise with it capture the imagination of many. This is like going to Africa and being fascinated by the elephants. After a while one discovers there are other creatures in the plains that command a certain interest. So it is with cities. A second approach is that of economic reach. Here one is concerned with the territorial extent of the interaction and command that particular urban economy exhibits. Sassen's world cities had reach that encompassed the entire globe. Other cities, such as Montreal or Barcelona, have a reach that extends throughout the continent in which they are situated. The smallest cities will be limited in their reach to 100 or 200 miles, although one local firm may have a reach that is international or intercontinental. The third approach looks to the economic function of the city in the global hierarchy of cities. Some cities are command centers while others passively accept the direction of the command centers – they have no choice. Financial and business decision-makers situate themselves in cities that have certain assets that are important to the process of making decisions. The fourth, and final, approach to size is that of the mentality of the city itself. Some cities simply "punch above their weight," because of the energy, imagination, assertiveness, and effective planning of their leaders, in both public and private sectors. Other much larger cities find themselves to be incapable of asserting themselves to be anything more than passive followers of more dynamic cities.

The importance of population size will differ between the US and the EU contexts. Comparable data are available for almost 300 metropolitan statistical areas in the US. In a subsequent chapter we will group cities into five classifications according to the number of inhabitants. In the EU, one finds fewer cities in excess of two million inhabitants and city size classifications tend to be greater at those of the smaller city populations. Comparable data however, are not available for large numbers of cities throughout the EU. Reach is primarily the result of the activities of the principal firms in the city's economy. One thinks immediately of the world-wide reach of the entertainment industry of Los Angeles, of the smaller Detroit and its automobile industry during the twentieth century, and of the much smaller Wolfsburg and Volkswagen. Other large cities, such as Mexico City, São Paolo, Mumbai, and Lagos lack this reach. Function can be the result of business and financial corporate decision-making centers that Sassen identified in London, New York, and Tokyo, but also in smaller cities that are the seat of institutions that dominate sectors of global society, such as The Hague (international justice), Nairobi (UN organizations), and Geneva (international diplomacy). Here population and reach are absent with no negative impact on the function of the city. Finally, many cities lacking the three other aspects of size manage to give themselves importance, or "size," by the effect of their own action. In the US and the EU many cities achieve this through the actions of universities that are situated in them. One thinks of Pittsburgh, with its prominence in robotics and information technology based at Carnegie-Mellon University, and other university towns such as Boulder (Colorado), Raleigh–Durham (North Carolina), Lund (Sweden), Cambridge and Oxford (UK), and Rotterdam (Netherlands). Other cities such as Lyon, Milan, Munich, and Boston have asserted themselves through their activities in fashion, culture, and international organizations.

On the other hand, many cities that have been negatively affected by economic misfortune, such as cities in the US industrial heartland, the British Midlands, the German Ruhr, and the industrial areas of the French-Belgian border have not been able to find the direction, leadership, resources, institutions, or energy to regain the "punch" they enjoyed for many decades.

It is clear that size is a more complex issue than it would appear to be at the outset. We have just presented some thoughts on the subject and will continue this discussion in greater precision as we go through this book. Any classification of cities by size will inevitably be somewhat arbitrary and can be contested by other researchers. The first thing that comes to mind is population; however, we will consider several other approaches to this question in a moment. In this effort we will focus in the first instance on US cities, because comparable data for them are relatively easy to obtain and relatively accurate. We exclude analogous analysis of the cities with the greatest populations – the 31 that have populations of over two million – arguing that these should not be considered to be small cities by any standard. However, one of the authors has studied most of these cities in other works, and we will include data for these largest cities in our analysis of how various factors vary by city according to population size (Kresl and Singh 2012). We will, however, exclude the smallest cities, those with a population under 100,000, on the grounds that they are likely to be primarily local or regional in their reach. Furthermore, it would be impossible to compile comparable data for these smallest cities. These smallest cities have their own fascination and place in the competitive world economy and warrant their own separate study. This leaves us with four categories of cities: (1) 100,000–250,000, (2) 250,000–500,000, (3) 500,000–one million, and (4) one–two million, plus the 31 largest US cities we are including for contrast. The number of cities included in each of the four categories is, respectively, 161, 74, 41, and 20, for a total of 299 US cities. We will use data for these categories of cities to examine several commonly held notions about the characteristics and capabilities of smaller cities, primarily in Chapters 3 and 4.

This classification can be linked to that of the McKinsey Global Institute's "middleweight cities" in its report *Urban America: US cities in the global economy* (McKinsey 2012). These are large metropolitan areas with the following populations: small middleweight – 150,000 to two million, midsize middleweight – two to five million, and large middleweight – five to ten million. The three categories of smaller cities in our study are similar to their small middleweight, with a higher threshold at the lower end.

Mega-cities

The UN has just published a forecast of the world's population, and concludes that, while 54 percent of humans live in urban areas today, by 2050 this will rise to two-thirds, with 90 percent of this growth taking place in Africa and Asia. The number of mega-cities will grow from 28 today to 41 in 2050, but only one-eighth of the population will reside in them. If all people had the same individual welfare function, we would all be living and working in the same city or in one that was identical in its essential characteristics to it – but we don't. Fully one half of total city-dwellers will reside in cities of fewer than 500,000 people and "(m)any of the fastest growing cities in the world are relatively small urban settlements" (United Nations 2014, p. 1). Surely, they cannot all be marking time until they have the opportunity to move to a mega-city. Indeed many or most of them prefer to stay where they are, and for sound legitimate reasons, such as family and friends, pace of life, employment, access to recreation and other assets, a good place to raise a family, and so forth.

Mike Davis alerted us to this demographic phenomenon a decade ago, concentrating his analysis on developing areas in Asia, Africa, and Latin America (Davis 2004). He saw a developing rural–urban relationship that led from the existing somewhat symbiotic one of rural areas generating population growth that would feed the needs for labor of the large urban centers, to one in which smaller cities, typically in the interior, would become starved for revenues and resources that could stimulate their growth and the mega-cities on the coast would become overpopulated with low-skill manual workers and to the creation of enormous slums. Indeed the title of his article was "Planet of Slums." One of the crucial factors was "the inherent tendency of silicon capitalism to delink the growth of production for that of employment" as urbanization "has been radically decoupled from industrialization, even from development per se" (Davis 2004, p. 3). This has become a standard depiction of the conditions of life in both rural areas and mega-cities in the developing world. The UN observes the "urbanization of poverty," with migrants from the countryside supporting the urban economy with labor in informal sectors, low-pay jobs in the clothing sector, and low-level service and maintenance work. In many instances their presence is so pervasive that the wealthy class seeks isolation and even protection behind walls and in gated communities (UN 2003, p. xxvi). It anticipates that slum dwellers will exceed two billion if no ameliorative policy initiatives are pursued. While slums are not limited only to larger cities, there is nonetheless an inexorable pull emanating from them to low-skilled and uneducated people situated in rural areas and small towns. This steady flow of people imposes burdens both on the rural area which loses younger and energetic workers and the large cities which have to devote resources to housing, health care, public security, and transportation, if the worst of the consequences are to be avoided.

While the focus of Davis and of the UN report is on the growth of slums and the negative consequences they have on the majority of humans, there is another more positive view of urban development that we will explore in this book. We are taken with the enormous potential there is for smaller cities to create for themselves places in the urban hierarchy, or the global economy, which will bring satisfying and productive lives to their residents. But first we will have to explore the reality in which smaller cities find themselves.

Population and demography

An element that will prove to be powerful in its impacts for smaller cities is population and demography. The fundamental issue here is whether smaller cities will be able to attract and to retain a sufficient number of workers with the necessary skills to create and to sustain an economy that is suited for the coming decades. This will entail the education and training of young people in the city, both native-born and immigrant, and the attraction of skilled and highly mobile younger workers, for whom life holds many options. This is a challenge to all cities, but larger cities hold a natural attraction to these highly desired workers due to their advantages in professional connection and advancement, in entertainment, in establishing a lasting social tie, among other things. Smaller cities have to work to present an attractive image, to create institutions and activities that are attractive, and to realize that as workers advance in age and career, and as they begin a family, smaller cities gain in attractiveness.

All cities are faced with a population that is aging. By 2050, some countries, notably Italy and Japan, will have populations in which the relationship between working and non-working individuals will be 1 : 1. Clearly there are serious fiscal consequences of this. Unless financial planning is done effectively, as it apparently is being done in the Netherlands with its pension system, each worker will be responsible for all of his or her needs plus the health and income needs of one senior. This could in itself present a powerful incentive for the younger worker to emigrate to a less burdensome place to work, live, and raise a family. Fortunately, in 2050 the age dependency ratio for the US will be about $1:2.5$, and, with its social security system being eminently capable of being made fiscally sound, young workers will be in a relatively good position. Nonetheless, among US cities the share of the population that will be of retirement age will vary dramatically. The least favored cities tend to be those that were strongest during the manufacturing age into the 1980s, while cities that have been able to position themselves well in the new technology-related economy of the twenty-first century will be in a relatively good position. However, given the mobility of individuals to seek out or to escape from cities that please or displease them, it would be impossible and preposterous to suggest which cities might have the highest or lowest worker : retired ratios.

A paradoxical conclusion reached by the authors of this book in another work is that there are positive benefits available to cities from an aging or senior population (Kresl and Ietri 2010). These benefits come from what seniors do with their time and their money upon retirement. Both the US government and the EU have declared that seniors in the coming years will be better educated, wealthier, more mobile, and healthier than has ever been the case (US Census Bureau 2006, pp. 1–2, Commission of the European Communities 2005, p. 9). We found that in many US cities and in some EU cities, seniors prefer to leave a residence in a larger house in the suburbs and to move to a city. These cities can be of all sizes, given that different sized cities offer different combinations of living environment, amenities, and assets. If all seniors had the same personal welfare function they would all live in the same city or at least in similar cities with attributes – but they don't. Movement into the city center or into a town generates an upgrading of the housing stock and prices, to some extent, and to a paradoxical rejuvenation of the city through aging. The lower downtown area of Denver, the area between the University of Virginia and the historic district of Charlottesville, and the mid-town area of Atlanta are all examples in the US. In the EU we can point to HafenCity in Hamburg and the Västerhamn area of Malmö. In addition to urban revitalization through residential decisions, it must be remembered that seniors no longer save – they spend. So their presence boosts retail sales, restaurants, and other business sectors. Media sources report that in the US individuals aged 50 and older have about 70 percent of total disposable income, amounting to 1.6 trillion dollars in spending – hardly an insignificant amount (Boyle 2013).

More specifically, seniors are also the strongest supporters of cultural institutions, with audiences for theater, music, art, and dance benefitting greatly from their presence. The final contribution we discussed in our work was the desire of seniors to participate in adult learning and other educational activities such as discussion and play-reading groups. These two activities are vital for a city that seeks to present itself as a center of learning, research, and culture. These "soft" determinants of urban competitiveness have become more important in recent years and having age groups other than the 5–25 year age cohort involved in these activities enhances the city's competitiveness.

City exposure and response

A century and a half ago, smaller cities were relatively protected from products of other cities. They used local products for the good of local consumers. The railroad brought many changes, such as standardized time, and travel for individuals, as well as both goods and consumers from distant cities (Cronen 1991). Few would dispute the assertion that the changes were, on the whole, beneficial and desirable. Most recently, changes in technologies of communication, transportation, and production have had the effect of destroying spatial distancing of cities and their economic actors. Of perhaps equal importance is the destruction of time, in the sense of the time that is available to respond to these changes in technology. The industrial cities of the post-World War II years were powerfully challenged during the 1970s to the extent that their existing economic strength was converted into an economic weakness in a matter of five to ten years, but their response to the resulting challenges often took decades. While the response was sometimes initiated by local public authorities, in other instances it was largely serendipitous. Sometimes the restructuring of the economy was path dependent, as with Chicago, while at other times it involved a break with the historical strengths, as with Pittsburgh. At other times, the recovery was not achieved for decades, if at all – in the US, Buffalo and Youngstown are examples. What this tells us is that smaller cities now confront greater challenges than has ever been the case, while at the same time the need for focused and determined action with regard to strategic economic planning and mobilization of local assets has never been greater.

The effectiveness of cities' response is affected by some issues within their control – such as effective planning, engagement of the principal actors in the local society and economy, effective governance, and mobilization of financial and other resources. However, in most countries in the developed world, national and sub-national governments are resisting engagement and have chosen to implement policies of austerity and of reduction of fiscal transfers to lower-level governments. In these conditions, economic recovery or development for many smaller cities will be profoundly challenged if not actually impossible. In later chapters we will discuss this situation and suggest some options for these cities that may increase their economic vitality and competitiveness. One option for smaller cities is that of forming networks that facilitate the sharing of ideas with regard to both problems and solutions, and that create structures for cooperative action and joint action. One difficulty is that in many large national or international city organizations the largest cities dominate activities and the smaller cities find that they get lost in the crowd. In many countries such smaller city organizations have been established, sometimes within larger structures. One such structure is the Small Cities Council of the US National League of Cities. This council includes over 150 representatives from member cities with populations of 50,000 or less. In the European Union, at the country level in particular, smaller cities have similar kinds of organizations. As an example, the German Association of Towns and Municipalities (Deutscher Städte- und Gemeindebund) has been operating an office in Brussels since 1991. In Italy the National Association of Italian Municipalities (ANCI – Associazione Nazionale Comuni Italiani) has a section specifically devoted to smaller cities – in that country, in 2012, more than 17 percent of the population lived in the 5,683 municipalities with fewer than 5,000 residents. However, another form of networking is the formation of a group of cities that have a common problem or task and that can be focused entirely on this inter-urban interaction. This can be very important, and we will discuss this in greater detail later in this book.

An issue very specific for the European case is the role and interaction of cities located in a cross-border region. This is quite common in the European area, where many countries are relatively small in size, and borders are very permeable for historic and cultural reasons and also thanks to the role of EU institutions. The most evident case is represented by the large cross-border area between France, Luxembourg, Germany, Belgium, and the Netherlands – one should not be surprised if Luxembourg's six months' presidency of the European Union in 2015 has set a priority on cross-border urban cooperation.

Also, many more geographically defined borders are seeing an improvement of cross-border networks of cities, thanks to better transportation (this is the case of the Øresund region between Denmark and Sweden), for historical reasons, or because of a common language, such as in many Alpine areas (e.g., the Italian-speaking Swiss Ticino and the neighboring Piemonte and Lombardia; the French-speaking or German-speaking areas in the west and center-east; the growing cooperation between Italian, Slovenian, and Croatian cities in the eastern part of the Alpine arc, where a mountainous border gives ends at the Adriatic Sea). Also cities in the new member states are making progress in developing cross-border agreements and projects. Second-tier cities are – for several reasons – key players in this growing feature of the EU cooperation: we will discuss this more in detail when presenting the European cases.

The dynamics of city size

Cities may be considered to be small on the basis of objective considerations. In addition to population, with which we have just dealt, size can be in terms of economic reach – how nationally or globally important is the city – or total output, or strength in some sector that is considered to be crucial for the contemporary or future economy, such as high technology, or information technology and computing, or biopharmaceutical activity. It can also have a position, or lack of one, in national or global decision-making and command – as a headquarters center. Sassen focused in her work on the three principal command centers: New York, London, and Tokyo. These are large cities but not the largest, and their prominence derives from qualitative factors relating to decision-making and command. Something other than merely population was at work. Capital cities from ancient Rome to relatively modern London have based their economy to a significant degree on inflows of goods, capital, labor, and ideas – of tribute in one form or another – from the far reaches of an empire. In the nineteenth century cities were important because of their prominence in manufacturing or transportation. During the twentieth this shifted to finance and then to high technology research and production. Clearly small cities will rarely have any global significance in these areas of economic activity. But perhaps of greater importance is size in terms of vision or aspirations. If small cities' leadership is convinced that the city cannot imagine a future in which it is an active actor on a larger stage, then the city will be condemned to insignificance and smallness. Other leaders have taken their small city from an event such as the industrial collapse of much of the historic manufacturing regions of developed North America and Europe, and the destruction of the base for their local economy, into a new era based on activities that are linked to new technologies and new activities.

While mega-cities seem only to get larger, many smaller cities have actually lost population. This phenomenon has been referred to as "shrinking cities" (Posey 2013). In North America, Japan, and Europe the collapse of the manufacturing sector in many traditional regions has led to significant population loss through outmigration, but in both Japan and Europe this has been exacerbated by declining birth rates. Thorstein Wiechmann and Karina Pallagst show how this population decline in Germany has been concentrated in the former DDR and in the Ruhr (Wiechmann and Pallagst 2012). Indeed, in the eastern part of Germany, of 15 major cities only four – Dresden, Erfurt, Potsdam, and Jena – have not experienced loss of population. In the US, the cities of the industrial heartland, which became the Rust Belt, especially Youngstown, Detroit, Pittsburgh, Buffalo, and Cleveland, have all experienced substantial loss of population as workers left in pursuit of employment elsewhere.

The counterpart, in recent literature, of the shrinking city is the "resurgent city." Paul Cheshire comments on a set of contributions to a special issue of *Urban Studies* by noting that the central point of agreement among the authors is the understanding that resurgence has to be seen as being a consequence of a previous decline (Cheshire 2005, p. 1232). Some of the shrinking cities of the US Rust Belt and the German industrial areas in the east and the Ruhr, during the 1970s and 1980s, have been successful in mounting an effort at resurgence during the 1990s and the twenty-first century, while others have continued to wallow in an economy that has become outmoded, non-competitive, and subject to increasing social pathologies. Since the largest cities continue to draw population from rural areas, the phenomena of shrinking and resurgence are a feature of smaller cities and will be discussed more fully later in this book.

Some words on methodology

The methodology that we will use in this book is driven by the availability of good, comparable data for large numbers of cities. As we noted above, data are available for almost 300 US metropolitan statistical areas in documents compiled by the US Census Bureau. One hundred and ninety-nine variables are available, and data will be taken from the 2012 edition of the *County City Data Book*, since in the most recent edition, that for 2014, most of the data are not updated. With this data we will be able to conduct a simple correlation analysis on variables for all 147 US cities of more than 250,000 inhabitants. We will not do a similar analysis for the additional 150 cities with population of less than 250,000. As cities become smaller in population they become increasingly idiosyncratic and do not fit easily into categories, and they also are decreasingly engaged in relations beyond their immediate economic space. For cities above this size, this rich data will allow us to examine several very interesting arguments with regard to the realities of large and smaller cities and to come to conclusions as to their validity. Basically, the question is: how do smaller cities differ from larger cities, and do these differences disadvantage them in some way, or do they perhaps work to their advantage?

Unfortunately, such a rich source of comparable data is not available for EU cities, and our analysis will be relatively limited when we study these cities. Despite the effort made by Eurostat in order to develop a common statistical framework for the EU countries, for detailed data at the urban level one has to rely on the 28 different national statistical systems. Eurostat has a sound database for the national and sub-national levels, with comparable data for the EU countries and regions, organized according to a common nomenclature. The NUTS system (nomenclature of territorial units for statistics) provides a classification of the European territory according to three levels (NUTS 1, 2, and 3), among which level 2 is the most relevant, as it corresponds to the regional scale in which the major policies are implemented, such as the cohesion policy supported by the European Regional Development Fund. At the urban level, the task is more difficult and homogenous data are available only thanks to the Urban Audit statistics, which still provide data for some topics (population, employment, etc.) but not detailed enough to allow us to reproduce in the EU the analysis that will be presented for the cities in the USA. For the European cases we will use more extensively the results of research projects: in doing this we will give high priority to the studies developed in the framework of the EU cooperation programs. This will provide us with comparable data and information, even if on specific regions or cases. Nevertheless, the different methodologies for the study of the two sets of cities will limit our ability to do comparative US/EU analysis.

Far richer, of course, is the analysis that is available for both US and EU cities in the scholarly research literature and we will be able to use this information for much of the analysis we will do. While smaller cities have not attracted the attention that has been given to mega-cities, global cities, and world cities, it is possible to gain insights from the existing literature into the place of smaller cities in the global urban hierarchy, and to discern the effectiveness with which they are able to engage themselves and their local economic actors in the more extensive economy of their nation, continent, and beyond. We will see that some economists and geographers have considered smaller cities, in both North

America and Europe, as centers of culture, innovation, creativity, and economic activity. Sadly, the knowledge of the authors limits their analysis to these two "industrialized" continents to the exclusion of fascinating material that would be found regarding other parts of the world.

The content of the chapters

After these comments that set the scene, so to speak, we will develop the main argument of the paper. What are small cities? And how do they function in the global economic space? Is it the case that smaller cities have been lost in the rush to celebrate the strengths and roles of large cities? This puts it too strongly, but certainly the great preponderance of research has been devoted to world cities, global cities, and mega-cities. In part this is because, although all cities do retain their own characteristics, large cities can be classified in convenient categories, and also in part because data are more readily available for them. Small cities are more idiosyncratic and below a certain size, depending on the country, usually fall beneath the radar of the data gatherers. So data-based research is more difficult with smaller cities and they are difficult to assemble in meaningful categories. It must also be said that they are of less interest to many researchers since they are usually, due to their size, limited in their reach to the region in which they are situated. This, however, is changing due to the impacts of advances in communications and transportation technologies that can extend the reach of the small cities. Changes in production technologies have also facilitated the inclusion of ever smaller cities in larger area economic interaction. While policy consultants seem to feel free to propose the same strategic plan for several large cities, this cannot credibly be attempted with smaller cities. Hence, they are usually left to their own devices. This will be the subject of Chapter 2.

A larger city is desirable for whom? The world economy needs centers of decision-making and control, large clusters of firms in the same activity, transportation hubs, corporate centers, and so forth. But what of the residents of the city? Is large always better? From the earliest studies of large cities, researchers noted that the benefits of size tended to be captured primarily by the wealthiest and most powerful residents, with the less powerful having to be satisfied with far less satisfying standards and conditions of life. Sassen observed:

> This new framework contributes to a reshaping of the sphere of social reproduction and consumption, which in turn has a feedback effect on economic organization and earnings. Whereas in the earlier period this feedback effect contributed to reproduction of the middle class, currently it reproduces growing earnings disparity, labor market casualization, and consumption restructuring.
>
> (Sassen 1991, p. 116)

More recently Scott concluded that the emerging system generates irrationalities that can be observed in the increasing spread of gated communities, in the concomitant deepening of urban social segregation, in the development of privileged and highly controlled enclaves for elite shopping and leisure pursuits, and in the increasing ejection of low-wage workers from inner city neighborhoods to peripheral urban locations that are today often far distant from relevant employment opportunities.

(Scott 2012, p. 173)

Finally, Piketty (2014) has captured the headlines with his analysis of income inequality and his forecast that it will become even more significant in the coming years, and that with absent corrective policies this will become inexorable. The crucial relation for him is that between income from labor and from capital. For us, the interesting question is the relation between the ratio of income from labor and of income from capital, and city size. That is, is income inequality projected to be more a feature of larger than of smaller cities? So, one of the issues we will have to confront, in Chapters 3 and 4, is the relation between city size and income inequality and the condition of different classes of its residents.

Another issue in Chapter 3 is that of small cities and sustainability. We will examine the relationship between small cities and five aspects of sustainability, an examination that will culminate in the question of the attractiveness of small cities to the skilled labor and creativity that are generally thought to be so important for the contemporary and future economy. What do small cities have to offer in the competition for talented, imaginative, and ambitious younger workers?

Finally, small cities can "punch above their weight" when they combine their strengths through networks. Large cities can usually host clusters of firms that can be internationally competitive; small cities have to form networks that are essentially clusters not limited by spatial proximity. Firms in networks create cluster-like structures, the cement of which is telecommunications and high-tech transportation.

The question of the specific advantages and disadvantages of smaller and larger cities is central to the argument of this book, and we will discuss both aspects of the attributes of smaller cities in Chapter 4. The issues of agglomeration, economies, connectivity, hard and soft determinants of competitiveness, networks, clusters, and so forth have dominated, and continue to dominate, this discussion. Large cities tend to be vertical cities, both for residences and for business. These vertical cities are able to achieve certain economies with regard to energy use that give them an advantage over the small cities. The simple fact that so many small cities are doing quite well competitively should be sufficient to make the point, but we must be more specific, if only to give encouragement to the leaders of small cities that have yet to achieve their "take-off." We will identify several aspects of their general situation that give small cities their advantage in some aspects of competitiveness vis-à-vis larger cities. While most of the small cities' advantages will be found to be in the "soft" category, such as amenities and quality of living, there are also some advantages in the "hard" category.

In Chapter 4, we ask the question: is bigger always better, or most competitive, or is there an optimal size for a competitive city? When do economies
of scale or of agglomeration become diseconomies? What does a city need in
addition to one or two good universities, an array of amenities (cultural, recreational, educational, etc.), public security (low crime), congenial neighborhoods,
and a set of talented individuals of sufficient number? Are Pittsburgh, Rotterdam, and Austin less competitive than Chicago or Mumbai? We will have to
consider whether size is linked with higher incomes and higher productivity, the
importance of a diversified economic base, the impact of urbanization on efficiency in production, and whether large firms and industrial complexes are
necessary for a competitive city. On the other hand, largeness often entails congestion, pollution, crime, and higher costs of living.

The rapidly evolved and evolving global economic environment places
burdens on small cities, especially those that are still dominated by traditional
economic activities that may no longer be competitive without major restructuring. But this new environment also offers them opportunities for competitiveness
enhancement and for exciting futures if they develop new economic activities
that take advantage of the unique attributes that are possessed by these cities.
Small cities are in a very difficult economic situation, to a considerable degree
because of the actions of other levels of government or the way in which social
practices have evolved. Nonetheless, in one text on urban economics, we find
the quote:

> for some industries/economic activities and not for others given that average
> costs appear to rise substantially in the largest conurbations there would
> seem to be a strong case for encouraging a settlement structure of medium-
> sized towns and cities rather than one involving only a few large cities.
>
> (Balchin *et al.* 2000, p. 76)

We will examine the veracity of this conclusion in Chapter 4.

In this book we will review the contemporary competitive landscape and the
place that smaller cities have in it. Small cities are relatively dependent upon
decisions, policies, and transfers of funds on the part of superior levels of government. The fiscal capacity as well as the willingness to engage in relationships
with small cities have been diminished in the past 15–20 years in both the US
and the EU. So while cooperation with superior levels of government is crucial
for infrastructure projects, a vast array of regulations, support for education at all
levels, and assistance in mobilizing actors in both the public and the private
sectors, small cities have in recent years been forced to be more entrepreneurial
and risk-taking on their own part. There are, as we shall see, many things small
cities can do on their own initiative, many of which are not at all costly to do.

To explore this we shall review (1) the new urban economic environment, (2)
the positive and attractive attributes, as well as the disadvantages, that are possessed by small cities, and (3) what they can expect from other levels of government. Following this, it will be possible for us to suggest an approach to strategic

planning that, if implemented effectively, will enable these cities to achieve the economic futures that are desired by their residents. Our analysis will be developed, in Chapters 5 and 6, through study of cities in the US and also in the EU. Due to the availability of comparable data in each geographic region, the analysis of each will be somewhat particular.

A similar approach will be taken to the issue of the relative competitiveness of smaller cities in the global context. Can these entities that are less well endowed with several attributes that are held to be important in competitive struggles over markets, jobs, and status hold their own against their larger counterparts? We will explore this question in Chapter 7 and Chapter 8, in recognition of the specific characteristics and realities that confront cities in the US and the EU. Do smaller cities have some advantages in this struggle that give them an edge in competition with larger cities? Many researchers have found that there is no significant correlation between city size and competitiveness in relation to larger cities.

In the final chapter, we will review the argument that smaller cities are important actors in competitiveness and that they warrant closer attention from researchers. We will demonstrate why this attention is warranted and we will also articulate a set of roles and functions smaller cities are uniquely prepared to fulfill.

2 Small cities in a world of mega-cities

We saw in Chapter 1 that much attention has been given to the largest cities in the world system – global cities, world cities, mega-cities, and mega urban regions have been the most widely discussed. They have an obvious impact on other cities and on the global economy, data are most easily available for them, they have devoted significant resources to planning for their place in the urban hierarchy, and a certain glamor attaches to them. Paris, London, Mumbai, Tokyo, New York – who has not had memorable experiences in them or anticipates such an experience? Major industrial corporations and financial institutions have their world headquarters in them. They typically host the World Cup or the Olympics or Expo. Who could not be fascinated with them? But we shall see in Chapter 4 that their size may not matter in the world of economic competitiveness. It can be argued that they are too large to be efficient or competitive and that, for many of them, efficiencies of agglomeration have been overtaken by diseconomies of agglomeration. Much of the current evidence suggests that the bloom is off the rose when it comes to city size. In this chapter we want to explore the place of smaller cities in the global hierarchy. Are they to be left on the sidetrack to suffer a slow decline and marginalization? Or do smaller cities have a function in this inter-city environment?

In Chapter 1 we noted that the UN estimates that 54 percent of the world's population resides in urban areas and that, of these, 50 percent live in cities of fewer than 500,000. The non-urban area population is forecast to drop to one-third of the total by 2050, so this leaves an even more substantial population living in smaller cities. Thus smaller cities are important today and they will continue to be in the future. The issues we will treat in this chapter are: Where do smaller cities fit in the global urban hierarchy? What functions can they fulfill? Can they act independently of the larger cities? Can they be important actors beyond the confines of their immediate region?

The hierarchy of cities

One of the consequences of the work of Christaller and others on Central Place Theory is the conclusion that in a large economic space there will be a hierarchical structure of cities from the regional capital city down to the market town

(Christaller 1966). The hierarchy is based on the development of a large concentration of certain high-level activities in what becomes the largest town, with the number and level of activities diminishing as one works through the structure from top to bottom. Corporate headquarters, a cluster of financial firms, a major transportation hub, a large number of high-level research centers and research universities, government administration, major health care institutions, and an appropriately skilled workforce would all be concentrated in the central city. It is also important that as city size increases so does the city's economic reach or the extent of the market it serves. Christaller then saw an ideal construct in which there is a principal or central city and then an array of smaller and less economically significant towns that grow larger in number as size diminished. One can imagine the smaller cities being principally local retail centers that, among other things, hosted traveling merchants for local residents.

An empirically verified approach to the question of city size is given by Zipf's Law, that demonstrated a "rank–size rule," in accordance with which the logs of city population size and city rank are arrayed in a straight line with a negative slope (Gabaix 1999). The largest city is twice the size of the second, and so forth in the progression one, one-half, one-third, one-quarter ... and so on. Zipf's Law has been verified for cities of greater than 100,000 in population, while Christaller applied his approach to smaller cities. While both Christaller's and Zipf's approaches amount to the same thing conceptually, Zipf's Law has been verified for many countries and such mathematical regularity is lacking among Christaller's smaller cities.

These approaches to city size and function lead us to the notion of the urban hierarchy, where cities are arrayed by size and different sized cities have different roles to play. The largest cities have the functions that were noted at the beginning of this section, partly because economics of agglomeration make certain functions more efficient and less costly, but there are many other reasons for this, including the fact that migrants tend to move to cities where the opportunities for work and a richer array of ethnic communities facilitate their integration.

The largest cities – the mega-cities, global cities, world cities, and world urban regions discussed in Chapter 1 – are at the pinnacle of the global urban hierarchy. New York, London, Tokyo, and so forth are always placed at the top of the international urban rankings, with other cities arrayed downward below them – Chicago, Shanghai, Singapore, Paris, Los Angeles, on down to the Stuttgarts and Pittsburghs of the world. At the top are the centers of global finance and corporate decision-making. Manufacturing no longer is a feature of the global command centers, although it usually is present. Regional linkages gradually take over from global linkages as city size diminishes. However, within this structure, as Peter Taylor is correct to stress (2009), horizontal relations have been developed among cities of similar or different sizes, in the equally trendy model of polycentrality. The option of network formation, and the reasons cities have for engaging in this process, will be examined in a later chapter.

Fujita, Krugman, and Venables find that Central Place Theory is descriptive of what actually happens in a space with various activities that, for some reason, aggregate in locations, and that after this process has worked itself out, the places follow a procedure that generates a structure in which there are cities of varying sizes, largely under the influence of economies of scale. Being economists, what they find wanting is discussion of the motives and actions of individual economic actors. They argue that "It is probably best to think of [central place theory] as a classification scheme, a way of organizing our perceptions and data. It is at best a description, rather than an explanation, of the economy's spatial structure" (Fugita *et al.* 2001, p. 27).

Capital cities and second-tier cities

The role of capital cities in a national or sub-national state setting, and the impact this has on the economic possibilities of smaller or second-tier cities, have received attention both in North America and in the EU. Do capital cities overshadow other cities in the geographic space, do they "suck all of the air out of the space," and do they actually hinder smaller cities in achieving their economic objectives? This varies, of course, from country to country in accordance with history, the structure of government, the constitution, and practice. North America and the EU differ dramatically in this regard and we will examine these differences shortly. But first, we must take a more general look at the issue.

In Europe, power was appropriated by an individual with sufficient force to allow him to dominate others. He (almost always a he) asserted authority, and this was accepted, after a bit of struggle, and he situated his base in a place that was defensible, in proximity to water and food and other resources, such as stone and wood for buildings. This strong point evolved over the years into a center of political and economic authority (Sutcliffe 1993). The site grew as other individuals gathered around him to curry favor, provide services, and obtain their own subordinate power and wealth. By definition as one moved farther from the center one encountered the periphery, *à la* Christaller. Here no significant centers of power that would challenge that of the center were tolerated. The individual at the center declared himself to be the sovereign or king, and often asserted that his power was derived from some supernatural entity, such as God. In order to buttress this power, the king developed his site into a center of law and justice, of political power, of ceremony, of culture, and of transportation and communication. Centuries later, this initial assertion of power and authority has coalesced into Europe's modern capitals – London, Paris, Madrid, Rome, and so forth on lesser scales. Each of these capitals has retained its dominant position in the economic life of the nation, in spite of the changes in technology, world markets, and international commerce, and the rise of finance as a key sector. The national capital "must somehow act as a national symbol and remain an important embodiment of national identity and power" (Rapoport 1993, p. 59), regardless what it does or does not achieve as an economic center.

In Canada and the US the situation was quite different. Canada was a British colony until it gained independence in the twentieth century. Toronto and Montreal represented the two major linguistic groups in the country, and while

Montreal was the economic center until the post-World War II period, each sought the status of national capital. The issue was resolved when Queen Victoria famously placed her finger on the map and declared that the capital would be Ottawa, a sleepy river town that had the advantages of being between the two larger cities, and far removed from the US border and the threat of military invasion. While Ottawa has maintained its position as the political center of the country, the two economic giants, Toronto and Montreal, continue to dominate industry, transportation, and finance. Now Calgary and Vancouver in the west have joined them.

In the US, Washington was declared the capital after a colony had become a democratic nation, and after the political heart of the new country had been situated for brief periods in eight other cities. Site selection was made difficult by the fact that neither the North nor the South would tolerate a capital city in the territory of the other. Since George Washington resided in the area, the location of the city on the Potomac River was amenable to all. It was thought at the time that the US would become a significant player on the world stage and that the capital had to be designed to represent this in its architecture. While the buildings of government are not tall skyscrapers that call attention to themselves, they do have massive footprints. A friend once stated that he thought the massive structures were there to intimidate the humble petitioner to government so as to tip the balance of power – perhaps. Washington did come to attain this status in the politics and affairs of the world, but the city has never achieved the economic importance of the EU capitals. Philadelphia and Boston were far more important and as the nation moved westward, Chicago, Los Angeles, Atlanta, and a dozen other cities became the economic powers of the new nation. This holds true at the level of the states where second-level cities such as Springfield, Albany, and Sacramento are clearly secondary to Chicago, New York, and Los Angeles and San Francisco. In the US, contrary to the EU, there was no economic center and periphery, and even in cultural institutions, education, transportation, and communication these non-capital cities have equaled and surpassed the assets of the nation's capital.

Beyond these different roles of capital cities is that of the impact capital cities have on the functioning of smaller or second-tier cities. It should be clear that in North America the reliance on market mechanisms for economic decision-making, in the US and to a lesser degree in Canada, free smaller cities from the dominance of the national, and certainly the state or provincial, capital. The powers of the central authorities are weaker here and smaller cities are left to their own devices to a degree that is not possible in the EU. In the US, urban policy and planning tend to come from the bottom up, while in the EU they tend to be top down. Smaller cities in North America have many more degrees of freedom in their actions than do their counterparts in the EU.

The fact that capitals impose a handicap on smaller cities in the EU warrants some discussion. In a recent study of 124 second-tier and 31 capital cities in Europe, Parkinson *et al.* found that the second-tier cities "can still generate dynamism for regions outside the capital and contribute to overall national growth. In many cases they punch beyond their weight" (2015, p. 1064). They find that while capitals have the largest city GDP in all countries but Germany and Italy, second-tier cities had the highest growth rate during 2000–2007 except for Greece, Portugal, and eight countries in Central Europe. In several Western European countries, multiple second-tier cities had higher GDP growth rates.

They argue that there are a couple of factors involved here. First, there is the issue of agglomeration. In the EU, since capitals are almost invariably the largest city in the nation, they therefore have the greatest economies of agglomeration. But they argue that economies of agglomeration often turn into diseconomies and that this then causes the large capital city to become inefficient: "Beyond a certain point, congestion, land scarcity, sprawl, marginalized human capital and infra-structure deterioration contribute to an area's decline. And investors and develop-ers may start to avoid them and move elsewhere" (Parkinson *et al.* 2015, p. 1064). This gets us to their second factor, investment. Capital cities have tended to get the lion's share of national urban investment. At some point, the marginal efficiency of capital in the second-tier cities rises above that of the capital. However, national policy as well as EU Commission policy has resulted in "over-investment in the capitals and under-investment in second-tier cities" (Parkinson *et al.* 2015, p. 1065). Germany is the grand exception to this, largely because of the system of shared governance and decentralization of both responsibilities and financial resources that is lacking in many other EU countries.

Camagni, Capello, and Caragliu concur, arguing that:

> Investment should be devoted to cities in order to make any of them, irre-spective of their size, be able to turn their risk of decreasing returns into agglomeration economies, by investing in renovating their functions and their way of cooperation.
>
> (Camagni *et al.* 2015, p. 1086)

One option for the second-tier or smaller cities is that of "borrowing size." We will discuss this in Chapter 4, but for now we should just note that smaller cities in proximity to a larger urban area can achieve the benefits of large size by simply attaching themselves to the beneficial assets of the larger entity, for example a hub airport or an efficient surface transportation, or a major research university, or they can achieve this through participating in multiple city networks.

In the EU while smaller cities do operate at a disadvantage re the capital city, this disadvantage can be overcome either through more intelligent policy by the national government and by the EU Commission, or through actions on the part of the smaller city such as borrowing size and networking.

The focus on large cities

In Chapter 1 we brought up the notion of mega-cities, and other forms of large-ness in urban areas, but did little other than mention some of the attributes that writers such as Sassen, Taylor, Hall, and Scott, found in them. Here we would like to take a closer look at our largest cities as a prelude to discussing their smaller counterparts. An insightful treatment of these largest cities has been given most succinctly by Jordi Borja and Manuel Castells. As is now standard, they see mega-cities as conglomerations of at least 10 million inhabitants; with this population the cities have the capacity to function as centers of economic, technological, and business dynamism; centers of cultural innovation, symbol creation, and scientific research; centers of political power; and connection points for the world communication system. In brief:

> Mega cities are rather more than gigantic territorial agglomerations of human beings ... They are in fact the nodes of the global economy and of the most powerful nations ... The alternative ecological dream of a universe of small communities living amid nature, connected up by electronic means, will be restricted to a small Californian élite or, more significantly, to the social and functional marginalization of rural areas the world over.
>
> (Borja and Castells 1997, pp. 27 and 30)

Mega-cities are seen as strategic nodes in a world of generalized urbanization. In this context they see, rather famously, the space of places giving way to the space of flows.

This is significant for our discussion of smaller cities because, while the space of places is globally fragmented, the space of flows is globally integrated. In a fragmented space the economic activities of smaller cities were more or less confined to the immediate economic region or to the area of their economic reach. In a space of flows, smaller cities have the opportunity to build a new relationship "between function and meaning through articulating the global and the local" (Borja and Castells, p. 44). Advances in the technologies of telecommunication, transportation, and production have facilitated this new conceptualization of global economic interaction. To a considerable degree, in this new world interactions have become scale free so that smaller and larger cities can interact with the smaller cities now able to participate in large city activities. More about this shortly.

Another approach to this new structure has been given by Peter Hall's metropolitan city regions, which are "contiguous Functional Urban Regions" and are similar to the consolidated metropolitan statistical areas used by the Census Bureau of the US (Hall 2009, p. 807). Hall identified several of these structures in Europe, including the greater south-east region around London, Randstad in the Netherlands, northern Switzerland, and Ruhr–Rhine–Main. These features can extend to a radius of about 100 miles from the center. Contiguity is the sole criterion and transportation knits the region together and facilitates the functioning of the space of flows. Within it functions will be distributed between high-level services in the center and secondary activities at the periphery. In some parts of the world these structures can extend for hundreds of miles. Scott comments that in a world of reduced national government transfers to cities, cities are forced to take on more initiatives by themselves. As a consequence cities are forming consolidated urban areas in all parts of the world and have now become "the core building blocks of the global urban system" (Scott 2012, p. 167). And as large cities become more focused on global interactions, smaller cities are left increasingly to their own devices. They must work hard to find ways in which they can insinuate themselves into the activities and networks that are being established by the largest cities.

The impact of large cities is, however, not all positive. From the beginning of the contemporary study of large cities we have seen them as having two characters, one positive and the other negative. In 1986 John Friedmann wrote an essay on "the world city" that began a discussion that has continued ever since (Friedmann 1995). From the beginning, Friedmann saw the large or world city as creating two distinct by closely related worlds.

On the one hand, these cities are the key nodes in the articulation of a global capitalist economy, but not without cost. They are the command centers, the home to the wealthy and powerful, the centers of economic decision-making, and the engines of global economic growth and development. However, they exist in a sea of impoverished and powerless regions throughout the world – the periphery to their center. The peripheral areas lack investment in physical and in human capital and as a consequence they can perform only menial labor-intensive and low-paid activities. The history of the world during the recent decades has been dominated by the frustration and unrest that deprivation in the periphery has generated.

On the other hand, within the large cities themselves this same relational dynamic is being manifested. Those who command and operate in the advanced sectors of the economy tend to live in the large cities in lives of luxury. All the consumer goods they want are available to them, elegant living quarters, extreme amounts of disposable income, and a mass of low-paid, low-skilled, and often recently immigrated workers to attend to their personal and business needs – from house-keeping to office cleaning (Sassen 1991, p. 335). Fritz Lange captured this well in his film *Metropolis*. Friedmann saw that in this situation "World city growth generates social cost at rates that tend to exceed the fiscal capacity of the state," and that "The overall result is a steady state of fiscal and social crisis … in which the burden of capitalist accumulation is systematically shifted to the politically weakest, most disorganized sectors of the population" (Friedmann 1995, p. 326). Clearly, this poses a challenge to create a response on the part of smaller cities.

The most dramatic representation of this new reality was given by Mike Davis in his article "Planet of Slums," and by UN-Habitat in its report *The Challenge of Slums* (Davis 2004, UN-Habitat 2003). UN-Habitat reported that 31.56 percent of the world's population lived in slums, with 43 percent of the total living in developing regions. In the developing world, agricultural reforms were in fact displacing rural workers who then streamed into rapidly growing cities in search of some sort of livelihood. These interventions have "actually increased urban poverty and slums increased exclusion and inequality, and weakened urban elites in their efforts to use cities as engines of growth" (UN-Habitat 2003, p. 6). Davis argues this will also create growing inequality "between cities of different sizes and specializations" (Davis 2004, p. 8). Davis's comment on inequality among cities of different sizes suggests implicitly that the impact on smaller cities will be negative. We will discuss this in detail later in this book. The essential point for now is simply that large cities are not necessarily uniformly beneficial to human welfare.

Glaeser takes a contrary view, arguing that slums are an indication of something positive. They are populated with individuals who are fleeing the stagnation and poverty of rural areas and they stream into the cities in search of a better life. Given their lack of resources, they settle in the cheapest areas of the city – its slums. But slum population is not fixed in any way. While there are continual streams of new residents, there is also a continual out-flow of others who have gained some education and skills and can then advance into the rest of the economy. In Glaeser's words:

> Urban poverty is not pretty – no poverty is pretty – but the favelas of Rio, the slums of Mumbai, and the ghettos of Chicago have long provided pathways out of destitution for the poor. In some cases, the dream of upward mobility is not coming true, but that is a reason to continue fighting for our cities, not to place our hope in rural life.
>
> (Glaeser 2011, p. 90)

There is, of course, no correlation between rural areas and smaller cities.

Aprodicio Laquian is convinced that

> if a conscious effort is taken to plan, shape develop, and govern mega-urban regions in a more effective way, it is possible to make them not only more livable and sustainable but to transform them into policy instruments for creating economic and social change in the nations-state and beyond.
>
> (Laquian 2005, p. 49)

Clearly a big topic and one that cannot be dealt with here.

There is a place in this world for smaller cities that can avoid these negative aspects while offering positive ones. Taylor, for example, quotes Rob Hopkins who sees smaller cities as "prime units of transition to a sustainable future" by changing their ways and creating more resilient places for living, and he then seeks to explore how these smaller cities "can be made compatible with a world of large cities" (Taylor 2013, p. 359). We will have more to say about this later in the book.

The life of a mega-city is not a smooth one and it is constantly being confronted with the development of diseconomies of agglomeration, as noted in the previous section, by the uncertainty of national government policy, and by the myriad changes in the larger society and economy. David Johnson has provided an interesting list of these challenges in a study of New York City (Johnson

1993). While seemingly secure in its status as the primary city in North America, the city has had to contend with the development of the information economy; the growth of power over policy of Washington; the deindustrialization of the US economy; the movement of many traditional Manhattan functions to suburban locations in New Jersey, Connecticut, and up-state New York; the rise of other centers of economic activity, culture, finance, and media, such as Chicago, Los Angeles, Atlanta, and so forth; and the influx of migrants from developing countries, their impact on the local labor market, and tension between these new immigrants and those established from an earlier inflow. Most of these developments have been felt by other mega-cities and they have responded with varying degrees of success. Explicit in this secular evolution of the large city is the potential for a beneficial impact on smaller cities as they receive firms and economic activities that are forced out of the large cities, and also of the workers and social institutions and functions that are part of this evolution. It is up to the individual smaller city to make itself attractive so that it can gain these benefits.

The new urban competitiveness environment

During the past 40 years, the global economy has been undergoing a steady transformation that is apparent to everyone. Low-skill, low-wage activities are moving from industrial economies to the economies of emerging nations and regions. Traditional activities in industrial economies are economically viable only if they undergo a comprehensive technological upgrading in order to remain competitive. The result for smaller cities is the need to reimagine the competitive advantages of their existing industries. New industries, with new products, new technologies, and new factor requirements will have to be developed, or existing industries will have to be transformed to meet the exigencies of the contemporary economy. This places an emphasis on creativity – both creativity in the development of new technologies of production and new products, and creativity in their application in economic activities. All cities can participate in this creative activity.

In the old economy of the nineteenth and twentieth centuries it was "hard" aspects that were important for competitiveness – proximity to a port, good rail transportation, proximity to a resource deposit, access to heavy industrial capital, availability of manual labor, some advantage in productive technique, and so forth. In the newer economy of the twenty-first century it will be the "soft" aspects that will be important for competitiveness – an educated labor force, public security, cultural and recreational facilities, urban amenities, access to high-speed communication, effective governance, effective strategic planning and mobilization of local assets, universities and research institutions, good health care facilities, and so forth.

Many of the locational and functional disadvantages of smaller cities can be overcome through application of the latest advances in technology. There are, of course, three major areas of technology that have important impacts on smaller cities and on their ability to participate in and to contribute to the economy beyond their economic reach area. We will examine each of these in order.[1]

First, there have been many changes in the **technology of production**. The River Rouge Plant of Ford Motor Company, completed in 1917, had a production line 1.5 miles long. Coal and iron ore went in one end and at the other end finished automobiles emerged. Such integrated production facilities are rare these days, with parts assembled in one location that were produced at hundreds or thousands of sites scattered throughout the world. This, of course, means that there are possibilities for many smaller cities to compete, and to be successful, by being the site for one or more of these production sites. With production activities now staffed by fewer workers, but by workers with specific technology-related skills, highly mobile workers can be assembled in a location in very short time, with city size no longer being a criterion of site selection.

The spatial reconfiguration of industrial production has been facilitated by the substantial changes in the **technology of transportation** that have taken place during the post-World War II period. Air freight, intermodal logistics, container shipping, and improvements in roads and trucking have brought all parts of the globe into relative proximity, thus making site selection more a factor of efficiency in production than of cost of transportation. Port cities have lost much of their advantage as smaller cities in the center of a large country can participate in production chains. For example, Apple produces inputs to its products in 95 countries, from 27 tons in Malta to 37 million tons in China, and over one million tons in another dozen countries. While a list of all of the cities is not available, it is clear that not all inputs are produced in large cities. For most of the hundreds or thousands of components of many products, from cell phones to automobiles and aircraft, production can take place in small-scale facilities in smaller cities.

Finally, this global production is knit together and supervised effectively due to changes in the **technology of communication**. Using the latest advances in telecommunications, firms in smaller cities and towns can video-conference with counterparts elsewhere, consult on projects and planning documents and designs, view and discuss images, work collaboratively in real time, and all of the other wonderful things that are now possible. For many activities, collaboration between or among participants hundreds of miles apart is as easy and effective as collaboration between the 10th and 19th floor of the same office tower.

These three advances in technology have transformed in a very positive way the capability of smaller cities and towns to participate in economic activities on the global scale. The spatial isolation of many smaller cities, and larger ones as well, has been overcome to a large degree by these technological advances, and others that functioned on the periphery of some large city have been able to reshape their economy, and its place in the larger economy, beyond the large city to which they were close. Many smaller cities were essentially based on resource extraction, and as the richness of the deposit diminished they have been able to restructure their economies in activities that had never before been open to them. Later in this chapter we will see how one furniture-producing city that was near to rich supplies of the right timber, High Point, North Carolina, has been able to become a furniture marketing center after furniture production moved to Asia. Not all of the advantages of large cities have been eradicated, of course, but it is now possible for smaller cities to engage in activities that were formerly closed to them. In the concluding section of this chapter we will examine how these technological changes have created a new place in the global urban hierarchy for smaller cities.

Large cities were usually the beneficiaries of streams of financial support from higher levels of government. Road and bridge infrastructure, research facilities, urban renewal, social housing, income support for disadvantaged populations, internationally connected hub airports, and many other things that contribute to the international competitiveness of our large cities were stimulated and supported by the inspiration and the infusions of funding that came from national and sub-national governments. Sadly for these cities, the higher-level government financial transfers and projects are being reduced under the pressures of the anti-tax and austerity movements that are having such a destructive impact on the rational functions of government. This will in all probability have a greater impact on larger cities in states in the South and rural states in the Great Plains that have been net recipients of federal transfers. In any event, the deterioration in the relationship between fiscal support to large cities and to smaller cities will work more negatively for the former due to their greater reliance on these transfers – yet another change in the new competitiveness environment.

The new place of smaller cities in the global urban hierarchy

As can be gathered from the discussion above, the fascination with mega-cities, and even just large cities, is beginning to wear a bit thin for many as reaction against them and renewed appreciation of the possibilities of smaller cities gain some strength. There are two approaches to examining the new place of smaller cities in the global economy. The first is what we get from theory and from general discussion. This was treated in the first few pages of this chapter. The second is what we learn from studying the actual experiences of smaller cities – it is this that will be the subject of our discussion for this final substantive section of the chapter.

With regard to the second, experiential, approach, in doing our research for this book we have arrived at several conclusions that are of relevance. In our study we included four sets of five US cities with populations in the following brackets: (1) two million plus inhabitants, (2) one to two million, (3) 500,000– one million, and (4) 250,000 to 500,000. The number of cities in the four categories are 22, 20, 33, and 70 respectively. A composite index of competitiveness was developed for these cities using the increases between 2002 and 2007 of retail sales, professional services, and manufacturing payroll, with the three variables being weighed 0.25, 0.4 and 0.35 respectively. With this data we did a correlation analysis of 20 variables relating to economic and social conditions in the cities. While the correlation coefficients were generally weak, it is of value to observe whether the coefficients for the cities and the 20 variables were positive or negative. Thus while the coefficients are not compelling, they are nonetheless indicative of the relationships.

The coefficients confirm the findings of other studies (Kresl and Singh 2012, OECD 2009, Ni *et al.* 2014, and Economist Intelligence Unit 2013) that there is no positive correlation between city size and competitiveness, indeed for all cities it is actually negative, but slightly positive for the two middle categories (cities between 500,000 and two million). This suggests that smaller cities have no disadvantage, vis-à-vis other cities, with regard to urban competitiveness. Another variable was constructed for "ambience," another composite variable based on several aspects such as restaurants, cultural assets and institutions, education, income, and so forth. The correlation between ambience and competitiveness is positive for cities of fewer than 500,000 inhabitants but is negative for larger cities and for all cities as well.

For some smaller cities the correlation coefficients were positive, while it was negative for larger cities as well as for all cities. These are: crime, migration, percentage of population aged 65 and older, and housing that is owner-occupied. The reverse, where the correlation coefficient was negative for smaller cities but positive for the three categories of larger cities, was true for: university graduates as a share of the population, professional, scientific, and technical workers as a share of the labor force, taxes per capita, and households with income in excess of $200,000.

One conclusion from this work is that small cities and large cities do differ in many important ways A second one is that some of these differences would be positive for smaller cities, while some of them would be negative in their impact. Clearly small cities warrant being studied in and of themselves.

At the most general level, and prior to reviewing the conclusions from our research, we can look to a study conducted by researchers at the University of North Carolina and published by UN-Habitat (2012) in which seven "lessons" regarding the planning process in 30 of our smallest cities were identified – each with a population of less than 10,000:

- community development is economic development;
- success is linked with being proactive and future-oriented and accepting of change and assumption of risk;
- successful strategies are guided by broadly held local vision;
- defining assets and opportunities broadly allows the city to capitalize on its competitive advantage;
- innovative local governance, partnerships, and organizations are crucial;
- a comprehensive package of strategies and tools is preferable to a piecemeal approach; and
- for long-term community development to be achieved, it is necessary to identify, measure, and celebrate short-term successes.

The seven "lessons" conform with what is generally seen to be the standard approach to strategic economic planning (Kresl 2007, pp. 27–31). These small cities were focused on one of the following four types of activities: entrepreneurship and small enterprise incubation-based, place-based, human capital-based, and industry or manufacturing-based.

In further research, we studied three city-size categories of US cities; those with populations of 20,000–50,000, 51,000–100,000, 101,000–250,000. Cities smaller than 20,000 were not included because they lack connection with the economy beyond their narrowest borders, and cities larger than 250,000 were not included because these cities were typically parts of metropolitan areas that were several times their size, so they could not be studied as individual cities. The cities were chosen with a bit of arbitrariness but also because they were not dominated by position in a larger metropolitan area and hence their policy responses to changes in their economic situation could be studied in and of themselves. These cities were responsible for their own economic evolution in ways that were not the case for larger cities.

A disadvantage of smaller cities is argued to be the lack of skilled and educated workers. However, one of the principal conclusions from our research is that a powerful factor in the success of many smaller cities is the presence of one or more colleges and/or universities, especially if this is paired with a regional health care facility. This is true even for cities as small as Lewisburg, Pennsylvania, with a population of about 20,000, and Ithaca, New York, population 30,000. In Pennsylvania this strategy is valid also for the two largest cities – Philadelphia and Pittsburgh. A relatively highly skilled, highly educated, and highly mobile workforce staffs these two sectors. It is things like urban amenities, as well as good jobs, that attract and keep these workers in these cities. Both higher education and health care provide economies that are stabile in employment and production, and cities that host them experience an economic stability that escapes other cities based on sectors, such as manufacturing and finance, that are more marked by cyclical phenomena. This activity has been recognized as being important for a competitive urban economy but it has been seen as being a feature of larger cities that seek to attract and retain Florida's "creative class" (Florida 2002). Our research confirms this for small cities as well.

A second disadvantage is that smaller cities have generally been thought to be deficient when it comes to effective strategic economic planning. They are thought to be lacking in access to skilled professionals in this area, they lack the necessary resources, they typically have little experience in charting a new course, and they are taken to be essentially too conservative and risk averse in their thinking to do successful planning. The work we have done on smaller cities shows that this is clearly not the case. Billings, Montana, and Boulder, Colorado – cities with populations of roughly 100,000 – are both examples of this. The actual needs for specialized skills in planning are perhaps not as great as the sellers of these services suggest they are. UN-Habitat has found that: "(T)here is no universally applicable formula for determining the right way to do community economic development. Decisions about what to do and why to do it have to be based on local conditions, context and capacity" (UN-Habitat 2012, p. 82). Hence, planning in smaller cities will be more site-specific and custom-made and local people often have sufficient knowledge of their city and its strengths and weaknesses as well as most of, if not all, the skills to plan and implement a strategy of competitiveness enhancement. Social capital tends to be stronger in smaller cities and this works to their advantage (Putnam 2002, pp. 117 and 138).

The third issue is that of branding and identity of the city. For the smallest cities these are not an issue since the cities function within a limited spatial area. The people who might be interested in the city tend to have good knowledge about it without an elaborate identity/branding effort. However, as city size increases so does the potential area in which the city economy has need for name-recognition and place-identity. As cities get larger, the competition for customers and clients in areas that are far beyond their own immediate economic space becomes more intense. Being known widely as a supplier of high-quality products or of goods in high demand makes it much easier to have good experiences with other economic actors. On the other hand, Ashworth tells us that identity-branding may be easier for smaller cities since larger cities are "multifaceted, multifunctional, and diverse" and getting these diverse actors to work toward one common strategy may be relatively difficult (Ashworth 2010, p. 231).

Fourth, while it is true that smaller cities do lack agglomeration economies, and the things that go with having them – airport hub status, the possibility of having multiple, mutually supportive industrial clusters, financial and corporate headquarters, and so on – with recent advances in the technologies of production, communication, and transportation, smaller cities have been able to overcome many of the disadvantages this brings, as has been shown above. One consequence of these technological advances is the facility smaller cities now have to participate in networks of other cities that have specific things in common. Networks are essentially clusters that lack proximity. With cities and their firms being able to fashion networks of cities in desired areas of economic activity, smaller cities can share knowledge and experiences, engage in collaborative projects, lobby together for policy changes, make joint approaches to potential funding sources, and enact many of the other activities that are possible for large cities by means of clusters. Needless to say, there remain things that only a large city can accomplish, such as being a world-class city of head offices, supplying advanced specialized services, and notoriety.

This informs us that smaller cities do have the capacity to create roles for themselves in a grander urban hierarchy than that which consists of their immediate surroundings. Clearly smaller cities cannot hope to become alternatives to large cities. They simply do not have the capacity to do this. In fact, they often function in the greater orbit of some large city, so much of what they can do has the possibility to fit into or complement the economic activities of the large city. In Chapter 7 we will see that some of the smallest cities draw benefits from a nearby city of under 250,000 inhabitants. So they both contribute to the economic region in which they are situated, that is dominated by a modestly larger city, and then also benefit from being situated there. Later we will discuss the benefits to be gained from "borrowing size" from a larger neighbor city.

Understanding that many smaller cities do have sufficient access to skilled and technology-oriented workers, can do adequate strategic economic planning, can engage in effective branding and identity development, and can use technologies to overcome their small size, what can they contribute to the global economy and what is their role or place in this system? Must they confine themselves to their immediate region or can they play a role in the larger global economy? In the past there was little impact smaller cities could have beyond their immediate region but, to take just one example, smaller cities that have assets that are important for tourism do sell their product in a market that extends to all corners of the globe. Advances in telecommunication and transportation have opened them to consumers on all continents. A visit to any one of hundreds or thousands of small tourist cities will show that their visitors come from everywhere. Can this be replicated in other sectors of the economy? A similar conclusion can be observed for cities that have cultural assets such as high-quality museums of art, architecture, and anthropology as well as festivals of music and theater. These smaller cities are clearly marketing themselves on a world scale.

We have noted above that smaller cities now fit into production chains that encompass scores or hundreds of cities of all sizes in the manufacture of automobiles, electronic equipment, consumer products of all sorts, apparel, commercial aircraft, and military equipment. There are hundreds of smaller cities that can be used to make this case, but the following six will do. Corning Glass Works, now Corning Corporation, has been in Corning, New York, population 11,000, since 1868. The company has gone through a couple of product changes and now is focused on five areas: display technology, environmental technology, life sciences, optical communications, and specialty materials. It has provided glass material for US space shuttles, glass for liquid crystal displays, and most recently Gorilla Glass, used as a scratch-resistant material for handheld devices. It has a cooperative arrangement with Sharp Corporation in Osaka, Japan, production plants in North Carolina, and its primary research laboratory in Corning. The company also founded, in 1951, and maintains, the Corning Glass Museum which contains 45,000 objects from 3,500 years of glass-making and draws 400,000 visitors from around the world.

High Point, North Carolina, with a population of 104,000 was long recognized as one of the premier furniture manufacturing sites in the US. This was principally due to the proximity of extensive forests and good rail transportation. The first factory was established in 1889 and within a decade almost 40 more were built. The industry was very successful through most of the twentieth century and grew to over 1,000 firms by the 1980s. Then in the 1990s globalization caused much of the production to be transferred to facilities in China and Latin America and High Point had to make a substantial transition from manufacturing to being one of the world's principal furniture-marketing centers. This transition was managed by the furniture manufacturers and property owners, in opposition to state development pressures to refocus the city's economy (Schlichtman 2009, pp. 110–111). The transition has been very successful with the city holding two furniture fairs annually, with about 12 million square feet of display space used by 2,300 exhibitors from over 100 countries and 85,000 visitors. The transition was accomplished by local business leaders and other entities in the community.

Columbus, Indiana, population 45,000, is the home to Cummins Engine Company. Founded in 1919, the company developed diesel engines and in the 1950s had more than half the market in the US. In the 1960s Cummins opened a plant in Scotland and by 2013 the firm had operations in almost 200 countries and territories, including facilities in India, China, Brazil, and the Netherlands. Recently the firm began to supply natural gas-powered engines to truck manufacturers. The firm has generated an inflow of foreign investment from many countries with 21 firms from Japan alone. In 1954, the Chairman and CEO, J. Irwin Miller, used Cummins funds to establish the Cummins Foundation (Columbus, Indiana 2012, p. 9). The Foundation's most public initiative was to support architectural fees for public buildings in Columbus. Over 50 projects were funded, with other companies and individuals funding other building projects. Currently the American Institute of Architecture has ranked Columbus number six in the US, behind Chicago, New York, Boston, San Francisco, and Los Angeles – this for a city of 45,000! So, Columbus has been an international actor both through its economy and through architectural tourism.

Dow Chemicals was founded in Midland, Michigan, by a Canadian chemist in 1897, producing only a narrow range of products. It expanded dramatically during World War I when it became a major defense producer. It expanded its production during World War II with a plant in Freeport, Texas, and now has facilities in the Middle East and Asia. Midland is a city with 42,000 inhabitants and was rated recently as one of the best cities in which to raise a family in the US. While it does not have the attractions of either Columbus or Corning, it is, nonetheless, home to a firm that has extended its reach to the entire global economy. The firm remains in Midland because of its history and the fact that it is the site selected by Dow's founder, Henry Herbert Dow; it has grown to be the second largest chemical firm in the world, by revenue, from its base in a city of 42,000 residents.

Wolfsburg, Germany, is a city of 122,000 and through its prominence in the automotive world has become the city in Germany with the highest per capita income. The city developed significantly through defense production during World War II, including military vehicles. Production of the Volkswagen expanded shortly after war, and the product line expanded steadily to include Audi, Porsche, Lamborghini, Ducati, and several other marks. As a consequence of the prominence of the auto industry, the center of Wolfsburg is Autostadt, an open-air museum in proximity to the various companies and dedicated to their products, and the largest hands-on science museum in Germany. More so than the other cities in this section, Wolfsburg is subordinate to the major company that is located there. That being said, the relatively small city is unquestionably linked to the global economy as are few others.

With 15,000 inhabitants, Sant'Elpidio a Mare, Italy, is only slightly larger than Corning. Nonetheless it is an example of the small firm model of middle Italy, as the home of Tod's, the maker of high-quality shoes and accessories for both men and women. The founder of Tod's, Dorino Della Valle, began his business in the 1920s and his son, Diego, expanded into sales in the US in the 1970s and then brought modern marketing strategies, but kept the handmade process. While manufacturing has been kept in the Marche region of Italy, marketing has expanded to include flagship stores in several countries, specifically 107 in Asia, 58 in Europe and 11 in the US. This is a classic example of a small Italian firm in a small Italian city that has extended its reach to encompass the world economy.

Final words

In none of these five cases was the city the primary actor through its strategic economic planning and the insights and energies of its local leadership group. In the case of Wolfsburg, it was government procurement agencies that promoted automobile production. In the other four cases, the impetus came from an entrepreneur or the head of a large company who decided to establish and promote some specific activity in the smaller city. But the point of this is simply to note that even in cities as small as Corning and Sant'Elpidio a Mare, the city had sufficient attractive assets in terms of skilled labor, transportation, capital, and energy to make the initiative a lasting success. Smaller and even small cities were certainly "not in the game." While these should not be looked upon as conveying some universal message for smaller cities, their experiences should be an inspiration to leaders in other smaller cities to seek out possibilities to achieve much the same result. The rest of this book will be an exploration of the possibilities and potentialities smaller cities have to do just that.

Note

1 This and the section that follows are based on the text of a conference paper given in Queretaro, Mexico, August 15, 2015.

3 What are the strengths and weaknesses of smaller cities?

Cities of all sizes are not interchangeable or without distinctive features. Some of these features are positive with regard to competitiveness and the economic success of any city, while others are negative. This is a point that is reiterated throughout this book, but it is also common sense that should be understood and accepted by all who give attention to cities. In this chapter we would like to be more precise with regard to these positive and negative aspects as they have impacts on economic performance and on the ability of the city to realize the aspirations of its residents. Ideally there would be a melding of the aspirations of the residents and the capacities and performance of the city's economy. Individuals have the option of movement and will presumably situate themselves for work and residence in a congenial setting. However, if the residential or working aspects are sufficiently attractive individuals will remain where they are and will work through individual and collective action to modify the aspects of work or residence that detract from their well-being.

Rarely will a city be in an unchanging state; it will almost always be in movement. Often, external forces such as the decline of an industry, political corruption, a natural disaster, or loss of one or more key individuals or institutions will generate a process of deterioration and decline. This becomes more important when the city is smaller as there are fewer alternative entities or actors to take the place of what has declined. Conversely, when something negative happens in a smaller city or town it is more immediately apparent to officials and economic actors that some collective action is required. Loss of a major employer can have a powerful and inescapable impact on a far wider community than simply those who are directly affected. It is here that the capability, professionalism, and competence of local leadership become apparent. Will the smaller city have the vision, the resources, and the personnel required to implement an effective policy response? Obviously, individuals will reassess their willingness to seek or to continue work and living arrangements largely on the basis of the effectiveness of local economic decision-makers in response to changing conditions in the city.

In Chapter 5 we will examine many of the specific aspects of smaller cities in an examination of the consequences of city size, or the lack of it. In this chapter we will limit ourselves to some more general characteristics of smaller cities, some of which hinder their economic performance in relation to larger cities while others are advantageous.

Some important aspects of the situation of small- and medium-sized cities

The disadvantages of smaller cities are much better known than their advantages. Clearly, smaller cities do not have the pools of specialized and skilled labor that are found in large cities, nor do they have internationally connected hub airports, access to large pools of capital, economies of agglomeration, "brand" recognition throughout the world economy, access to media and publicity, and so forth. But neither do they have the problems with congestion and pollution that are found in many big cities, or the high living and housing costs, and the social pathologies that afflict many larger cities. Small cities are not always examples of Norman Rockwell's America and there is no one template for them. Some of them are abandoned manufacturing or mining towns and isolated places where the major export is their young people. These are indeed places where people live "lives of quiet desperation." Others are Rockwellian quiet places, where traditional economic activities continue as they have for decades. These places are "good places to raise children," where incomes are considered to be adequate, and where the standard of living and of engagement is enhanced by innovations that are done elsewhere.

But at the same time there are many smaller towns that have thriving economies, lively cultural and social scenes, and access to recreation and natural beauty that are very satisfying to millions of people. Many of the most successful smaller cities and towns are home to one or more universities and/or colleges that not only offer cultural activities but host centers of entrepreneurial activities and of start-ups. These towns are quite attractive to firms in many industries. They are attractive to young skilled and educated workers and are very efficient places for firms to locate for certain activities. These can be as competitive and engaged in the mainstream of innovation and creativity as any city.

With most small towns the distinction between the place of work and the place of residence are blurred. Workers often live in the same small town just a mile or two from work. In large cities, even in the outer suburbs where firms have established corporate campuses for their economic activities, the vast majority of workers live several miles distant, as is evidenced by the enormous parking lots that are adjacent to the production facility. In many instances, most famously Silicon Valley and San Francisco, the firm provides some form of bus or other transportation for its workforce. One of the attractions of smaller cities is not having a commute of one or two hours or more, allowing the worker to enjoy a more satisfying relationship with spouse, children, and neighbors. Income may be somewhat higher in the large city but it comes at the cost of time and commuting cost, both of which will be subjectively evaluated by the worker.

In the two sections that follow we will examine the disadvantages and the advantages that are part of the condition of smaller cities. The disadvantages have been widely discussed and are more intuitive than the advantages, so they will be dealt with more briefly. It is the advantages that are often ignored and that require a more detailed and more extensive treatment.

Potential disadvantages for smaller cities

Elsewhere in this chapter and in the next we will detail many of the aspects of a small city that work to its disadvantage – the lack of economies of agglomeration and the things that go with this, such as a major airport, access to a wide variety of professional services, an established identity among other cities, and so forth. Here we want to focus on the difficulty smaller cities have in doing effective strategic planning and in reaching beyond their immediate region and insinuating themselves in the interactions of the global economy.

Strategic economic planning is something in which every urban economy needs to be engaged. The pace and extent of change in markets, consumer taste and the modes in which they make their purchases, the actions of other competing cities, the impact of technological advance, and the emergence of new competitors on other continents combine to force change upon every economic entity and to compel it to respond effectively. To fail to do so is to be left behind and out of the game. The choice is to adapt, enhance competitiveness, and penetrate markets or to become marginalized and to stagnate relative to other smaller cities. The question becomes that of the capability of smaller cities to take charge of their economic evolution and of their place in the hierarchy of cities. We will have more to say about small cities and strategic planning in the next section of this chapter but for now we must highlight a couple of their disadvantages.

These disadvantages of smaller cities in strategic planning stem largely from two aspects of their situation.

One of these aspects, we should note, is that smaller cities typically lack experience with designing and implementing an economic strategic plan, so this is an activity that is quite new to them. Another aspect is that, due to their size and inexperience, they lack the trained staff and access to professional services that are vital to any successful planning initiative. As has been noted elsewhere, these services are readily available in the broader market, but it is not always the case that professionals from "outside" have the necessary intimate knowledge of the city and its history and familiarity with its social structures and principle actors. These factors are contributory to the following five disadvantages of smaller cities.

First, in comparison with large cities, smaller cities lack recognition and perceived distinctiveness. This is understandable since there are a couple dozen large cities and hundreds of smaller cities. Everyone can identify the characteristics of New York, Chicago, and San Francisco, but how many can do this with Provo, Charlottesville, and Madison? In addition to sheer numbers, these smaller cities have not devoted much effort, historically, in distinguishing themselves from each other. They have not had to play on a national, let alone an international, stage. Many smaller cities have begun to devote resources to efforts of "city branding," that is, to identifying and publicizing the ways in which they are different and, indeed, superior to their counterparts elsewhere in the country. Schlichtman urges smaller cities to "engage in active differentiation, by the exaggeration, embellishment or even the creation of peculiarities, to garner competitive advantages" (Schlichtman 2009, p. 119). Another writer stresses *"uniqueness* and *authenticity,"* and that smaller cities must "have the ability to 'tell their own story'," but that they must "also be ready to learn from other places" while recognizing they need to "avoid formulaic borrowing" – the result must be authentic (Bradford 2004, pp. 6 and 8).

Second, they lack vision as to their achievable future. This may be in large part due to the fact that they have done so little thinking about the future. Many smaller cities have had economies that have been dominated by a single industry, and in many instances by a single company. Times were generally good so there was no need to think of changing course. But then the single industry or firm suffered difficulties and had to greatly reduce or even eliminate its operation. Now it was necessary for the city to consider its future and to plan for it. This is, needless to say, difficult for smaller cities that have always been traditionalist and conservative in their thinking. Sinclair Lewis's *Main Street* comes to mind.

While path dependency is perfectly acceptable as a strategic approach being past bound is not. One team of researchers has reminded us that "new growth paths in regions do not start from scratch but are strongly rooted in the historical economic structure of a region" (Neffke *et al.* 2011, p. 261). Path-dependent development simply means that the city's future economy will be directly linked to its past economy. Schlichtman's High Point, North Carolina, is an example of a small city that evolved, under some duress, from being simply a manufacturer of basic furniture to a manufacturer of high-quality specialty furniture and one of the world's principal furniture-marketing centers. A much larger city, Chicago, has a contemporary economy that is a good example of path-dependent development. Nineteenth-century rail and lake transportation, financing of the grain trade, and basic steel manufacturing have been transformed to air and truck, as well as rail, transportation, transacting in currency futures and derivatives, and specialized steel and high-technology manufacturing. Achieving a path-dependent development requires the necessary specialized skilled labor and professional services, as well as other specific amenities and production assets. Not all cities can accomplish this but many can, and have.

Traditional small-town risk aversion is another handicap. Often the decline of a dominant industry or firm is a gradual event that takes place over a decade or more. The city's leaders do not want to signal that they see weakness in the existing economy for fear of exacerbating an already weakening situation. So they do not act. This, of course, only makes things worse as they do not fashion a creative response to the deteriorating situation.

Third, they lack experience with strategic economic planning. As we will argue below, this is a very complex and involved activity. Properly done, it requires the participation of a large number of individuals representing all sectors of the city's society and economy. If one just initiates a process it is likely not to be successful. Ideally a city should initiate a planning initiative every couple of decades, in which case many of the individuals involved will have had experience from the previous exercise. In addition to familiarity with the process of planning, one should also know the city and its residents well. This will facilitate development of a plan that realizes the ambitions of the residents of the city and it will also make it easier to engage the energies, ideas, and commitment of resident-participants in the planning process. It is easy to call on an outside consultant to set the objective, to set up a structure to implement the plan, and to suggest how to engage residents and to monitor their performance in carrying out the tasks of the plan. But often consultants come to the project with a plan and its objective already in hand, with inadequate understanding of the real peculiarities of the city. As was written in one study: "(T)here is no universally applicable formula for determining the right way to do community economic development. Decisions about what to do and why to do it have to be based on local conditions, context and capacity" (UN-Habitat 2012, p. 82). Hence, strategic economic planning is always a challenge for a smaller and inexperienced city administration.

Fourth, they lack their own resources, both financial and in trained specialized personnel. We will discuss the financial constraints further in Chapters 5 and 6 when we examine the situation with national and sub-national governments and their capacities to assist city governments. But for now it is sufficient to note that superior levels of government both in North America and in Europe are less willing and less able to provide financial support to initiatives at the city level. In the United States, cities are limited to sales taxes and property taxes and to borrowing to generate funding, principally for public schools and basic services. These funding options are invariably met with significant resistance on the part of tax-paying residents. Therefore, any proposal for expenditures, including for a strategic economic planning initiative, must be clearly thought out and compellingly in the interest and to the benefit of the community.

Fifth, they are often spatially disadvantaged. The global economy and the "system" in which it resides are challenged powerfully these days by notions of sustainability, that is the likelihood that they will be able to function effectively and efficiently in the decades to come. Much of the most negative evaluation is lodged against the sprawl cities of North America and cities of the less developed world, but also against smaller rural cities and towns. The essential critical comment that is made is that these cities build themselves horizontally rather than vertically (Glaeser 2011, chapter 7). Vertical residences in tall apartment or condo buildings are much more efficient with regard to use of energy for heating and air conditioning than are the same number of residential units spread out in suburbs and smaller cities, especially those in rural settings. Residents in large, densely populated cities use far less energy in transportation, since they have access to relatively efficient public transportation and they can walk to shops, restaurants, parks, and cultural venues. Many dwellers in smaller cities can walk to these places but most of them are usually forced go to by automobile since they lack efficient public transportation. Hence, many smaller cities have a decided cost disadvantage with regard to activities that require local travel when compared with a center city, although hardly so when the comparison is with a suburb.

In spite of all of this, Ashworth argues that identity-branding initiatives may be easier for smaller cities than for larger ones. He notes that larger cities are "multifaceted, multifunctional, and diverse" and it is difficult to combine many stakeholders, interests, and goals into one strategy (Ashworth 2010, p. 231). Presumably he would also find this to be a characteristic of strategic economic planning.

Potential advantages for smaller cities

Smaller cities are distributed throughout the national economic space and in any national economic space some cities are favorably situated while others are "beyond the fringe." While distance can be overcome with the internet, other telecommunications, access to a major express highway, and occasional travel for face-to-face contact, it is nonetheless true that location can be a major competitive advantage for some smaller cities. Proximity to a large city will give access to an international hub airport and to the whole array of service and product inputs that will be available at the efficient large city price plus transportation cost, a cost that is usually negligible for what is needed for the current high technology economy.

Many other smaller cities are still linked closely with access to a raw material that may be used in production of wood, metal, leather, textile, or other goods. For these traditional activities **location can be a powerful advantage** for the city or town. Schlichtman examined the experience of High Point, North Carolina (population 100,000), a city that was known widely for its furniture-making firms. They were initially located there for access to vast supplies of hardwood timber, a rail service that was begun in 1894, and, of course, to a labor supply. Over the decades the city evolved from being just a center of furniture production to being a major world center of furniture display and distribution; High Point now hosts a semi-annual High Point Market with 100,000 exhibitors from producers around the world. Many firms closed due to competition from new producers in Asia and other places, while those that remained retained their competitiveness by focusing on high-quality hardwood furniture. Schlichtman argues that "almost any niche market can potentially develop a critical mass in a global economy that it could not reach in a regional economy." Cities that are in any way distinct should "engage in active differentiation, by the exaggeration, embellishment or even the creation of peculiarities, to garner competitive advantages" (Schlichtman 2009, p. 119).

Conversely, the countryside is replete with ghost towns, or their equivalent; towns that were created because of access to a mineral deposit or some other raw material, or land that lost its fertility – the American West is littered with them. The coal-mining towns of Pennsylvania, where one of the authors lives, offers many prime examples of this, including one town that renamed itself Factory-ville, in hopes of luring a factory! Extraction of coal brought jobs and wealth for a few decades but then the veins became less competitive and no activity to build on this or to replace it was pursued. While the times were good there was no need for it, and when the times turned down there were no revenues to support a transition to another activity – the classic resource trap.

Another sort of Pennsylvania town is Lewisburg, the economy of which was built on access to cherry hardwood for furniture-making and canal transportation for movement of timber and grains. The furniture factory, Pennsylvania House, closed its doors in the early 1980s, and many of the workers took their skills and established wood-working, furniture, and milling shops in the area. Since this time, this city of 20,000 has refashioned its economy so that it is now based on two major employers and economic actors, Bucknell University and a medical complex that is centered on its hospital and an extensive list of medical special-ist services. The economy is no longer based on access to timber and canal trans-portation, but on knowledge, professional services, and creativity. In contrast with many small cities in central Pennsylvania, Lewisburg is an example of a thriving small city economy that has inserted itself in the modern economy. Many other small cities are fashioning strong economies based on education and regional health care, as are the state's two largest cities, Pittsburgh and Philadel-phia, although each of these cities has major additional economic strengths. It is worth noting that Lorentzen and van Heur state that:

> Artistic resources clearly also do exist in small cities, but it may be quite difficult for public authorities to capitalize upon them, because cultural net-works are often very flexible and eclectic. Traditional planning methods have difficulty dealing with artistic communities of this kind.
>
> (Lorentzen and van Heur 2012, p. 12)

The point is that in many successful small cities local authorities do little if any-thing to plan for (high) cultural activities – it is all the provenance of one or more local universities and/or colleges. Each of them has its departments of music, theater, dance, and art. Each is likely to have performance facilities and a theater for films. In many smaller cities it is the university/college that supports the local (high) cultural activities. Bars and clubs provide a local pop and country music life. Local authorities have only to plan for a local crafts fair and other similar events.

While hardly a ghost town, Buffalo, New York, gained its early twentieth-century industrial prominence due to access to cheap hydro electricity from Niagara Falls that was used to power steel production and manufacturing. Once long-distance electricity transmission lines became efficient, the advantage of Buffalo in these activities disappeared, as hydro power was transmitted to fac-tories located elsewhere in the region, and the city entered a decline that has con-tinued until very recently. The city was not successful in grounding an economic revival on the Canada–US Free Trade Agreement and has been slow to find another base for its economy to supplement education and health services. This history is similar to that of many cities in the industrial centers of North America and Europe of a century ago.

Clearly, location can be a competitive advantage that sustains a city's economy or it may be a factor that fails it in the long run.

It has been widely noted that **cultural assets and recreation** can attract and retain a highly skilled and well-educated labor force (Florida 2002, chapter 10). A more contentious issue is whether this pairing of assets can be made available in small cities as well as their larger counterparts. In a study of Darwin, Australia, Brennan-Horley showed how the creative activities in a city of 125,000 population could be mapped by city district, thus enabling one to then demonstrate that it is incorrect to see smaller cities as "provincial, 'uncreative' and hence easily explained" (Brennan-Horley 2010, p. 175). Creative activities were carried out by firms that were small and medium-sized, in contrast with the globally connected firms in larger cities. In the city they were concentrated in specific districts depending upon what assets they needed for efficient production. Some firms need the office space and general connectivity with other firms in the city center; others sought out a site in a beach district, or in a suburban location.

McGranahan, Wojan, and Lambert, in their study of rural growth, stress "the potential contribution of the outdoors as a means to attract the creative class and recharge knowledge." While tourism is the mainstay of many rural towns, "The ability of high-amenity places to attract the creative class as long-term residents combined with rapid innovation in telecommunications make the attraction of 'learned people' a viable substitute to attracting fee-paying tourists" (McGranahan *et al.* 2001, p. 551). This is exactly the strategy that has been pursued by scores of small cities and towns throughout the US during the past two decades. It is up to each of these cities to chart its own course toward the objective of an economy that is rich in cultural assets, creativity, and amenities such as outdoor recreation. McGranahan *et al.* then make the curious contrary comment that "the creative class might be associated with effectiveness in limiting growth in order to preserve landscape and other qualities that drew them in the first place" (McGranahan *et al.* 2001, p. 551). The evidence offered to support this contention is that growth in the highest amenity counties slowed during 2000–2005. Obviously there can be a variety of reasons for such a slowing of growth, and they do not comment on the growth of other counties. Glaeser *et al.* offer a dynamic that leads to a similar conclusion. They argue that people move from unhappy places to happy places so that unhappiness is one element in a city's or region's decline. When individuals move to a happier place they generate rising rents and congestion that eliminate the pleasures of living and working in that place. As they destroy the aspects that drew them to this place they are offered the higher wages that one sees in larger cities, "presumably as compensation for their misery" (Glaeser *et al.* 2014, p. 30). More will be written of this in the concluding section of this chapter.

In the United States, through the nineteenth century, most of the institutions of higher learning were established by religious organizations. Therefore it was the tradition to locate **universities and colleges in smaller cities** in rural areas far away from the large city and its diversions, temptations, and sins. Even Harvard University was located in rural and distant Cambridge, and Columbia University was beyond the pale, far from the southern tip of Manhattan. The legacy of this is that, today, hundreds of small cities and towns are blessed with institutions of higher learning. They tend to educate far more students than can be accommodated by local firms and most of them are attracted to the employment opportunities in larger cities. This having been said, it is true that the presence of a university or college makes a town very attractive to younger skilled workers, especially to those with young children, to seniors who seek out small town amenities and lifestyle, and to entrepreneurs with small and growing firms whose workers seek recreational and other small town aspects. In other countries and on other continents, higher education and learning tend to be big city activities, and smaller cities and towns do not have this attractive feature.

This means that many smaller cities and towns can actually function as learning regions and as centers of innovation. In many cases the city has grown in size as a function of the growth of the university; one thinks of Ithaca, New York (Cornell University), Waco, Texas (Baylor University), Evanston, Illinois (Northwestern University), and Provo, Utah (Brigham Young University). This growth is stimulated by the research activities of faculty who often initiate start-ups of new firms linked to their work – a symbiotic activity that benefits everyone. This is the sort of thing that Mayor Bloomberg initiated with the Roosevelt Island Technology Center with Cornell University and the Israel Institute of Technology. It is a phenomenon that is suited to cities of all sizes.

Small size is also seen by many observers to be beneficial in facilitating creation of structures that are effective in generating social capital, start-ups, public–private sector cooperation, planning, innovation, and effective governance. Putnam tells us there are two forms of structure that are relevant for **formation of social capital**: strong ties and weak ties (Putnam 2002). Strong ties are linked to family and kinship; they tend to be strong but exclusive in that they include only a very limited set of individuals. Weak ties are based on things such as knowledge and association; these can be developed over time to be effective for whatever the task is. Anyone can join as long as he/she has characteristics that will be beneficial to the group. It has been argued that when people move to a small city or town they tend to do so with long-term residence in mind, while those who move to a large city are more likely to abandon it for another. This is said to be due to the fact that one moves to a small town for aspects such as "natural beauty, cultural amenities and tolerance" whereas large city residents are more likely to see the city as relatively undifferentiated from other similar-sized cities and they are more responsive to a higher wage offered elsewhere.

Putnam states that: "Altruism, volunteering, and philanthropy ... is by some interpretations a central measure of social capital," and that all forms of altruism are demonstrably more common in small towns. All of this is better "when the scale of everyday life is smaller and more intimate" (Putnam 2002, pp. 117, 138, and 205). This leads him to hope for a time when

Americans will spend less time traveling and more time connecting with our neighbors than we do today, That we will live in more integrated and pedestrian-friendly areas, and that the design of our communities and the availability of public space will encourage more casual socializing with friends and neighbors.

(Putnam 2002, p. 408)

A group of researchers stresses that the attributes of a smaller city or town exert "the *retaining* effect rather than the attracting effect" (Andersen *et al.* 2014, p. 130). Social relations become embedded in the fabric of the smaller society. The point of this is that when individuals live in smaller cities they come into closer contact with a far larger percentage of the people who will be important to them in some way than they are likely to in a large city. With these contacts, one can say, they reduce the notion of "six degrees of separation" to just one or two. Establishing a productive connection with others is less time-consuming and uncertain than it is in larger, amorphous urban spaces.

Another recent research study concluded "that the formation of successful new enterprises was a principal means through which the creative class/ entrepreneurial synergy led to growth" (McGranahan *et al.* 2001, p. 546). Hence the capability of smaller cities to encourage **start-ups** and to engage in **innovation** is of primary concern for their economic vitality and competitiveness. Silicon Valley is the prime example of a region that has been supremely successful in both. Situated between two large cities of roughly one million inhabitants each, San Francisco and San Jose, Silicon Valley proper is composed of several smaller cities of between 65,000 (Palo Alto) and 150,000 (Sunnyvale) with a major university (Stanford), access to major airports, and all of the amenities that are desired by a technologically skilled workforce. Such a grouping of economically competitive small cities has been described as an economic micro-region, a space that has the capability to introduce policy that will attract and retain mobile investments and enhance competitiveness of the firms in the area. The essence of the micro-region is the need for transactional proximity. The greater the complexity, uncertainty, and uncodifiability of transactions, the greater the need for a functioning economic micro-region (Gray and Dunning 2000, pp. 411–412).

A Silicon Valley type area has also been described as that of the "small world," that is, "social networks that cut across individual firm boundaries" that explain a crucial element in the success of Silicon Valley, "effective management of innovation in an environment of ongoing knowledge exchanges" (Thatchenkery and Heineman-Pieper 2011, p. 91). These authors stress that one of the features Saxenian (1994) highlighted in her studies of Silicon Valley was the large numbers of highly educated immigrant workers who rather naturally established social networks, interconnected firms, and international business and technology networks. The social space of a smaller urban area, in which immigrants function would be seen as an immigrant ghetto in a large city. The result here was an environment that was highly conducive to start-ups and innovation.

Krätke gives us further evidence that large cities may not have an advantage over smaller cities when it comes to the knowledge-intensive manufacturing activities that are so closely identified with start-ups and innovation. His study concludes that while there is a highly significant relationship between these manufacturing activities and the "proportional size of the scientifically and technologically creative workforce," there is no significant relationship with "the share of skilled professionals in the fields of financial services, management, and consulting" (Krätke 2011, p. 57). It is this latter cohort of the labor force that is supposed to be one of the competitive advantages of larger cities. None of this is to say that smaller cities are superior to larger cities when it comes to start-ups and innovation; rather it is to suggest that the assumed disadvantage of smaller cities must be rethought.

One of the techniques that have gained much interest in recent years is that of **public–private sector cooperation**. This can range from a simple relationship between local government and a small number of local business and social entities to a highly complex structure with multiple levels of government or city administrations and numerous business, university, social, and interest group entities. The objective of this structure is that of improving local policy determination and implementation, problem-solving for the firms involved, ensuring government assistance in achievement of private sector objectives, and promoting innovation, as well as ensuring that the actions of the private firms are not in conflict with the obligations of the public sector authorities. Landry has written that "The business community is entrepreneurial, has drive and is forward-looking ... The community in turn is proud of their products and the reputation they bring to the place" (Landry 2011, p. 522). Each entity brings distinctive expertise to the venture and all participants must benefit from this interaction. The operation of this sort of structure can be made clear from the experience of one very well-known example – the Research Triangle in North Carolina.

The Research Triangle concept was adopted in 1955 when a local businessman took the idea of a research area that would stimulate economic growth in the Raleigh–Durham–Chapel Hill metro area to the governor of North Carolina. At first the partnership was between the state government and the three universities in the area – Duke, North Carolina, and North Carolina State. The universities were to provide talent, and knowledge that was in keeping with their operational mandates. A Research Triangle Committee was formed a year later. A New York investor initially provided some funding but soon balked due to the lack of local investors. A local banker was asked to take over the management of the initiative and immediately saw the need to broaden the structure from just state government and universities to one that involved private sector companies. In 1959 Chemstrand Corporation established its research facility there but it was only in 1965 that IBM made its decision to put a research facility there, and this was the development that put the project on the path to become one of the principal research parks in the United States. One pair of researchers has concluded that what is involved here is "a process of social sequential learning" that stimulates development that works for the benefit of all participants and for the common welfare as well (Leyden and Link 2013, pp. 179–184). More generally, it has been written that public–private partnerships "appear to anchor multiplex, cross-cutting knowledge networks to the extent that they are constituted with the principles of inclusion and participatory governance" (McDermott 2013, p. 81). In this regard, it is noteworthy that the Research Triangle became successful only after the government–universities structure was modified to include private firms.

This experience is a model for so many other public–private partnerships that have been established in the United States as well as in many other countries. It should be noted that, in 1980, the population of the Raleigh–Durham–Chapel Hill metro area was just over 600,000 – hence, this very successful initiative can be seen as a smaller city project.

With regard to **planning**, smaller cities have both advantages and disadvantages specifically related to size. We will examine the advantages here and the disadvantages in the next section of this chapter. To begin with, a fundamental question: Does planning have positive impacts? Planning initiatives are undertaken with great enthusiasm and commitment, but opponents of government action argue that economic development should be left to market forces and that intervention by the state will only get in the way. A rather dispassionate study was conducted by Erickcek and McKinney, who have demonstrated that evidence "suggests that deliberate policy may have led to the growth differentials of ... metro areas" (Erickcek and McKinney 2004, p. 25). Their study, using data for 267 US metropolitan statistical areas with population of fewer than one million, was to determine whether city planning initiatives had a positive impact on the change in personal income over the decade of the 1990s. They used a model to predict growth during this decade and found that more than expected growth occurred in two of eight types of urban areas – "university/government/ business complexes" and "growing new economy places"; it was below what was expected in "old economy places in slow decline," "sprawling places," "company towns left behind," "college towns leaking graduates," and "company towns left behind but still socially stable"; and was what was expected in "private sector dependent places." The definitions of places are not clearly specified here, but they give a rough idea of the sorts of places in which active public policy has a positive impact.

There are several caveats that should be issued with regard to strategic economic planning. First, is the recognition that today's competitive strength may be tomorrow's social pathology. This is the case is some of the types of cities, above, for which planning had little impact. Industrial centers that were based on manufacturing labor and housing and other city features that accompanied them found that these assets were of little benefit and even a hindrance in the contemporary economy. Turin, Italy, attracted relatively unskilled workers from the Italian south to work in the Fiat factories. Youngstown, in the US, attracted similarly unskilled workers from Appalachia for the steel mills. In both instances the cities were ill prepared for the post-heavy industry economy that confronts them and many other cities, and the workers from the earlier economy have become the source of social pathologies – unemployment, deteriorating neighborhoods, sub-standard housing, delinquency, and crime.

Pittsburgh emerged into the new economy not through planning by the city but through actions of its two major universities, Carnegie-Mellon University and the University of Pittsburgh, that developed information technology, medical technology, and health care on their own initiatives. Turin, however, began a formal planning initiative by the city government in 1998 that culminated in the Winter Olympics in 2006 and several international Congresses. Part of the effort was the construction of a subway system, expansion of the airport, various beautification and neighborhood improvement schemes, restructuring municipal government, and investments in the local university system and technology-sector. The result has been a resurgence of Turin's economy and place in the European urban system. Montreal is another example of a city that aggressively used the authority of the municipal government to restructure its economy. The multimedia, fashion, film, and information technology sectors have all been stimulated though the city's initiatives to create facilities for them in suitable districts of the city. So planning can work, as can serendipity in the case of Pittsburgh.

But do smaller cities have advantages in doing this? If we are to answer this we must briefly examine what is involved in a planning initiative that will enhance a city's competitiveness and its ability to shape its own future. There are five principal elements in economic strategic planning (Kresl 2007, pp. 27–31). The first is development of an understanding of the city's true strengths and weaknesses. Smaller cities in particular tend to have a collective understanding of how they compare with other cities. Usually the set of cities used for comparison is limited to those in the region in which the city is situated, and this is dominated by understandings that are based on the city's economic history. As one researcher has put it: "Cities need an internally generated and well-articulated narrative of identity before they can be recognized externally" (Modares 2014).

A labor force, for example, that was suited for the past competitive strength, is very likely not at all suited for what the future needs. The same can be said of the city's educational and training institutions. The future economy will demand skills that will differ dramatically from what has been demanded previously. On the other hand, a skilled labor force seeks certain amenities for work and residence in which the city is well endowed but that were not seen as valuable in earlier decades. A competent assessment of these strengths and weaknesses is an absolute necessity before any planning can proceed.

The second is the involvement of the major institutions, organizations, social communities, and individuals in all aspects of the process of designing the plan and setting its objectives. This is crucial because it is necessary to gain the wishes of all participants with regard to the future economy and society that will be established by the planning process. If the plan is to be a success it must realize the aspirations of the city's residents. There are many examples of plans, designed by a mayor and his closest associates, usually with input from the business community and prominent residents, that fail to meet their objective. One example is that of Dresden in the early 1990s. A small group centered on the mayor designed a plan with little or no involvement of the community and with little publicity. Its objective seems to have been little more than keeping some firms from leaving the city. A subsequent plan done in 2003 involved many committees representing sectors of the community, a specific set of four targeted sectors of the economy, and approval by the city council (Dresden Wirtschaft und kommunale Amt 2003, pp. 15–36).

The third is the design of a plan that will have as its ultimate objective an economy that realizes the aspirations of the residents of the city. Too often an outside consultant is eager to suggest a plan that has already been developed for another city that may have little in common with the city undertaking the planning initiative. It may be true that the "economy of the future" will have certain characteristics that suggest bio-pharmaceutical or information-communications technology or some other technology-intense sector should form the basis of the local economy. Not only does such a plan have little to do with the assets or aspirations of the city, but if all cities adopt this plan they will all be in competition with each other for the same sales. In designing the plan, bottom-up is usually better than top-down.

Beyond the economic specialization of the city, residents will have preferences with regard to a variety of amenities and other features of the city. The degrees of economic inequality and of homelessness vary dramatically among cities. In some, residents are seemingly blind to people living in cardboard boxes along major roadways while in others this is intolerable, and public shelters and decent food are provided to the indigent. Some populations seek maximum per capita income above everything else, while in others the work–leisure trade-off is such that they prefer to work 1,450 hours per year (Norwegians) while others work 1,950 hours (Americans and Japanese). These different preferences will have impacts on the way the economy is designed and functions. Some populations demand that resources be allocated to cultural facilities while others are quite indifferent to concert halls, museums, and theaters. The list goes on, of course, but it should be clear that different populations have different preferences and aspirations. It is these particular preferences and aspirations that should govern the specification of the objectives of the plan.

The failure of a plan can be the result of the fourth component, the inability to engage and to mobilize the talents, energies, and insights of the city's residents. A successful plan usually has many committees and broad support throughout the community – the business community, of course, but also universities, social groups, low-income individuals, cultural institutions, professional societies, and so forth. A resource as rich as this cannot be ignored and excluded from implementation of the plan. After studying the successful planning exercise of Huddersfield, United Kingdom, population 130,000, Landry concluded that success required "giving scope to people's creativity and harnessing their capacity to solve problems. This was the true source of urban competitiveness" (Landry 2000, p. 83).

The fifth is obvious but nonetheless requires attention – the monitoring of performance and the evaluation of how various actors have functioned. If one participant in a planning initiative fails to perform adequately this may reduce the effectiveness of other participants. In a smaller city, personalities who are known to many are involved, and news travels fast. Hence, individuals should be put in positions in which they can use their knowledge and skills, and the friends of the members of the planning committee should be carefully screened before being brought into the process. A study of small city economic development in the US concluded that "residents are always the most important resource and communities with limited resources cannot afford to exclude anyone from planning or development effort" (UN-Habitat 2012, p. 81).

Final thoughts

So, were does this leave us? Should we expect smaller cities to be able to find a place for themselves in the global urban hierarchy and to compete with counterpart and with larger cities? There is no doubt as to their attractiveness and their value to human society. As one recent UN-Habitat report put it:

> The generic features of small and medium-sized cities – particularly their human scale, liveability, the conviviality of their neighbourhoods, and their geographical embeddedness and historical character – in many ways constitute an ideal of sustainable urbanism ... Small and medium-sized cities are, therefore, essential for avoiding rural depopulation and urban drift, and are indispensable for ... balanced regional development, cohesion and sustainability.
>
> (UN-Habitat 2012, p. 4)

This conclusion was seconded by McKinsey and Company in a report on US cities in the global economy:

> The true vigor of America's urban economy comes from a broad base of dynamic middleweights and the relatively high per capita GDP they achieve. There are just over 255 middle weight cities in the United States, compared with just over 180 in Europe. And they generate more than 70 percent of US GDP today, compared with just over 50 percent in Western Europe.
>
> (McKinsey 2012, p. 3)

This informs us that smaller cities are beneficial and indispensable, but are they competitive? This is the question we broached in this chapter.

The weaknesses or disadvantages of smaller cities are well known and have received rather minimal treatment here – we did not think that a longer exegesis was necessary. Clearly, smaller cities lack agglomerations, at least in the common understanding of the term, and they have shortcomings that hinder them in doing effective strategic economic planning; however, there is nothing that makes this activity impossible for them. Many smaller cities have surmounted these difficulties and have had very successful planning experiences. More will be said about this in Chapter 7.

What required greater attention is the several advantages or strengths that characterize smaller cities and towns. We highlighted the following factors as having some benefit for smaller cities: location, cultural assets and recreation, higher education, social capital, innovation, public–private sector cooperation, and planning. This is not to say that larger cities do not have strengths in these areas, but rather to argue that smaller cities do have capacities in these areas that work to their advantage.

In the next chapter we will examine the impact of size on urban competitiveness and economic viability. Again the question will be whether smaller cities are disadvantaged here because of their lack of size.

4   Is size important?

We have just examined the place of smaller cities in the global economy and their economic characteristics. This gets us to the extremely important issue of whether cities have to be large to be successful in achieving the aspirations of their residents: that is, can smaller cities be competitive in the economy of today and tomorrow? Are mega-cities too large to be able to adapt to the changing demands of global markets? Are their advantages overwhelmed by the congestion, pollution, crime, and corruption for which they are so famous? Are there lifestyle or livability advantages for smaller cities that offset their lack of economies of agglomeration and of scale? These are very important issues that warrant serious examination.

In this chapter we will begin with a review of the arguments researchers have proposed for the consequences of size (large or small). Then we will examine whether there is such a thing as an optimal size for a city – can a city be too small or too large to satisfy the aspirations of its residents? We will then propose the notion of an economic core for an urban economic space and how it relates to the actual size of the city. Finally, we will attempt to resolve some of the issues raised here through data that has been accumulated for 145 US metropolitan statistical areas.

The consequences for a city of large size or of the lack of it

The recent fascination with mega-cities and with our largest cities as global actors has generated an examination of what it actually means to be large from the standpoint of economic performance and social relations among the cities' population. In fact, a good review of these aspects can be found in a textbook on urban economics that was published some years ago (Balchin *et al.* 2000, chapter 2). For now, we will simply enumerate the proposed advantages and disadvantages of size, and will use our data to try to verify or to disprove some of them later in this chapter.

Data we will provide later in this chapter will confirm that city size is positively linked to **higher incomes** (and productivity). Larger cities have higher concentrations of more generously paid higher-level corporate executives and larger professional services firms. It is also true that industries such as finance in which a large percentage of employees are well paid tend to concentrate in larger cities. Sadly, city size may also be linked to inequality, as Joel Kotkin has written: "As a result of changing economic conditions, there is now a greater disparity in core cities like New York, Chicago and Los Angeles than in most American communities" and they "tend to boast areas with the highest concentrations of inherited and rentier wealth in the nation, as well as some of the greatest concentrations of poverty" (Kotkin 2014, p. 2). Nathaniel Baum-Snow and Ronni Pavan demonstrate that about one-third of the increase in wage inequality is accounted for by city size alone (Baum-Snow and Pavan 2013). This is largely due to concentration of higher skills in larger cities. So it is in the largest cities that the question of "for whom is the city created" is most relevant and pressing – all residents or primarily higher skilled workers?

The higher income in large cities must be linked to another factor of large cities, that of a higher cost of **housing**. If the large–small city differential in housing cost exceeds the differential in incomes, then workers may be no better off in the larger city. This is exactly what two researchers examined in their study of city size, skill intensity, and housing cost. The issue is whether the higher incomes generated by higher skill intensity ratios in larger cities can be linked as causal factors to higher standards of living, or higher real income. Broxterman and Yezer concluded that while "cities with high house prices have higher wages" and "cities with higher rates of house price increase have faster rates of wage increase," housing cost is shown to be the primary causal factor. So in large cities high incomes are more or less offset by higher housing costs, leaving workers no better off than if they were in smaller cities (Broxterman and Yezer 2014). Additionally, it must be acknowledged that many of the highest priced condominiums and apartments serve primarily as stores of liquid assets (through purchase) and as places to store valuable objects, rather than as places of residence for those who live and work in the community (Satow 2015). These are often owned by foreign individuals who spend little if any time in this high priced housing. The *New York Times* published a five-part series of articles on this phenomenon (Story and Saul 2015). This seems to be a phenomenon that is common to all major internationally connected cities, such as London, Miami, Paris, and Singapore. Even though these buildings are lightly occupied – perhaps only 25 percent – their construction and presence increase costs for other residents in the city.

It is undoubtedly true that there is **greater choice** for both consumers and producers in larger cities. The situation has deteriorated for many smaller cities because of the dynamic centered on big-box stores. In many smaller cities and towns a big-box retailer will locate an outlet there. The consequence of this is a sometimes slow and sometimes rapid deterioration of the viability of smaller retailers who have been in business for many years or decades. The town is then left essentially with the single big-box retailer. Years later the big-box retailer finds that it cannot meet the competition from counterparts in neighboring towns and closes it outlet. Now the smaller town is left without either its traditional small shops or the single large retailer. This is usually a considerable blow to the vitality of this town.

A counterforce is, of course, the rapid rise of internet shopping. Currently e-commerce totals about $300 billion out of total US retail sales of over $4.5 trillion, or only 6.7 percent (*Internet Retailer*, www.internetretailer.com/trends). However, e-commerce is concentrated in books, clothing, consumer electronics, and household goods, so small town shoppers may be able to do quite well shopping for these goods on the web. E-commerce is projected to grow to almost $500 billion by 2018 and will make further inroads in specific areas of retail. So the disadvantage for small town customers, consumers as well as firms, may be steadily diminishing.

Agglomeration economies have long been seen as central to city growth and to efficient production. Cities used to be large because urban industrial plants were large and they needed to be close to certain other specialized firms and to services such as transportation. Think, for example, of Pittsburgh and the Homestead Plant, Detroit and the Big Three, and Chicago and its Southeast steel district – all large and with huge labor forces needing housing, and many related goods and services. In recent decades much of the industrial production and economic activity in general is done in smaller-scale facilities and in facilities that may be just spatially dispersed elements narrowly focused on their task in the company. In fact, Packalen and Bhattacharya have published a paper in which they demonstrate, using evidence from millions of patents granted between 1936 and 2010, that while

> agglomeration did indeed have a considerable positive impact on the adoption of new ideas as inputs to the inventive process throughout most of the 20th century ... [the] advantage of larger cities may now be declining ... [and] the advantage of locating R&D resources in large cities over locating the same resources in smaller cities thus seems to be much smaller now than it has been in the past.
>
> (Packalen and Bhattacharya 2015, p. 8)

As a consequence, in developed countries large urban industrial areas are now located in close proximity to residential or commercial districts, and the impetus for agglomeration has changed. Now many smaller facilities tend to be highly specialized sub-entities of large corporations. Others are highly specialized but independent. Each type of facility needs to be close to other firms that have the professional services, input products, specialized labor force, research facilities, and so forth. This describes a process of agglomeration, in which many activities are grouped together for positive mutual interaction, or economies of agglomeration. Elvery has shown that "the productivity gains from agglomeration are larger for skilled labor than unskilled labor" (Elvery 2010, p. 377). Hence, agglomerations by industry may sort themselves out with regard to their suitability for cities if appropriate size.

On the other hand, if these firms operate in close proximity they may create diseconomies of agglomeration, as they overstress the local skilled labor market, local research facilities, and other inputs. Additionally, an individual firm or sector does not have to have access to all inputs, so an effective agglomeration might be one which is rather limited in size, depending on the specific needs of the firms involved. So while agglomeration requires that a city achieve a certain minimal size for all of the relevant activities to be grouped together, this may be accomplished in a city that is rather limited in population, that is, in size. A very large city may have a large number of agglomerations, many or most of which can operate efficiently with no contact with the others. Does an ITC agglomeration need to be near an agglomeration in fashion or bio-pharmaceutical activity? Probably not.

Economies of scale are both a mechanism and a reason for smaller firms to grow into larger firms. With firm size many things, as all economists know, can be done more efficiently and at lower cost. This occurs as a matter of course – up to the point at which economies turn into diseconomies. The economies are due to bulk purchases, more efficient use of space, lower cost of transportation, and lower cost of capital, among other things; the diseconomies occur, for example, when the organization becomes too large and complex for efficient decision-making, when lack of coordination and planning result in duplication of efforts, and when additional inputs can be obtained only at higher cost, because of supply constraints. For many firms the optimal scale of production can be achieved in a city of moderate size. Even the classic steel production and heavy manufacturing, of aircraft for example, could be done in cities of just a few hundred thousand population – a mega-city was never needed. Cities such as Omaha, Nebraska, Milwaukee, Wisconsin, and Gary, Indiana, were fully competitive in their industrial activity.

It is almost true by definition that large cities have a far more **diversified economic base** than does any small city. However it is not the case that effective diversity is a positive function of city size. A city of one million inhabitants is likely to have all the economic diversity that most economic agents would need – mega-cities may have no advantage here. Each economic actor will have a specific set of other actors that are required for its efficient operation. An additional factor is the accessibility that the internet provides to firms in smaller cities for inputs, advice, professional services, and the whole array of diverse aspects that are required for their operation. So a diverse economic base provides benefits but a very large city is not required for a firm to gain access to them.

Commuting time and **congestion** stand as one of the primary disadvantages of working and living in a large city – though not for everyone, of course. Highly paid workers can afford an apartment of some sort in reasonable proximity to their place of work. A short ride on a bus or subway is little inconvenience, and walking a few blocks is refreshing and healthy. The average commuting time in large cities is just over 30 minutes each way, and 26 minutes average for all cities over 25,000 in population. Many tout walking and bicycling as good alternatives to commuting by car, but for small, medium, and large cities, the percentages of commuters who walk or bicycle are roughly 1 percent, 0.5 percent and 0.25 percent each, respectively, of all commuters. Commuting times of one hour or more each way are greatest for commuters who work in the

District of Columbia (27.4 percent), New York (18.2 percent), and California, Illinois, Maryland, Massachusetts, and New Jersey (all 10–12 percent) (McKenzie 2013).

There have been two primary responses to the commuting and congestion problem. First, an early response was to move corporate activities out of the city center to corporate campuses in outer suburbs. This dramatically reconfigured commuting patterns as workers commuted from suburb to suburb rather than from suburb to city center. Second, many cities began to invest in light rail lines that would link nodes within populous suburbs and the city center. Atlanta and Denver are two such cities. Travel for retail tended to shift from stores in the city center to shopping centers reachable principally by car. However, neither of these responses has been sufficient in its impact to reduce the demand for additional lanes in existing expressways, and most large cities are still marked by traffic that during rush hours barely moves. None of this is a problem as city size diminishes, hence avoidance of commuting long distance is a benefit of living in a smaller city.

Environmental contamination, or **pollution**, is not the consequence of activities in the city itself, but is often brought to the city by wind or water. Beijing is one of the classic examples of a city with a terrible environment and, while much of this came from dense automobile and truck traffic, a major part of this is blown in from the west of the city from coal-powered industrial and power-generation facilities and from grazing that kills grass cover. Pittsburgh is a city that has done a commendable job of cleaning up its sources of pollution, such as the now-disappeared steel industry, but it is now ranked the eighth most polluted city in the US, largely because of airborne contamination from coal-powered electricity generating plants in Ohio to the west of the city.

Smaller cities and suburbs actually have heavier use of automobiles and their accompanying exhaust pollution than do large cities. The latter typically have more extensive systems of public transportation and in more densely populated large cities residents are more likely to walk to shop, to work, or to leisure activities. Hence, pollution is generally worse than in large cities.

The **crime** rate is widely thought to be lower for large cities than it was 20 years ago (Walters 2014, chapter 2). In the data we will present below there will be a negative correlation between city size and crime, except for the smallest cities, those with populations of between 250,000 and 500,000. Big city mayors have made much out of this phenomenon. But has it really been reduced in large cities? In a report, for the internet site *Citylab*, Sarah Goodyear has referred to a study by John Eterno, Arvind Verma, and Eli Silverman that stated that during the years that Michael Bloomberg was mayor of New York, 55.5 percent of 1,770 retired police officers reported that they had "personal knowledge of (at least one) instance in which crime reports were changed to make crime numbers look better than they were" (Goodyear 2014, Eterno *et al.* 2014). While this refers to only one city and is based on responses to a questionnaire, it does cast doubt on the data that show crime rates in decline. It is, of course, perceptions that motivate individuals to move their residence, and many studies have given perception of a lower crime rate in small cities as being one of their principal attractions.

The cost of **public services** – such as police, fire protection, the legal system, and recreation – is a concern for businesses. A policy research group at Rutgers University studied the relationship between city size and efficiency in provision of public services. Their conclusion was that the cost structure is in the shape of an inverted "U," with the cost of public services rising with population size for cities of fewer than 25,000 and more than 250,000, with the relationship level for cities between these two sizes (Holzer *et al.* 2009, p. 1). Increasing size is linked with public works and other capital-intensive services, but efficiency diminishes with city size for labor-intensive services such as police, fire, and public education, which account for about 80 percent of public services. While the difference in the cost of public services is not enough to deter a firm from locating a facility in a city that is larger or smaller than 25,000–250,000 it may be a consideration for firms in some specific sectors of the economy. The Rutgers study did not attempt to measure the quality of public services for cities of different sizes.

Residents **with lower incomes** do not fare as well with increasing city size as do higher-income individuals. In large cities, as the economy evolves from fabrication to professional services, the average skill and education levels and income all increase. In almost all cities this entails a process of gentrification, in which the wealthiest individuals purchase whatever property they want, and the lower-income residents are forced to move to a less desirable location. This process of gentrification can also be seen as one of class cleansing. Mass-market retailers fail and shut their doors, and low-income people are left with fewer places for shopping. Many of them move out to the inner ring of older suburbs, but when they purchase residences that have been vacated by higher-income middle-class residents, the viability of the local shopping malls is put into question. Then we see scores of malls closing their doors, leaving low-income residents, again, with diminished opportunities for shopping. This story has become quite commonplace, to the degree that we can take it to be a consequence of the improvement in the economy of larger cities. Researchers into city economics have long seen this disadvantaging of the lower-income population of a city to be an almost inevitable phenomenon. Tomaney concludes that, given the income inequality that is seemingly inherent in cities of large size, it is necessary to "promote development outside the metropolitan regions which were the winners in the era of neoliberal globalization" (Tomaney 2010, p. 778).

It is also the case that this evolution is positive for some industries/economic activities and not for others. Small-scale manufacturing has largely left under pressures from the development of higher technology, professional service, and financial activities. Gilles Duranton and Diego Puga argue that cities will shift from specialization in a sector of activity to specialization in a function, generating a structure of separate business centers and manufacturing cities. "Business centers are few and large whereas manufacturing centers are more numerous and smaller in size" (Duranton and Puga 2005, p. 365). Clearly there is a positive role for smaller cities in this restructuring of economic activities.

An issue that is commanding much attention these days is that of cities and sustainability. The most common reference to sustainability is that of **the environment**. That is, does a city operate in a way that will lead to the non-viability of it as a place of residence and of work? Not all of the environmentally damaging aspects of a city are of its own doing. Pittsburgh cleared up its steel-related pollution when the mills shut down. Nonetheless it is one of the top ten US cities for pollution because of the airborne pollution that comes to the city from coal-powered power plants in Ohio. Other agents of pollution come to the city via a river that brings contaminants from distant mines and manufacturing sites.

There are, of course, several other approaches to city sustainability. The first is **ambience**, factors that make the city attractive to the desired workers as a place for work and for living. Clearly, larger cities have more options for entertainment, dining, and culture. However, given the seating capacity of a city's cultural venues and the fact that a small number of people attend them frequently, many of whom are out-of-towners, it is not the case that in a city of 10 million residents many of them ever attend a cultural event. The percentage is probably significantly higher in a smaller city, especially a city with one or more universities. Small towns are generally closer to sites for outdoor recreation, such as boating, hiking, hunting, and fishing. Larger cities close the gap a bit with their ample supply of gyms, exercise facilities, climbing walls, and squash and racket ball facilities. There would probably be a slight advantage to smaller cities with regard to ambience.

Another, and very important, aspect of sustainability is that of **demographic** sustainability. Specifically, a city must be able to attract and retain the younger, skilled, creative, and educated workers who will be the backbone of the economy in the coming decades. This generally means that, in addition to interesting work, the city must provide the soft determinants of competitiveness that are so important today. Ann Markusen and Greg Schrock note that: "the specialization of labor is deepening and is not confined to the largest cities" (Markusen and Schrock 2006, p. 1318). In addition, while seniors can have several positive impacts on a city's economy, young immigrants from the rest of the nation and the world are needed to slow down, if not halt, the aging of the city's population. Many smaller university towns are very attractive to desired demographic cohorts, although non-university small cities and towns would appear to have a disadvantage when it comes to demographic sustainability. In many small towns the chief export seems to be younger people but this is not true of all small towns.

The final aspect of sustainability we will examine here is that of **economic** sustainability. When we look at the work that has been done on shrinking cities and on resurgent cities, it becomes clear that the greatest gamble is played by cities that are primarily single industry cities (Wiechmann and Pallagst 2012, p. 272). While larger cities tend to be more diversified and are less susceptible than small towns to a disastrous downturn in one industry, the experience of the manufacturing and steel cities of the industrial areas of North America and Europe makes it clear that this is not always the case. Narrowly focused cities such as Detroit, Buffalo, Youngstown, and Pittsburgh are examples of larger cities that were not able to survive the downturn in manufacturing of the 1980s.

Pittsburgh has resuscitated itself due to the chance development of robotics and computer science, and medical technology and health care at its two principal universities. On the other hand, Chicago was more broadly focused in its economic activities and manufacturing and steel, transportation, and finance were able to modernize their activities and keep the city from following the path of more narrowly specialized cities. Many smaller cities that were specialized in favored sectors have done very well.

Size is no guarantee of long-term sustainability. As Edward Glaeser and Joshua Gottlieb put it:

> In 2000, real wages weakly declined with city size. The natural interpretation of this is that these cities have become much more attractive places in which to live. Some part of this increased attractivity may be the result of declining crime rates. Another portion of this increase seems to be due to rising incomes and education levels which increase demand for urban amenities like museums, restaurants and concerts.
>
> (Glaeser and Gottlieb 2006, p. 1297)

The issue of sustainability is complex and difficult to sort out, but there does not appear to be an advantage for larger or smaller cities here.

Is there an optimal size for a city?

Given these advantages and disadvantages of large size, one can ask whether there is a best or optimal size for a city. That is, is there a size at which the advantages of size are maximally greater than the disadvantages? What is the optimal size for a city? How negatively will a few extra million residents be for a large city? Is Tokyo with its 37 million a good model for other cities? Begović suggested that optimal city size would probably be below 500,000 (Begović 1991) while an OECD study suggested that optimal city size for short-term productivity effects would be about six million residents (OECD 2006, chapter 1). Camagni *et al.* (2015, p. 1083) found, with enviable precision, that the optimal size for a city was 714,973, "the maximum point of the benefit curve function." No one has found 30 million residents to be the best size for a city. The conclusion offered in a report, *Hot Spots 2025*, issued by The Economist Intelligence Unit was:

> The top ten most competitive cities in 2025 [will] range from the world's biggest, Tokyo, with an estimated population of 37m, to some of the smallest, such as Zurich, estimated population 1.4m. Indeed, there is no correlation between a city's size and its competiveness ranking in the Index ... Given that average costs appear to rise substantially in the largest conurbations there would seem to be a strong case for encouraging a settlement structure of medium-sized towns and cities rather than one involving only a few large cities.
>
> (Economist Intelligence Unit 2013, pp. 3 and 76)

This has been found to be the case in studies of US cities (Kresl and Singh 2012) and Ni *et al.* (2014) have found this to be also true for Chinese cities, as has Jaime Sobrino for Mexican cities (Sobrino 2003, pp. 378 and 379). Large cities must be alert to the possibilities that economies of agglomeration will change to diseconomies. Jane Jacobs (1992) offered us the vision of a large city retaining or regaining its viability through the rather natural development of neighborhoods or districts that have powerful identities and congeniality for their residents. They are in effect the equivalent of towns in which big city residents can escape many of the negative aspects of big city life and retain what is so attractive about smaller scale living spaces.

Figure 4.1 is the modification of a figure by Alonso that is found in a popular textbook (Balchin *et al.* 2000). It makes clear the difficulty one has in asserting that some particular city size is convincingly "optimal." Here we can identify four different city sizes that could be considered to be optimal. The first is at point A, at which average cost of city size intersects average benefit from below;

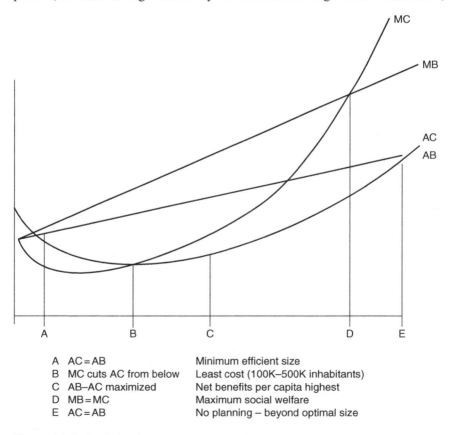

A	AC = AB	Minimum efficient size
B	MC cuts AC from below	Least cost (100K–500K inhabitants)
C	AB–AC maximized	Net benefits per capita highest
D	MB = MC	Maximum social welfare
E	AC = AB	No planning – beyond optimal size

Figure 4.1 Optimal city size.

Source: Alonso 1971 (reproduced by permission of the publisher).

this is the minimum efficient city size since at smaller size, average cost exceeds average benefit. The second is at point B at which marginal cost intersects marginal benefits; this is the least cost city size since marginal cost equals marginal benefit. The third is at point C at which the difference between average benefit and average cost is greatest; here net benefits per capita are the highest and this can be considered the optimal size from the standpoint of the residents. The fourth is at point D at which marginal cost intersects marginal benefit from below; this point gives maximal social welfare, since the marginal cost of an additional resident exceeds the marginal benefit. With no planning or control, population would probably increase to point E since additional migrants would themselves face average benefits and average costs. This gives good justification for the imposition of planning and some controls.

It can be imagined that this figure might include both the 500,000 of Begović, say at point A, the six million of the OECD, say at point D. Is one looking for minimum efficient size, least cost, net benefit per capita, or maximum social welfare? If city leaders wish to target one city size as a long-term policy objective, how are they to choose among the various optimal sizes? One may benefit residents while another may be the objective of the business community. This is not to suggest that the city can choose between 500,000 and six million residents, but a more sensible question is whether the city ought to seek to attain a larger or smaller size over the next couple of decades. As Joel Kotkin has noted: "Increasingly, the key formula is not about achieving size, but efficiency" (Kotkin 2014, p. 4). This question is linked to the next one we will consider – the economic core of a city.

There are some possibilities for a smaller city to overcome what difficulties lack of size may bring. For example, in large cities firms may be able to produce products more cheaply due to access to inputs made by other firms in close proximity, due, as noted above, to economies of agglomeration. However, it is possible for firms in small cities to "borrow size" (Alonso 1975, p. 200). That is, the firm can still purchase the low-cost, efficiently produced input from the original big city firm, with the only cost disadvantage being that of transportation. This might be offset for the small town producer by what he/she perceives to be the lifestyle advantages of the smaller town. Or as some Dutch researchers have put it: "Small regions can compensate for the lack of internal economic mass by establishing relevant connections with larger regions" whereby "they may achieve productivity and welfare levels, comparable to those of agglomerated regions" (Thissen *et al.* 2013, pp. 57–58). There would, then, be no disadvantage to locating in the smaller town. Perhaps the key here is the establishment of networks with other cities, some of which may be considerably larger, from which the benefits of agglomeration could be appropriated by the smaller city (Camagni *et al.* 2015, p. 1085).

Additionally, both the small town and the small town firm have the option of participating in one or more networks. Networks are essentially clusters that may lack proximity but are viable due to advances in telecommunications and internet operations. Firms form the network because they have common challenges;

they may be in an isolated or peripheral location, and would benefit from collaboration and joint projects with firms in similar situations. They can collaborate on solving technical and production problems, in joint marketing initiatives, in new product design, and so forth. Firms in this situation can capture some of the potential benefits of being in a cluster situated in a larger city. Johansson and Quigley argue that "for many transactions, an established network reduces the effective distance between nodes, reducing the transaction (or transport) costs that would otherwise be prohibitive. When collocation is infeasible, networks may substitute for agglomeration" (Johansson and Quigley 2004, p. 175). Another researcher concluded:

> as they grow, network economies increase the benefit of all those who are "connected" giving a "win–win situation." This is why less-favored regions cannot afford not to be connected and regional policy has to cope with the so-called 'digital divide' between those regions that are connected and have the ICT skills, infrastructures and the knowledge access, and those that are not.
>
> (Cuadrado-Roura 2009, pp. 194–195)

In short, networks are essential for smaller cities and towns, especially for those that are close to a large city.

The economic core of an urban economy

By definition large cities differ from small cities because they have larger populations. But what is the effect, or better yet the advantage, of a larger population? We have discussed above the advantages and disadvantages of large size for a city. But let's look at the question in a slightly different way. If we assume we have a city of, say, one million residents, would it necessarily be more or less competitive with another 500,000 residents? Of course, it depends upon what the additional residents actually do. Are they more like an additional 20 pounds of muscle on an athlete or like an additional 20 pounds of fat. If the latter, then larger size would not be likely to add to the performance of the athlete, unless he is a sumo wrestler!

A city is competitive because one or more of its major industries is well structured and managed, and because it can then meet the competition in national and international markets with firms located elsewhere producing the same product. This industry, or these industries, involve the firms that produce these goods or services plus the many other firms that assist them in their activity. This will include some business services, transportation services, parts suppliers, engineering and other consultancies, educational institutions, research facilities, and so forth. This complex of firms and activities can be thought of as the city's "competitive core" – the city is a competitive city because of this complex of firms. But this core is nested in a larger set of economic activities that have nothing to do with the activities of the competitive core.

A good example for this is the US city of Pittsburgh. This was for more than a century one of the primary centers of steel production and manufacturing in the country. Its demise was triggered by the oil and gas price hikes of the 1970s. In 1970, manufacturing employment was 293,689 out of a workforce of 919,011, or 32 percent. What did the other 68 percent do and how was it related to manufacturing? The support sectors listed in the previous paragraph might bring the core percentage up to 40 or 45 percent of the workforce. By 1989, 29 steel plants had shut their doors. Today the Pittsburgh economy has virtually no steel production and total manufacturing employment has shrunk to about 140,000 or 47 percent of its 1970 level. The new competitive strengths of the economy are computer science, robotics, and information security, based at Carnegie-Mellon University, and medical technology, and regional health care based at the University of Pittsburgh. The employment of this new competitive core is difficult to estimate but let's assume it might be about 50,000, with another 20,000 completing this core. Would the Pittsburgh economy with either of the two competitive cores, in 1970 or today, have been more competitive with another 500,000 or one million workers in beauty salons, auto repair shops, convenience stores, supermarkets, big-box retail outlets, the informal economy, and so forth?

Would a mega-city be any less competitive if it lost half of its population that had no connection whatsoever with its competitive core? The UN wrote: "The world is faced with the reality that many large- and medium-sized cities are increasingly becoming areas of impoverished urban exclusion" (UN-Habitat 2003, p. 230). Mike Davis continued in this vein: "Mumbai (Bombay) ... is projected to attain a population of 33 million, although no one knows whether such gigantic concentrations of poverty are biologically or ecologically sustainable" (Davis 2004, p. 2). Slums have value as the first residential location for poor, unskilled migrants from the countryside. But, this aside, there can be no presumption that thousands or millions of slum dwellers add to the competitiveness of the city. In itself, size need not add anything positive to the city's economy or to its competitiveness. Indeed, the presence of this feature of urban life may well diminish the attractiveness of the city's economy to the needed inflows of skilled workers and investment capital, and may have negative impacts on ambience, public security, congestion, public health, and so forth. This could have been crucial for Pittsburgh, reliant as it now is for skilled and educated workers in computer science, health, and education for its economic vitality. Any city must develop policies and strategies to ameliorate the negative aspects of slums and social exclusion, but this is quite aside from any notions of competitiveness and of the vitality of its competitive core.

Smaller cities and creativity

Charles Landry alerted us to the importance of creativity in the emerging modern competitive economy (Landry 2000). Creativity is not at all limited to arts and cultural activities but is found in all aspects of human endeavor, and certainly in computer science product development, city planning, and logistics. It pervades everything we do. Shortly after Landry, Richard Florida focused on the creative class and its importance for urban economies (Florida 2002). While Florida has tended to focus on larger cities, Landry stressed that creativity can be found in cities of all sizes, and Anne Lorentzen and Bas van Heur, in a study of smaller cities, stressed that the creative industries in these cities were "engines of economic innovation" (Lorentzen and van Heur 2012, p. 2).

We have already noted that smaller cities are a mixture, as are all other cities, of aspects that are attractive and unattractive. Smaller cities are thought to have advantages with regard to access to quality health care and education, public security, and recreation. It is also the case that it may be easier to build social capital relations; Avi Friedman argues that "reduced population size can also affect social attributes in small towns and potentially lead to greater familiarity with and closeness between residents. Having fewer places to meet will result in more frequent chance encounters, for example" (Friedman 2014, p. 181). This set of positive features will be attractive to workers in certain fields of activity, albeit not to all. The classic manufacturing work was hard and physically demanding and generated little demand for recreation and cultural institutions; the emphasis was placed on quiet relaxation and perhaps also on hunting and fishing. When the economy evolved into one of office work, finance, and professional trades, skills were more portable and agglomeration economies demanded that the good jobs should be concentrated in large cities – smaller cities were thought to be "out of the loop" and second tier. In the current economic climate, dominated by research, telecommunications, and technology, workers are highly skilled and highly mobile – they can work wherever they want. They seek both interesting work and a living environment that is congenial both to themselves and to their families with young children. It is here that Joel Kotkin, discussed below, sees an "anti-urban impulse" (Kotkin 1990). Suburban living is often seen as rather boring and sterile, and with an enormous variety of conditions in our hundreds of smaller cities it is possible to find a place that seems to be ideal. Scott corroborates this with his finding that there is "a slow but definite long-run process of diffusion of corresponding forms of human capital down the metropolitan hierarchy" to smaller cities (Scott 2013, p. 247).

Smaller cities often have one or more universities and colleges with all the lifestyle features these entail; lower housing costs, an increasingly powerful draw for smaller cities, good restaurants and bars (as a consequence of the expansion of culinary institutes and cooking schools), and access to outdoor recreation. Not all smaller cities have these attributes, of course, and many are as sterile and boring as the archetypical suburb; but many of them have become very successful. One thinks immediately of the university towns Boulder, Madison, Austin, Raleigh, and Salt Lake City, but the map is filled with smaller successful, although less widely recognized, cities and towns. Creativity, as Landry sees it, pervades all of these successful smaller places. In a study of cities and creativity, the Martin Prosperity Institute, of the University of Toronto, found that the top ten ranked cities were: Ottawa, Seattle, Oslo, Washington (DC), Amsterdam, Tel Aviv, Copenhagen, London, Calgary, and New York –

clearly the largest cities do not dominate the list (Martin Prosperity Institute 2015, p. 2). Half of these cities have populations ranging from 450,000 to 1,200,000.

Research on small cities in Canada concluded that "the presence of amenities, the absence of a blue-collar work culture and the presence of a large elderly population are positive predictors of large cultural worker populations in small urban areas" (Denis-Jacob 2012, p. 110). A study of Wollongong, Australia, argued that here, too, a small town with strong working-class legacies was linked to "skepticism towards culture, art, leisure, work and creativity" (Waitt and Gibson 2009, p. 1243). It would, of course, take more study to demonstrate the generality of this relationship beyond the city cultures of Canada and Australia. With regard to a retired or an elderly population, it is clear that this cohort of the population of today and the foreseeable future is a positive force for support of cultural and educational activities in cities large and small (Kresl and Ietri 2010, chapter 4). Both the US Census Bureau and the Commission of the European Communities have stated that the seniors of the coming years will be healthier, wealthier, better educated, and more mobile than has ever been the case (US Census Bureau 2006, pp. 1 and 2, Commission of the European Communities 2005, p. 9). The summary thinking on the issue of small cities and creativity is that "there is ample opportunity for smaller cities to step up and compete with their larger neighbors" (Lewis and Donald 2010, p. 48), but that their situation is "embedded in various complex and competing understandings of place identity (notably, class and industrial legacy), city size and proximity" (Waitt and Gibson 2009, p. 1244). Small size need not be an impediment to development of a local economy of creativity. Indeed, Bradford offers the suggestion that "pursuit of the creative vision is more urgent and in many ways more feasible for smaller communities than for large cities" (Bradford 2004, p. 9). We will close this section with another quote from Landry: "Whilst (smaller cities) cannot compete with global hubs there is a vast range of global niches and strengths to be captured. And indeed very large places often become dysfunctional and so reduce their creativity potential" (Landry 2011, p. 525).

Empirical evidence regarding city size

As discussed above in Chapter 2, in order to gain an empirically based understanding of some of these issues related to city size we gathered US census data for 43 variables for 145 US metropolitan statistical areas. The cities were grouped in four size categories, from 250,000 inhabitants to two million. We excluded smaller cities in part because of the work that would be involved in obtaining the required data for the 162 cities between 100,000 and 250,000, let alone for hundreds of smaller cities. There was also the fact that these smallest cities were less connected to the larger national or international economy and would be less likely to share common forms of relationship and interaction. They might in fact warrant a separate study of their own specific situation. With the 145 cities we did study, we sought to identify the ways in which size related to a variety of important variables that were of interest to us.

As a second step we constructed an index of urban competitiveness based on the same approach that was taken in studies published by Kresl and Singh (2012). The equation used was a weighted composite of the growth in professional services between 2004 and 2009, the growth in manufacturing payroll between 2002 and 2007, and the growth in retail sales between 2002 and 2007, weighted by 0.4, 0.35, and 0.25, respectively. This methodology is discussed in greater detail in Kresl and Singh (2012). Unlike these earlier studies, here we did not obtain data to do a regression analysis of the determinants of urban competitiveness, this not being the objective of our work. Within this limited study, we have gained some valuable empirical verification of aspects of the importance of size in the economic activities and performance of urban economies.

Table 4.1 presents the simple coefficients of correlation between population (city size) and 20 of the variables we selected as being of interest with regard to the situation of smaller, and larger, cities. This is not a regression analysis in which we would be interested in the statistical significance of an estimating equation. A regression analysis would give us an understanding of causation – the variables in the estimating equation explain or determine the values of the dependent variable. Here we are looking for only coincidence – do two variables move in the same direction? Hence, we present only the correlation coefficients rather than include the *p*-values which have little relevance here. Whether the two variables are positively or negatively correlated is sufficient for the purposes of this study.

Correlation analysis has, to begin with, reconfirmed the conclusion of others that there is no linkage between city size, expressed in population, and urban competiveness (Kresl and Singh 2012, OECD 2009, Ni *et al.* 2014, The Economist Intelligence Unit 2013). The correlation is certainly not robust, and is actually negative between city size and urban competitiveness for all cities as a group, as it is for cities with two million inhabitants and between 250,000 and 500,000. It is positive only for the two middle groups, between 500,000 and two million inhabitants. This indicates that smaller cities have no disadvantage with regard to urban competitiveness in relation with other cities.

In earlier studies, Kresl and Singh included "culture" as a variable (Kresl and Singh 2012). This was shown to be a significant determinant of competitiveness, and we thought of including it in this project. But the index we found for culture was quite dated and would not be relevant today. The difficulties in analyzing the cultural sector are discussed in a report on cultural vitality in communities that was done by the Urban Institute. They compiled data for seven aspects of cultural vitality, each composed of several variables; they examined only the top 50 metropolitan areas and did not give a composite ranking for the communities (Jackson *et al.* 2006). This is all the more relevant since many cities have made major efforts to enhance their cultural assets and institutions in the past decade, and data for even five years ago would not give a true picture of the situation in the cities included in this study. The next best thing was "ambience," taken from the *Places Rated Almanac*. In addition to the "lively arts," this index includes "good restaurants," "bookstores and reading," "visible history," and "people."

Table 4.1 Correlations with city size (population)

Variable	All cities	2 million	1–2 million	500,000	250,000
Competitiveness index	-0.041658	-0.150113	0.034671	0.093362	-0.194390
Crime	-0.109350	-0.035916	-0.165899	-0.165899	0.062680
Poverty	-0.107962	0.121082	-0.048364	-0.048364	-0.083971
Unemployment	0.007915	0.093627	-0.062872	-0.062872	0.217297
Ambience	-0.394171	-0.457160	-0.165230	-0.069053	0.071959
Owner occupied	-0.320530	-0.604596	-0.349798	-0.349798	0.241972
Physicians	0.722883	0.638797	-0.099731	-0.099731	-0.035190
Population growth	-0.097973	-0.143686	-0.101158	-0.101158	-0.103041
Migration	-0.276035	-0.569841	-0.152844	-0.152844	0.015327
University graduates	0.269379	0.073270	0.329985	0.329985	-0.014273
65 and older	-0.112165	-0.129665	-0.092522	-0.201436	0.051540
Income per capita	0.074590	0.034740	0.348939	0.348939	0.081549
Households $100,000 or more	0.360642	0.361610	0.484179	0.484179	0.124990
Households $200,000 or more	0.292220	0.455543	0.432155	0.432155	-0.029269
Earnings from labor/earnings from capital	-0.043164	0.054388	-0.054388	-0.096145	-0.034290
Government transfer expenditure per capita	-0.068797	0.180121	0.096145	-0.330649	-0.331413
Federal grants per capita	-0.117475	-0.308033	-0.330649	-0.155052	-0.118810
Taxes per capita	0.472841	0.718730	0.242077	0.242077	-0.044529
Debt per capita	0.159298	0.245052	-0.069991	-0.069991	-0.026552
Professional, scientific, and technical employment/total employment	0.337620	0.349745	0.337620	0.437059	-0.009258

The last category is comprised of data for age, diversity, education, income, political values, and religion. Ambience is a component of the soft determinants that have gained in importance in recent years, to the detriment of hard determinants. Ambience is positively correlated with competitiveness for all cities and for the cities of less than one million inhabitants; for those over one million the correlation is negative. Ambience and population (city size) are positively correlated for cities of less than 500,000 inhabitants but negatively for all larger cities and for all cities as well. The mean values for ranking of ambience, as expected, decline sharply from 37.8 for the largest to 194 for the smallest cities, but the coefficient of variation rises from 47.87 for the smallest to 78.59 for the largest cities. Thus, the findings for ambience for all cities indicated that the situation of smaller cities is dramatically different from that of the largest, but this is not necessarily to the detriment of smaller cities. While the rankings for ambience for the largest cities are the highest, the variation among these cities is far greater than it is for smaller cities.

Given the recent interest in income inequality in all societies, we wanted to relate this to city size. Thomas Piketty has published an important study of this inequality for the past three centuries through application of a model that is based on the earnings from labor and those from capital (Piketty 2014). He shows the increase in inequality, especially during the past two decades. We have created a variable that is the ratio of earnings from labor (wages) to those from capital (interest, rents, and dividends). The correlations between this variable and city size lack robustness and are of interest only because the coefficients are positive for the largest (over two million in population) and the smallest, 250,000 to 500,000 in population); they are negative for all cities and for the two middle-sized categories. So from this we cannot state that income inequality is greater or smaller in large or small cities.

We can identify several variables in which the correlation for the smallest category of cities is positive, in contrast to their being negative for the other categories of cities as well as for all cities. These are:

- crime;
- ambience;
- percentage of housing that is owner-occupied;
- migration; and
- residents aged 65 and older as a share of the local population.

So for the smallest cities these variables rise with city size, while they diminish for all others. Conversely, for the following variables, the correlations are negative for the smallest cities but positive for the three other city sizes. These are:

- university graduates as a share of the population;
- professional, scientific, and technical workers as a share of total employment;
- taxes per capita; and
- households with income of $200,000 or more.

The values for some of these variables would be considered to be positive aspects of smaller cities, such as ambience, migration, and taxes per capita, while the values for others, such as crime, university graduates, and professional, scientific, and technical workers, would be considered to have negative impacts. But the main point to be made here is that in these nine variables the smallest cities are decidedly different than their larger counterparts, albeit the differences may in some cases be rather small. It should also be noted that both the smallest and the largest category of city differ from the two middle categories with regard to unemployment and the Piketty variable. The largest cities differ from the others with regard to the correlation between city size and physicians per 100,000 residents, and debt per capita. For all city categories, there is a positive correlation between city size and taxes per capita, households with at least $100,000 income, income per capita, and a negative correlation between city size and population growth, and federal grants per capita. Again, many of the variables lack robust positive or negative correlation with city size but they do attest to the fact that cities of larger or smaller populations are different from each other. Smaller cities do appear to have both distinct advantages and distinct disadvantages with regard to larger cities.

Only with regard to government transfer expenditures per capita do the two smallest city sizes differentiate themselves from larger cities. This is not the case when we correlate variables with urban competitiveness. In Table 4.2 we present the correlations between the competitiveness index we created and 16 variables representing aspects of city economies. Here we note that the two smallest city categories are differentiated from larger cities with regard to ambience, where their coefficients are positive and larger cities negative, and with regard to:

- physicians per 100,000 residents;
- universities;
- university educated; and
- debt per capita;

where their coefficients are negative and those of larger cities are positive. With the Piketty variable, the coefficients for the three smaller city categories are positive whereas that of the largest cities is negative. All four categories of cities have positive correlations with regard to:

- crime;
- migration;
- population growth; and
- professional, scientific, and technical workers.

They have negative correlations with regard to government transfers per capita and the 65 and older cohort of the population. However, it must be noted that here the coefficients are even less robust than they were with regard to city size.

Table 4.2 Correlations with the competitiveness index

Variable	All cities	2 million	1–2 million	500,000	250,000
Ambience	0.035701	-0.094286	-0.034424	0.232347	0.192632
Government transfer expenditure per capita	-0.085145	0.229356	-0.497174	-0.329321	-0.028140
Crime	0.044422	0.107015	0.065390	0.000045	0.099940
Migration	0.135799	0.487544	0.256316	0.371487	0.206095
Poverty	-0.075438	-0.390488	-0.295959	0.076392	-0.017415
Physicians	0.037552	-0.084510	0.164273	-0.059005	-0.353374
Unemployment	-0.071364	-0.603425	0.019266	-0.000460	-0.075315
Universities	-0.061810	0.137722	0.041211	-0.248026	-0.065922
Population	-0.041658	-0.124365	0.034671	0.093362	-0.194390
Population growth	0.285810	0.466128	0.365944	0.500074	0.248181
University educated	0.025932	-0.015961	0.158103	-0.088828	-0.105578
65 and older	-0.107840	-0.097842	-0.406055	-0.136377	-0.021764
Taxes per capita	-0.059598	-0.105008	-0.030211	-0.265038	0.021610
Debt per capita	0.022047	0.226586	0.334270	-0.076526	-0.008922
Earnings from labor/earnings from capital	0.018420	0.166829	0.007816	0.098242	0.082129
Professional, scientific, and technical employment/total employment	0.019091	0.477691	0.019091	0.078875	0.113062

Interpretation of the coefficients for urban competitiveness is rather more tenuous than they are with regard to city size. In both cases a fuller multi-variable regression analysis would have thrown some of these variables into greater significance than has been shown here, and would have caused us to exclude others. All we can do with this analysis is to demonstrate that smaller cities are indeed different in many aspects, and that some of these differences work to the benefit of the smaller cities.

Kotkin's alternatives to the large city

Joel Kotkin has offered a set of three alternatives to the largest of our cities; smaller cities that afford combinations of assets that give one or more satisfying places in which to work and to live (Kotkin 1990, chapter 2). He begins his argument with the notion of "the anti-urban impulse." Individuals do not seek isolation as much as they do interaction on their own terms. These individuals have a far more nuanced understanding of where they want to locate themselves and of the criteria they will take into account. He offers us a set of three alternatives to the large city: (1) midopolis, (2) nerdistan, and (3) small towns. Each in its own way enables individuals to escape from a situation in a large city that they now find to be less congenial and less supportive.

The **midopolis** is essentially the outer ring of suburban development of a large city. The core gradually diminished as a preferred place for work and residence. First the urban dwellers sought more space, better schools, and lower taxes, and then they were followed by companies, particularly in the science-based economy of research and telecommunications, and in cities such as Boston, New York, Chicago, Los Angeles, and San Francisco. Boston's I-128, northeastern New Jersey, and Silicon Valley are examples of this. As the technology economy developed, the midopolis proved to be inadequate for many firms and they gravitated toward major university towns, such as Austin, Salt Lake City, and Palo Alto. These **nerdistans** were attractive to young, unmarried workers with graduate degrees in technology fields who find the urban core a bit too frenetic and disordered, and the midopolis too boring to be attractive. Contact among technology workers hundreds of miles apart is now as easy as is contact between the 10th and 20th floors of the same high-rise building, and many of them have participated in the **revenge of the small towns**. Advances in telecommunication have reduced the attractiveness for some of these workers of a hub airport, and the necessity to congregate in even a nerdistan. Lifestyle preferences are drawing them to smaller cities in close proximity to mountains, forests, beaches, and other recreational features. Not all technology workers have the identical preferences for relations with cultural institutions, crowds of similar people, recreational opportunities, and high-speed travel – if they did they would all live in similar places. But the alternatives presented by Kotkin make it clear that this is not the case. Cities that are big but not the largest of our cities, specialized university cities and towns, corporate campuses on the edge of large cities, and small but connected towns are all at least as attractive to many technology workers as are our largest mega-cities. Each category of urban work and residence option has its own attractiveness. There is clearly room for all of them.

Final thoughts on city size

In this chapter we have examined the advantages and the disadvantages that attach to city size or to the lack of it. The advantages of agglomeration are generally recognized, often as a key or essential element in competitive success; smaller cities are then thought to labor under a severe handicap. We have tried to make it clear that this is not necessarily the case. Large cities suffer under significant disadvantages because of their size. An internationally connected airport is to varying degrees offset by the disamenities of congestion, pollution, and lack of community. While these can be dealt with so they do not hinder competitiveness in many instances, they appear to be intractable. Favored large cities experience substantial inward migration of individuals from rural and/or isolated communities and from other cities that are suffering from loss of a major employer or industry – one thinks of steel and heavy manufacturing as well as supplies of raw materials. Technological change has also knocked the props out from under the economies of many cities of all sizes.

We have examined the concept of city size and whether there is such a thing as an optimal city size. This proved to be a very elusive concept and one is left with the understanding that there is a great range of city sizes that can be considered, if not optimal, capable of achieving success in competing for jobs, plant locations, and skilled labor. Perhaps more important is the notion of the economic core of a city. Certain sectors or activities will be the heart of a city's competitiveness and they may consist of a rather small portion of the labor force of the city. Several hundred thousand other residents who work in activities that have nothing to do with the city's competitive economy would make a medium-sized city into a large-sized city but would do nothing to make it more competitive or more significant economically. A rather small city with a couple of universities, a technologically savvy labor force, and a good set of urban amenities may very well be more competitive than a city twice its size.

Many of these notions were supported by the correlation analysis we presented. Some of the variables we examined worked to the advantage of larger cities but others did for smaller cities. Importantly, this work supported other studies that found no correlation between city size and competitiveness. In many instances there was little or no difference in the correlation of individual variables and large and small cities. In many areas we examined, a disadvantage that attached to being a smaller city has been eradicated over time through advances in the technologies of production, transportation, and communication. Large firms disaggregated their functions into smaller entities that could most effectively be done in locations other than large cities. Cheaper transportation made it easier for small cities to "borrow size," to use Alonso's term. Better communication has made it easier for smaller cities to establish and participate in networks that enable them to participate in "clusters" that lack proximity. All of this has worked to the advantage of smaller cities.

There is no need to reiterate all of the points that have been made in this chapter. Suffice it to say, the world does not belong to the largest cities, in fact with extreme city size may come diseconomies and deterioration of an initial advantage. But it behooves the leaders of smaller cities to work to make their local economies capable of competing on a continental or global basis. In its study *How Regions Grow*, the OECD stated:

> The new regional approach is based on the principle that opportunities for growth exist in the entire territory, across all types of regions. The aim is to maximize national output by encouraging each individual region to reach its growth potential from within.
>
> (OECD 2009, p. 5)

We concluded the chapter with Kotkin's cautionary comments that there are effective alternatives to the largest cities and that the smaller cities are seen by many young and skilled workers and by many seniors as attractive alternatives to the large cities that have captured so much attention in recent years.

5 Public policy and small cities in North America

Cities are situated in multi-scalar structures of national and sub-national governments, each of which has its own capacities, authorizations, ambitions, and responsibilities. Large cities often rely on the political clout they are able to muster to get the funding and other support they seek for projects that are often international in their impact. To be sure, they have local projects having to do with urban renewal, crime prevention, recreational and other facilities and structures, and economic development, but they also host sporting, cultural, and business-related events that capture the attention and the participation of entities and individuals from all over the world. These initiatives require the participation and sometimes the co-sponsorship of sub-national and national governments, and even international bodies for events such as international sporting events, world Congresses, heritage site development, cultural expositions, and so forth. Even with activities the consequences of which are limited to the national space, given the assumption that there exist positive externalities that benefit individuals, firms, and other cities and regions, those promoting these ventures invariably seek financial support from national and sub-national entities defined by a scale that captures these benefits. Large cities tend to reach in all directions for financial assistance in their projects.

In European nations, the capital city tends to be the dominant city economically and all other cities lag considerably behind, as is shown recently in research conducted for an ESPON project (Parkinson *et al.* 2015). However in the majority of EU countries the GDP growth rate of the capital is lower than for many second-tier cities, indicating a dynamism that may cause this structural relationship to change in the future as non-capital cities come into their own economically (Parkinson *et al.* 2015, p. 159). Capital cities have several advantages that have traditionally put them in favorable positions: the national political agencies have considerable power and resources, and decision-makers seem to prefer to make expenditures that make the place in which they live and work as vital and congenial as possible. These cities are also the locations of many of the nation's premier educational institutions and research agencies, and they and their research staffs naturally attract investments from the business community. Being close to political power is also attractive to foreign companies when they locate their national or, in some cases, continental head offices. Finally, capital cities generally have the most advanced transportation, communication, and other infrastructure in the nation. For these reasons, capital cities in the EU tend to dominate their national economic spaces. However, Parkinson *et al.* warn us that

> national governments which concentrate attention and resources on their capital cities risk increasing uneven development with whole regions and cities missing out on chances to enter the new economy. Second-tier cities although less able to act on the global state, can still generate important dynamism for regions outside the capital and contribute to overall national growth. In many cases they punch beyond their weight.
>
> (Parkinson *et al.* 2015, p. 1064)

In the US the situation is quite different. Historically, there has been a powerful urge to separate political and economic power. So while Washington is the political capital, and has captured some investments and activities that seek to be close to political power, the economic power has always been first in Philadelphia and then in New York City. Other large cities such as Chicago and Los Angeles, and more recently, Houston, Seattle, Atlanta, San Francisco, among others, have developed their own national presence and international competitiveness and strengths. This separation of economic and political power holds true even within states: Chicago and Springfield in Illinois, New York City and Albany in New York, Los Angeles/San Francisco and Sacramento in California, are only three of dozens of such examples. The way is then open for non-capital cities in the US in a way that is not the case in the EU.

Another factor that aids non-capital and second-tier cities in the US is that while in the EU government policy and spending, at the EU and at national and sub-national levels, dominate much of the economic scene for cities, government has had, and continues to have, a far less important role to play in the US. In fact, in 2008 while 30 percent of local government revenues came from the state government, the federal government share was only 4 percent (Congressional Budget Office 2010, p. 3). Cities do, of course, require government funding for very important specific projects, and we will elaborate on this later in this chapter. For specific projects of local transportation infrastructure, natural disaster recovery, social housing, small business development, education at all levels, and assistance to low-income residents, the cities need outside money, most of which must come from superior levels of government. But if all cities must compete on the basis of their objective characteristics, capital cities in many states are at a disadvantage in that they were often situated in rather isolated places, the principal advantage of which was that it was relatively convenient for horse travel between home and capital by the legislators – Harrisburg, Pennsylvania, and Springfield, Illinois, are two good examples of this. Many of these capital cities find it difficult to meet the competition of smaller cities with good universities/colleges, proximity to larger markets, access to interstate highways and larger airports, and less of a bureaucratic mindset for decision-making.

Historically, US cities, including some rather small ones, also have recourse to a far a greater degree than EU cities to cooperation and assistance from the business sector and from universities. While many large firms seek out concessions from municipal and state governments, such as tax breaks, development grants, and regulatory relief that will enhance their position in the market, before committing to a decision on location, many others simply move to a location that makes business sense. Smaller cities are rarely in a position to be able to offer much in the way of financial assistance, but they can cooperate with zoning changes, local infrastructure improvements, and similar measures that can be very important to business investors. Universities, both public and private, have been very active in developing "eds and meds" strategies for smaller cities, and university faculty and departments have been instrumental in developing agricultural programs from wine to avocados to bio-fuels. In addition, many small firm start-ups in the technology sector have been the result of faculty realizing the commercial potential of their research in the market. We will examine some of these activities in Chapter 7 when we look at some smaller US cities.

Smaller cities have to learn how to achieve and to maintain their economic vitality in competition for support for initiatives that may be largely focused on their immediate region. A national or sub-national government entity may announce a competition for funding for some project for local development, infrastructure, housing, or recreation or cultural facilities, and each city must design a proposal and submit it in a competition with many other similar cities. In Chapter 3 we examined the capacity of smaller cities to be successful in these sorts of initiatives.

This chapter will focus on three specific aspects of the economic situation of smaller cities and their economic planning initiatives. Of crucial importance in these initiatives is the funding that is available from superior levels of government and the willingness of the political process of each to entertain government support for projects of city governments. This has become increasingly under question in recent years, and we will examine state and national level funding and participation in detail in the first section of this chapter under the rubric "fiscal federalism." A separate question is what one could reasonably expect a superior level of government to be able to accomplish with regard to supporting city initiatives; that is what are the capacities of these levels of government to offer financial assistance as well as of smaller cities to use it effectively? This will be discussed in the second section of the chapter. In the final section we will examine what cities can reasonably be expected to do and what their capabilities for action are. Do smaller cities have the experience, skills, and local resources to engage successfully in strategic economic planning?

This chapter is paired with Chapter 7 in which we will examine the experiences of three sets of smaller cities in the US and the extent to which these cities have realized the potential for action that will emerge from the discussion of this chapter.

US fiscal federalism – then and now

Financial relations between national and sub-national governments are difficult and complex everywhere. There are many reasons for this, some local and others more general. Essentially, the issue is the nature of the specific responsibilities of each level of government to work to achieve the three Musgravian objectives: stability of output, equity in the distribution of income, and efficiency in the allocation of resources (Musgrave 1959, chapter 1). While the attention that must be given to each of these objectives is a continuing necessity, in the shorter term each may require increased or reduced effort by individual levels of government. The business cycle and periodic booms and busts generate extraordinary work on stability of output; demographic changes and macro-economic events make equity in income distribution a continual problem, and the allocation of resources must be responsive to both short-term and long-term changes in demand for goods and services.

On the spending side, each level of government has by law access to certain specific sources of revenues. The situation is made complex by the fact that, over time, the streams of revenue that each source generates will increase at different rates. The most general and the most responsive is the taxation of personal and corporate income. Income taxes in the US have varied from 90 percent for individuals in the 1950s, to 35 percent today, and they could be increased to high levels overnight if there were the need and political will to do this. Since most citizens pay this personal income tax and most businesses pay the corporate income tax, tax can generate an enormous stream of revenue. This wonderful source of income is the primary source of revenue for the US federal government and many states have levied income taxes, but it is not available to municipalities. These sources of funding are summarized in Table 5.1.

One of the problems with this distribution of funding sources by level of government is that not all of the sources grow at the same rate of increase or with the same degree of reliability. One of the mainstays of municipal finance, the property tax, has remained rather steady historically, but between 2006 and 2010 the recession and the financial excesses of this period caused property values to plummet by 27 percent. There was no immediate impact on property tax revenues because the impact is usually not felt for about three years, but by 2011

Table 5.1 Sources of revenue by level of government, 2010 (percentage)

Level/source	Income*	Sales	Property	Transfers	Other	Payroll
National	46/13	–	–	–	9	32
States	15/2	22	–	37	24	–
Municipalities	2/0	6	30	38	25	–

Source: Tax Policy Center, *The Tax Briefing Book*, May 7, 2013.

Note
* Personal/corporate.

they had begun to decline – by 3.9 percent followed by a decline of 2.1 percent in 2012 and 0.4 percent in 2013 (National League of Cities 2014). This weakness is anticipated to continue for the near future. Municipal sales tax receipts have always been more volatile, dependent as they are on current economic conditions. Growth in receipts plummeted from 6 percent in 1998 to −5 percent three years later, and from 2 percent in 2008 to −8 percent in 2010 before soaring to 6 percent two years later. The combination of these two primary sources of municipal funding creates considerable instability of revenues. Municipalities vary in the degree to which they utilize these two sources of revenue, with all using property taxes and about half using sales taxes as well. State aid to municipalities varies dramatically. While the average is 18 percent of general revenue, seven states offer 30 percent and eight of them offer 6 percent or less (National League of Cities, 2015, p. 20). Federal government transfers to municipalities are only 4 percent of their total revenues, but state governments receive substantial transfers of federal funds for a variety of uses, including health care, education, highway construction, housing, and public assistance; much of this is spent in municipalities with their direct participation. Furthermore, there are several aspects of the federal tax code that work to increase funds available to municipalities.

Arguably the most powerful impact the federal government has on local governments' economies is through its macro-economic policy (Kenyon 2003, p. 170). When Washington chooses not to use its monetary and fiscal policy options, because of ideology or indifference, the entire economy may suffer from rapid inflation or from recession or depression. Recessions have sometimes disastrous impacts on local sales, property and income tax receipts, and inflation can have a negative long-term impact on city finances. In fact, Ingram and Hong identify this as the "root cause of municipal fiscal crises" (Ingram and Hong 2010, p. 23). New York rather famously had its difficulties in 1975, and more recently both Jefferson County in Alabama and Orange County in California defaulted on their debt. This has happened to only 54 of 18,400 municipal bond issuers between 1970 and 2009, but it is certainly troubling to those municipalities to which this happens (Congressional Budget Office 2010, p. 9). In response to the then current major recession, Congress passed the American Recovery and Reinvestment Act in 2009. This act gave substantial short-run relief to state and local governments that were suffering from the decline in revenues from their sources, sales, income, and property taxes; however, this is not expected to have a significant impact on the projected budget deficits for these governments (Government Accountability Office 2010).

For the coming decades, the forecast for state and local finances is rather grim. While the macro-economic situation has a major impact on this, the looming cost issue is projected to be rising health care costs for state and local governments.

Finally, there is the important issue of "unfunded mandates," whereby the federal government enacts programs that require action by lower levels of government, but does not supply the funding to carry them out. Examples of this would be environmental regulations requiring, e.g., treatment plants for waste-water, the Safe Drinking Act of 1996, restoration of toxic abandoned industrial sites, Americans with disabilities, health care (Medicaid), and mandates for education policy and practice. It has been estimated that when Homeland Security issues a terrorist alert, New York spends an extra $5 million per week and Los Angeles pays $1 million. These mandates shifted billions of dollars of expenses to the levels of states and municipalities and caused considerable neg-ative response from these levels of government. Some relief was given by the Unfunded Mandates Reform Act of 1995, although there were several exemp-tions that kept this from giving local governments complete relief (Nivola 2003, pp. 1–3, 8).

What we learn from this is that municipal finances have elements of variabil-ity that negatively affect this level of government, and that municipal govern-ments are dependent upon the good will and financial capability of higher levels of government. The willingness of these levels of government to work support-ively and predictably with municipalities is something that we will now examine.

The decline of national and sub-national governments as actors in competitiveness

In this section we will examine four aspects of this worrying situation that federal government finances cause for municipal governments: (1) fiscal dif-ficulties tied to debt reduction and austerity; (2) the political attack on govern-ment from the conservative right wing; (3) the political gridlock that exists in Washington between the two houses of Congress and between them and the executive branch; and (4) the issue of divided loyalties between rural and urban policies in state capitals.

A prescient forecast of **fiscal difficulties** was offered in 2003 by Daphne Kenyon who wrote: "A critical issue in the coming years will be the temptation for the federal government to react to its declining budget surpluses by cutting grant-in-aid to state and local governments" (Kenyon 2003, p. 164). The fiscal difficulties are largely self-inflicted by government in Washington. The scenario begins with the cutting of regulations that exerted some control over what finan-cial institutions could do in the market. Abrogation of the Depression Era (1933) Glass–Steagall Act, through legislative action and Alan Greenspan-led Federal Reserve reinterpretation of the act, formalized the transformation of US banking from a rather boring deposit and loan management enterprise to the much more exciting world of investment banking, derivatives, sub-prime mortgages, and variable rate mortgages. It can be argued that this was the proximate cause of the housing bubble and financial crisis of 2006–2007, and the dramatic recession that followed it.

The response of many in Congress to recession is always to cut taxes to induce wealthy individuals to spend more of their money, and to balance the federal government budget by cutting social program expenditures. While the latter invariably has its full, anticipated impact, the former usually remains simply a promise to be kept. Budget deficits may be avoided, but so too will their stimulatory effect. This anti-Keynesian approach to macro-economic stabilization policy removes the one policy tool that is available to policy-makers. State and local governments are often required to balance their budgets and in practice they have tended to take a pro-cyclical position. In fact, in 2010 75 percent of federal grants to state governments were used to cover state budget deficits rather than to fund new projects (Henning and Kessler 2012, pp. 14–15).

Absent counter-cyclical policy at the federal level, a robust recovery from the Great Recession has not been possible. Monetary policy conducted by the independent Federal Reserve Bank, a small stimulus package the Obama administration has been able to coax out of Congress, and some actions the president has been able to take have succeeded in reducing unemployment and increasing GDP growth, albeit more weakly than should have been the case. While unemployment in the US is less than half that of the Euro area, 5.4 percent versus 11.1 percent, and GDP growth is double, 2.3 percent versus 1.1 percent, there is concern that wages in the US have not grown significantly and that many workers are still not back in the labor force. The recovery, absent adequate fiscal policy stimulation, is generally considered to be anemic.

This macro-economic weakness has had, and continues to have, strong negative impacts on state and local finances. This will be detailed in the section that follows.

The **right-wing budget attack** on federal and state government has its origin in the belief that the private sector can do what needs to be done to manage a modern economy with little or no participation by government. Ranging from the rational position of Friedrich von Hayek and other free-market economists to the less rational ideological writings of Ayn Rand, this approach has mobilized many in the Senate and especially in the House of Representatives to seek to introduce policies promoting "small government" without regard to what data or economic reason tell them. As Kevin Kruse argues, in the post-World War II years the business community mounted an attack on the New Deal legislation of the Roosevelt administration through legislation to remove restrictions on what America's oligopolistic industries could do to take advantage of their market power vis-à-vis consumers (Kruse 2015, chapter 1). Once their income streams had been augmented, they sought to reduce taxation of wealthy people. Personal income tax rates have indeed fallen from about 90 percent in the 1950s to 35 percent today. This was done under the guise of a policy of Christian libertarianism. In the front of the initiative was the promotion of religion, and of social issues such as anti-abortion, anti-LGBT, anti-welfare, and anti-government health and education. Promotion of these social issues was simply a front to get the population behind the small government initiative.

In 2011 Congress passed the Budget Control Act that instituted spending cuts (sequestration) of $1.2 trillion between 2013 and 2020. This policy, which was directly counter to what would have been proposed by John Maynard Keynes, was done in the midst of the most severe recession the country had faced since the 1930s. Unemployment rose significantly, incomes fell, and state government budgets were negatively affected through loss of revenue. Cuts in spending for social programs also shifted the burden for provision to needy individuals to state and local governments.

This has manifested itself most recently in the Paul Ryan budget proposals. Ryan's objective is that of cutting federal government spending by $5.5 trillion over the next decade. There will be no new tax increases and with defense, disease prevention, border control, the FBI, veterans' health care and some other similar items not being cut, the entire burden will fall on state and local programs such as education, roads and bridges, public health, law enforcement, and alleviation of poverty. One trillion dollars are expected to be gained from cuts in unspecified programs such as food stamps and welfare – programs that benefit the lowest income citizens (Weisman 2015). It was estimated that grants to state and local governments would fall by 22 percent, by $28 billion in 2014 alone, and when combined with the reductions through sequestration the loss could be $247 billion from 2013 through 2021 (Leachman *et al.* 2012). In Ryan's own district in Wisconsin, Janesville, the president of Forward Janesville, John Beckord, attributes the recovery of the city's economy from loss of a major GM plant and 5,000 jobs to expansion of Interstate 90 that enabled the city to restructure itself as a major distribution center for major companies, situated as it is between Chicago, Milwaukee, Madison, St Louis, and Des Moines. Without federal grants to state and local governments the city would in all likelihood be wallowing in inactivity (Lizza 2012, p. 12).

What the Ryan proposals do not reduce directly they accomplish by transferring responsibility to state governments. Since the majority of state legislatures and governorships are held currently by conservative Republicans, it has been left to them to do the rest of the attack on expenditures for social programs which they have been doing with enthusiasm.

The atmosphere in Washington has become dominated by **political gridlock** at least since the beginning of the Democratic Obama administration. Senate minority leader Mitch McDonnell set the scene when, shortly after President Obama's inauguration, he stated that his primary objective was to see the failure of the administration and its replacement by a Republican one. In the House the rise of the ultra-conservative Tea Party group brought in a substantial group of representatives who espoused the anti-government Christian-libertarian philosophy of lower taxes, especially on the wealthy, reduced social expenditures, and cuts on staple items such as social security, Medicaid, and Medicare, as well as reducing the federal role in education. In general, states should be able to manage most programs and since, as noted above, much of state government was in the hands of Republicans, the attack could be continued at this level. Exacerbating this situation is the fact that a great many of the Congressional districts have been "gerrymandered" so that urban, low-income and minority populations are underrepresented in the Congress, and the Tea Party representatives can be assured of continued re-election as long as they keep to the party line on policy. The result is that the House and Senate have been gridlocked in inactivity, with the naming of post offices after past political leaders being the dominant result of recent sessions. At one point in 2013 it got so bad that there was a government shut-down, the cost of which has been estimated at $24 billion, 0.06 percent of GDP, and a loss of 900,000 jobs (Islam and Crego 2013).

Gridlock caused the population to have a powerfully negative view of politics in Washington, except for the local representative who was articulating the dominant view in his gerrymandered district. There was an incentive to increase gridlock when the Democrats were dominant in the Senate and the Republicans were in the House. However bad things were, at least the blame had to be shared, it was argued, by both parties. Since this meant that the president was unable to get legislation through both houses he was seen as inept as well. There is some hope, now that the Republicans have control of both the House and the Senate, that they will see that gridlock and inaction will increasingly be seen as caused by them, and that the party may see that it is now in its interest, with a presidential election coming in 2016, to pass some legislation, even in collaboration with the president.

State and local governments have been powerfully affected by the inability of Congress to pass legislation and by the hostility of powerful Tea Party voices in the party to vote against urban issues and policies, whether for large cities or for small.

Both Washington and state capitals exhibit **divided loyalties** when it comes to funding projects. Cities have difficulty getting the appropriate share of funding from superior levels of government because of the powerful position in government of agricultural and natural resource areas. One of the concrete problems is the over-representation in legislatures of these districts and the under-representation of urban areas. Small states tend to be rural and large states tend to be urban, or to house the nation's major urban centers. Hence in the Senate and the House in Washington, agriculture and resource issues get greater support than do urban issues such as passenger rail travel, housing, industrial site restoration, welfare, immigrant services, and so forth. In fact the 38 million residents of urban California (Los Angeles, San Francisco, San Diego, and Sacramento) have two senators while the 38 million residents of 22 small states have 44 senators (Liptak 2013).

Senator Ted Stevens (Republican), who chaired the Senate Appropriations Committee, during 1997–2005, was famous for his energetic sponsorship of the "Bridge to Nowhere" that would serve a small community in rural Alaska. There are, of course, many other examples as egregious as this. In the House, Congressman Bud Shuster (Republican), Chairman of the House Committee on Transportation and Infrastructure (1995–2001), did much to authorize construction of wonderful four-lane expressways in his district in a rural part of Pennsylvania, while Philadelphia and Pittsburgh were denied funding for their transportation projects. Again, there are many examples of rural districts being favored over cities. In its study of the Pennsylvania economy, the Brookings Institution found that rural and agricultural areas had consistently been over-funded, while cities had been under-funded. Their conclusion was that "Pennsylvania should turn its focus back to its towns, cities, and older townships as a way of reenergizing its future" (Brookings 2003, p. 110). Attention to agriculture and rural districts was depriving the economy of the investment in education, infrastructure, small business assistance, urban renewal, low-income housing, and other economic and social programs that were crucial to the long-term competitiveness of the Pennsylvania economy. The same is true for other more urban states, such as California, Illinois, New York, New Jersey, Ohio, and Michigan, and increasingly for evolving states such as Texas, Colorado, and Georgia.

The conclusion one has to draw from discussion of these four troubling aspects of US fiscal federalism is that state and local governments are receiving less in the way of fiscal transfers for programs that have historically been shared by all levels of government, that unfunded mandates are still being issued to their financial detriment, that Congressional indifference to weak macroeconomic performance is reducing state and local revenues, and that the traditional partnership has been frayed significantly. The specific consequences of this will be clearer when we examine what cities should legitimately expect from higher levels of government and what they can do by and for themselves.

What can smaller cities expect of other levels of government?

Each level of government has the capacity to assist smaller cities in distinct ways. In the US this is partly due to specific items in the US Constitution, in part due to legislative actions and decisions by the president or a governor, and in part due to the effectiveness of action at that level. It is clear that the national and state governments have different roles vis-à-vis cities. After examining national and state governments we will consider the options and responsibilities of cities.

The **national government** has constitutional responsibilities that have powerful impacts on cities. One of the most important is that of keeping the international borders and inter-state commerce open to the free flow of goods and services. Economic theory tells us that trade restrictions enable city economies to specialize in activities that will not be sustainable in the long term. Either producers in other countries will out-compete them, or technology will make these products or their mode of production obsolete. In either event the city economy will enter a process of slow decline. Freeing trade offers the producers in all countries the opportunity to specialize in the things they do best and to leave the industries they do not do well. This may be a frictionless transition on the chalk board, but in reality many workers are deprived of employment and income. Trade liberalization was made palatable to workers and their unions when, in 1962, President Kennedy included Trade Adjustment Assistance. This initiative offered workers and firms damaged by freer trade funding for development of new skills, relocation assistance for workers, and restructuring funds for firms. Typically, Congress has failed to fund trade adjustment adequately and those damaged by freer trade have had little recourse but to struggle on their own. Hence, when the Trans-Pacific Trade Pact was put before the Congress in

2015, labor and their representatives in the House and Senate rebelled against it. Only promises to fund it fully brought them around.

Open inter-state commerce is even more important for the smaller cities, since this often plays a more powerful role for them than does international trade.

The Inter-state Commerce Act was passed in 1887 to curb the market power of railroad companies that had begun to form trusts, cartels, collusive arrangements, and other measures to dominate markets. In the first Article of the US Constitution (Section 8), Congress is given the power to regulate commerce among the states, as well as with foreign countries. Smaller cities have a strong interest in trade liberalization and in open borders with other countries and especially among the states, since their local and regional markets do not allow them to achieve the economies that are necessary for their survival and for high incomes based on productivity.

Of perhaps equal importance is the authority the national government has in harmonizing regulations and economic practices throughout the territory of the US. A patchwork quilt of separate state or even local regulations would have the potential to stymie economic interaction among city economies.

Beyond these regulatory responsibilities of the national government, fiscal federalism mandates that Washington participate, using its efficient taxation on incomes, in funding of local projects, such as conference centers, sports stadia and recreational facilities, educational building and initiatives, health facilities, cultural projects, urban renewal, and low-income housing. On a larger scale, Washington also contributes to highway maintenance and construction, air and rail transportation, waterways, irrigation, and forest management. All of these programs have powerful impacts on smaller cities since dramatic increases in sales and property taxes for full funding of local projects often have the effect of making the city less attractive to skilled and mobile workers, and as a site for production by firms. Considerations of economic efficiency argue for strong national government participation in the funding of local projects, such as those identified here.

One unsettling aspect of federal transfers is that with regard to states, the net tax-transfer relationship is so disparate. At one end, the tax-transfer ratio for Delaware is over 200 percent of its GDP, and for four other states, Minnesota, New Jersey, Illinois, and Connecticut the ratio is over 100 percent. At the other end, West Virginia, New Mexico, Mississippi, and Puerto Rico all gain at least 200 percent of their GDP in transfers, and another dozen bring back over 100 percent. The consequence of this for smaller cities is that, since much of the federal transfers to states are spent on city projects or passed on through to them, the federal government's relationship with cities varies considerably depending upon which state the city happens to be located. A city in Connecticut will have a dramatically different relationship than will one in New Mexico.

Finally, commenting on the period during which the Carter, Reagan, and H. W. Bush administrations were introducing a "new federalism" with the federal government increasing its participation in local initiatives, Pagano and Moore argue that this introduced a new element of instability into local finances, as the federal interest waxed and waned. This led to many of the resources city govern-ments had to default and bankruptcy (Pagano and Moore 1985, chapter 5). A contributory element in this movement toward city financial difficulty was the great pressure on city governments, by local boosters as well as by the national government and the international organizations involved, to support efforts to host events such as the Olympic Games or the football (soccer) World Cup. Zim-balist has found that there is little to support the notion that these events can work to the financial and economic advantage of the city:

> In the short run the increasingly massive costs of hosting cannot come close to being matched by the modest revenues that are brought in by the games … the main legacy consists of white elephants that cost billions to build and millions annually to maintain, along with mountains of debt that must be paid back over ten to thirty years.
>
> (Zimbalist 2015, chapter 7)

Often the national government disappears when the debts come due.

State governments often participate with the federal government in infra-structure, social, educational, and cultural programs. It must be said, however, that of total revenues of local governments, only 4 percent consist of aid from the federal government, while 30 percent come from the state governments, although some of the state funds are transferred from the federal government (Congressional Budget Office 2010, p. 3).

Many state agencies and commissions provide funding for local projects including recreation and cultural programs, forest and game lands maintenance, town development, rural roads and other infrastructure, business development, senior programs, and so forth. Through its department of economic or com-munity development, a state government can give vital assistance to the coordin-ation of economic and political actors. The department can bring together specialists in various activities with local officials, share the experiences of other cities, participate in the planning and execution of economic development plan-ning, and assist in energizing the local business community. State development funding can be used to get local projects off the ground and can signal the value of the initiative to other potential funding agencies.

Many state governments try to equalize expenditure per student in elementary and high schools so as to offset the disadvantage of students in poorer districts. In part, this disadvantage comes from the difficulty school boards in poorer dis-tricts have in generating revenues through property taxes – the properties in their districts are lower in price and their owners have lower incomes. One example of this is the state of Vermont, which introduced equalization in 1997. The wealthier districts fought this initiative, wanting to retain their advantage. The compromise was to allow the wealthier districts to top up the funding above what the equalized state funding provided (Vermont Department of Education 2011). Equalization, to the extent that it is implemented, can bring considerable advantages to smaller and poorer towns, especially those in rural areas, since education is one of the primary factors in generating economic growth and enhancing competitiveness.

Finally, state agencies can give assistance to smaller towns in developing the effectiveness of, or enhancing the performance of, structures of local governance. The state can be an agent that helps to bring together representatives of government, business, universities, social agencies, low-income residents, seniors, and minorities in a structure that will greatly assist in the development of effective economic and community planning. Many civil servants have been operating in this area for an extended period of time and have a great deal of knowledge, many acquaintances, and access to strategic economic planning professionals, as well as to potential sources of funding.

Two researchers for the Brookings Institution have written, in this spirit, that:

> federal and state governments act as partners with their cities and metropolitan areas around common issues of national significance. In some cases, cities and metros lead and states and the federal government follow. In other cases, it is the reverse. But in either case, mutual respect and comity hold.
>
> (Katz and Bradley 2013, p. 184)

What can smaller cities do?

As is clear by now, the superior levels of government have very extensive impacts on the economies of smaller cities. The full range of infrastructure and social and economic programs is affected by the decisions and capability of these levels of government to provide steady and predictable support for effective planning at the city level. As we have seen, that level of financial support is not at all certain and many cities have experienced serious difficulties when anticipated support was not forthcoming or was withdrawn. Parkinson *et al.* comment that "Cities perform better in those countries which are less centralized and economically concentrated and where cities have greater powers, resources and responsibilities" (2015, p. 1061). Perhaps this uncertainty of stable funding is one of the reasons for this.

Local governments have to work in collaboration with the superior levels of government due to the lack of sufficient funding obtainable from the sources at their disposal, primarily sales and property, and in some cases income, taxes. The big items such as transportation infrastructure, hospital and school construction, for example, are far beyond the means available to local authorities, and in many cases they bring broader regional benefits. However, local authorities' role in the process is crucial since they must ascertain what projects will benefit the community and how they link with other aspects, such as economic or community development or competitiveness enhancement, and with other cities. This opens the discussion to the role of local authorities in effective economic-strategic planning.

It is clear that the smaller city must initiate the process of planning and must begin by establishing a structure of participation that generates a course of development that will be enthusiastically supported by all, or almost all, of the principal entities in the community – business, education, social, government, age groups, health care, recreational, and cultural. This has been referred to as the "urban knowledge architecture," and the need for both consensus and inclusiveness is central to it (Nomninos 2013). This step is widely discussed and seen as necessary but it is usually not carried out effectively. Local powerful entities that have enjoyed a decision-making position for decades can be instinctually ill disposed to open the door to new partners in planning for the future development of the economy and the community; excluded groups have no stake in the planning process and have no interest in participating in it. The exclusion of their voices makes it virtually impossible to achieve the desired results. This is the first challenge in any planning process.

Once the city has decided to embark on a strategic economic planning process to enhance competitiveness, or perhaps just to maintain the vitality of the local economy, there are several important issues that must be confronted and dealt with. Here is a list of ten of them (Kresl 2007, p. 28):

1   How can the strategy of the planning exercise be set?
2   How can planners determine the best means of achieving the strategy of the plan?
3   Which entities can assist the effort, and which can hinder the planning process?
4   What can local governments control or affect or realistically hope to accomplish?
5   What do state and national governments control or affect?
6   How can local actors be most effectively mobilized?
7   How can costs be contained?
8   How can local government be made most effective?
9   What criteria should be used to assess success? How long should the evaluation period be?
10   What links to external entities, such as other similar cities, are useful?

Full discussion of these ten issues would take us far afield, given the focus of this discussion, but the reader can fill in much of the missing text through a few moments of reflection. Needless to say, these issues absolutely must be considered by those in the community – and not just those officials who are directly involved in the planning process. It is, however, worthwhile exploring briefly the nature of the first of these issues, that of determining the path that is to be pursued in the initiative.

The most important thing planners must do is gain an accurate understanding of the basic situation of their city's economy. First, they must have an objective assessment of the specific advantages and disadvantages, and strengths and weaknesses in comparison with the economies of other cities. Historic strengths may no longer be important in the contemporary economy; weaknesses often develop slowly over time and are not noticed. Are the industries and activities that are important today going to be as important in a decade or so? Second, they must take an objective look at the competition. Has technological change altered the economic space within which they operate? Is freer trade opening the city to competition from abroad? Should they be fearful of the impact of China, India, and other developing economies? Or should they try to work with them?

Third, the new era may require the increased participation by new leaders and leader firms. These must be integrated into a structure of decision-making that may cause tensions with the current leadership. However, without their participation, planning may be a fruitless activity. Fourth, they must explore the potential of industrial clusters and of participation in national or international networks. Networks can be thought of as clusters that are not limited by proximity; they can be extremely useful for smaller cities in which a cluster in one industry may not be feasible due to lack of size. Fifth, they must reflect on the possibilities of cooperation with superior levels of government. We have discussed at length the benefits and limitations of this, in the current fiscal and political situation, but there are beneficial programs and funding to be found.

As a final note, it must be observed that in the highly competitive environment of today and the near future, it is often the first city to initiate action and to move to develop strength or competitiveness in an area that gains the advantage. Inaction usually condemns a city to missing opportunities and marginalization. In all but the most dismal and hopeless situations, local action can lead to an improved situation tomorrow.

6   Public policies and small cities in the European Union

Large size is certainly not among the key features of the European urban system. If we consider the ranking of the top 30 largest cities in the world, we will find the first European cities only at the very last positions – given that only London has a metropolitan area of more than 15 million inhabitants and Paris has more than 10. The entire Rhine–Ruhr metropolitan region has slightly more than 10 million, but here there is a multi-polar network of more than 10 cities in four districts, where most of the single cities are well below 600,000 residents, except Cologne with approximately one million. Other continents are dominated by mega-cities, but the European territory is characterized rather by a relatively smaller size and by a predominantly polycentric structure in which cities are seen as a multi-polar network replicating at different geographical scales. This is usually accompanied by the idea that the more polycentric the territory is, the more cohesive and balanced it will be in its development.

In this framework, the keywords of discussion on the European "urban agenda" entails the idea of a European Union as a network of cities in the world economy, cities developing cross-border cooperation, integrated transport connections, integrated territorial development, cooperation in governance, collaboration on smart solutions, etc. We must underline that, when we mention "urban agenda" in the European Union framework, we refer to a long-lasting discussion with alternate fortunes, entailing an incredibly large number of documents, position papers, meetings, statements, interactions, that – to simplify a critical position – have not been translated yet into a concrete policy.

We will present this European reality in this chapter. It is in fact useful to explain how this differs from the urban reality in the USA when it comes to the analysis of the relationships between the city and other levels of government. In the European Union the discussion on the "urban agenda" involves the European Commission, the 28 member states (with very different levels of commitment on the subject), the individual cities and their provincial or regional authorities (differing in each state), a large number of other stakeholders, in particular when dealing with cross-border cooperation and integrated territorial development, which are in turn claimed as the key areas in which cities are involved. After introducing the issue of the "urban agenda," we will focus on how the discussion has recently been progressively focusing on the role of second-tier and small and medium-sized cities. This has been possible thanks to some research contributions provided by large cooperation projects involving scholars from many European countries, developed in the framework of the European Union cooperation programs, and thanks to a specific emphasis given on the subject by the latest (and current during the writing of this book) three six-month presidencies of the Council of the European Union.

Before discussing the role of second-tier cities in the policy discussion, we will devote a few pages to outlining the principal features of the European urban structure that might be of interest. We will not replicate here an exhaustive description of the European urban system, but we will rather discuss the role and position of second-tier and small and medium-sized cities in the European urban geography with regard to their demographical features and to their contribution to the formation of national and European GDP and GDP growth.

The geography of European second-tier cities

We do not need to replicate here a general outline of the structure of urbanization in Europe – which is well described in a number of sources, among whose we suggest the informative *Report on Economic, Social and Territorial Cohesion* produced regularly by the Directorate-General for Regional and Urban Policy (European Commission 2014). In a purely discursive way we could summarize some of the general features in the following:

• the urbanization pattern in Europe is as diverse as is the territory of the European Union itself: densely urbanized areas, large capitals, rural lands, islands, remote Nordic regions ... to cite only a few of the heterogeneous features of the European countries, which clearly have an impact on urbanization;
• the prevailing structure of many countries and regions is polycentric: rather than being dominated by a large urban pole, the structure is rather a multi-polar network of smaller cities;
• the peculiar urbanization structure in Europe depends on physical constraints, but above all by the long-time historical evolution of urban diffusion in the continent, in particular in the central area, from the southern part of the United Kingdom to northern Italy.

In this context, the presence of a significant structure of second-tier and smaller cities is confirmed by the demographic data, such as the share of the national population living in the capital cities. In most European countries, less than 20 percent of the total population reside in the capital cities, and remarkably, in a group of larger countries, the capitals have less than 10 percent (France, Belgium, Denmark, Romania, Slovakia, Spain) and some less than 5 percent (The Netherlands, Italy, Poland, Germany). Only in Malta do almost 50 percent of the population live in the capital city, Valletta, but Malta is a small island with evident geographical constraints. Only in Latvia, Estonia, Cyprus, Ireland, and

Greece does the capital city have a relative demographic importance of between 25 percent and 30 percent.

Despite this, it must be noted that in 2012 fully 71.7 percent of the population of the European Union lived in an urbanized area (European Commission 2014). We will not discuss this in detail, but given the peculiar pattern of urbanization in the European Union, there has been a great effort by Eurostat and others to elaborate a common definition of urban areas, using both geographical and functional methodologies in order to be able to categorize regional and sub-regional territories according to their prevailing urban or rural features. This is relevant for making available place-based information to inform policy-making when discussing the largest strategies affecting the entire European territory.

As we mentioned above, only a few cities in the European Union have a significant size. Only 30 cities have more than one million inhabitants; 41 have more than one-half million to one million; 101 with 250,000 to 500,000 residents and finally 383 with 100,000 to 250,000. Capital cities and important economic centers can be found in any of those categories and also in the very large number of European cities with fewer than 100,000 residents. This, combined with the information provided above, confirms the idea that second-tier cities are very relevant for the European framework – despite, as we will see, the fact that they have not been always considered as they should by policies.

The 2014 *Report on Economic, Social and Territorial Cohesion* (European Commission 2014, chapter 14) provides extensive discussion of the demographic features of the European cities. Among the most interesting aspects for our discussion, we would mention those related to age distribution. There are some general trends, such as the presence in some capital cities of a larger share of working-age population. This might lead one to consider that second-tier cities have a larger share of older population, and therefore an expected strong impact of age-related expenditure – or the eventual benefits, as we previously discussed.

Another aspect relevant for the thesis presented in this book is the different availability of housing in larger or smaller cities. In a perception survey conducted in 79 cities in 2012 (European Commission 2013) a question was included asking about satisfaction with the ease of finding good housing: it must be noted that among the less satisfied were the residents of larger capital cities, while among the most satisfied we find smaller second-tier cities in many countries of very different areas of the European Union.

This brief presentation of the European context needs to be completed also with regard to economic data. Considerations are limited as a consequence of the lack of homogeneous data for the 28 countries, in particular for the post-crisis years (2011 and later). However we are able to refer indirectly to some studies published on the issue.

After their analysis in the ESPON SGPTD project (see below), Parkinson *et al.* (2015) are able to argue that in some countries, the federal states in particular, second-tier cities have outperformed the capital cities with regard to their GDP growth. They also see the good performance of many capital cities as a consequence of a disproportionate concentration of investments at the expense of second-tier cities, which will unavoidably lead to an unbalanced territorial development in many countries, in Central and Eastern Europe in particular. In another study, Evans compares the share of national GDP produced by capital and by second-tier cities, confirming the remarkable contribution of the latter to the national GDP: on average they contributed 23.2 percent to national GDP in 2009 versus the 34.8 percent contributed by capital cities (Evans 2015). As to this figure, there is a relevant difference between a group of countries in which the capital cities prevail (Hungary, Latvia, Estonia, Ireland) and a group in which the largest contribution is provided by second-tier cities. In Germany for example second-tier cities have 45.7 percent of the GDP vs. 5.2 percent for the capital; in Italy 38.8 percent vs. 8.8 percent; in Spain 34.6 percent vs. 18.1 percent; in Poland 38.9 percent vs. 17.5 percent. Poland represents an important exception to the Central and Eastern European model in which, in general, capital cities are largely more relevant.

In their study Camagni *et al.* (2015) analyze data for 136 metropolitan areas in the European Union, considering the trends for cities larger than one million inhabitants versus those ranging from 200,000 to one million. They study the GDP growth rates from 1996 to 2009 and are able to verify that in the periods of economic growth the largest cities perform better, but that in periods of economic slowdown the smaller cities grow faster. This becomes even clearer when referring to the growth of the per capita GDP, showing that during the recession the second-tier cities contribute more to their national economy than do the capitals.

Two other studies, by Dijkstra *et al.* (2013) and by David *et al.* (2013), on the data up to 2009, substantially agree on three features of the European urban system that are relevant for the policies and for our discourse. First, the European territory entails such a large variability of contexts that it is almost impossible to outline general trends for the entire area. As a matter of fact, in the various studies we read, cities are usually grouped in macro-areas. Second, despite the heterogeneous context, we can see a general trend: there is no evidence that the size of the cities is correlated with better performance or competitiveness. Third, policies emphasizing the role of larger urban areas could lead one to not consider properly the very relevant contribution to economic growth represented by the less urbanized areas of many countries.

These conclusions are to a large extent coherent with what has been developing in the policy discussion in the recent years, which we will try to briefly summarize in the following.

Cities in European policies: the "urban agenda" of the European Union

As was mentioned above, the European Union has not achieved the target of building a real European urban policy. This is a relevant aspect. In a broader context, in which the 28 countries engage periodically in working together toward common objectives in various policy areas (cohesion, agriculture and fisheries, infrastructures, etc.), an operational urban agenda would provide the individual countries with a common perspective for the development of cities. And, as we will see below, some scholars argue that, in the presence of an urban policy at the national or European level, second-tier cities would be able to contribute more to economic growth.

There are several reasons for the lack of a cohesive European urban policy. First, there is the lack of an explicit mandate by the member countries for a common policy on this topic. The second is the territorial diversities that characterize and differentiate the European cities. Atkinson highlights how the complexity of the European urban system makes the definition of common responses almost impossible (Atkinson 2001). Although the majority of European cities have been facing similar changes, such as deindustrialization, urban sprawl, and, more recently, the economic downturn, it is clear that the differences in the national contexts make each case unique. A third reason is the structural deficiency that is related to the lack of a common lexicon for urban issues, useful in order to conceptualize the problems and to thus implement a common action. This depends largely on the fact that many countries do not have an urban policy at the national level.

Despite these obstacles, since the 1980s European countries have been multiplying their efforts in the urban area, elaborating strategic documents and a common theoretical framework (Dukes 2008), and even more importantly experimenting with new practices in the management of urban issues.

In this slow although progressive construction of a common vision for the cities, it is possible to recognize a twofold point of view and way of acting on cities. On one hand, cities are recognized as being the places in which the largest number of European citizens lives. On the other hand, cities are seen as the strategic nodes for European economy. It is possible to recognize a shift in this approach, in particular by observing the implementation of Structural Funds. Until the late 1990s the European Union had mainly promoted programs for cities as places for living, with policies intended to foster quality of life, sustainability, and physical and social regeneration. Since 2000–2006, interest progressively shifted toward a vision of European cities and their contribution to economic development and competitiveness, with policies less oriented toward improving the urban ambience per se, and more toward stressing the key factors in the cities' attractiveness. The structure of European policies is very well articulated, but it is possible to outline two categories with special regard to the urban areas (Parkinson 2005). First are the mainstream policies, in the context of the European Regional Development Funds. These are characterized by the fact that cities are not the actors of the promotion of policies, as the European Regional Development Funds are managed at the regional level. It must be noted that in the 2014–2020 period, urban policy has been explicitly introduced among the priorities to be developed in the regional operational programs and in the national strategies. In the past the EU promoted specific programs such as the Urban Program, in which cities themselves were required to be active in the definition of policies and the management of funds, eventually competing at the European Union level with other cities in order to access the funding opportunities. The cancellation of the Urban Program in 2007 has been accompanied by criticisms, underlining the fact that the suppression of policy instruments devoted to cities poses a threat to the visibility of urban issues and the contribution of cities in the elaboration of strategies (Atkinson 2007). Moreover the competences acquired by local administrators and functionaries in managing European funds in their cities may be lost after several years of effort in their acquisition.

Second, concomitant with this shift in the orientation of Structural Funds, there has been a growing emphasis on cities as strategic determinants for the national economies and for the competitiveness of the European territory as a whole. This is no news to the representation of the territorial structure of Europe, as the role of the cities has been emphasized for decades in shaping the center–periphery vision in which we see the central area, from southern UK to northern Italy, as the economically strongest of the continent, while the surrounding periphery lags behind. In many visions during the 1990s (e.g., the European Spatial Development Perspective in particular; Committee on Spatial Development 1999) cities of the peripheral areas (such as the Mediterranean or the Atlantic area) are seen as poles for economic growth and thus as engines for a more balanced territorial development. The concept of "polycentric development" enters into the European discussion and policy-making, emphasizing the idea that a multi-polar urban network should be promoted by policies, rather than the less balanced predominance of a single large urban core. There is no space here for summarizing a very large debate on this issue: from our point of view we could just underline that the issue of polycentric development has been proposed sometimes at different geographical scales with poor attention to the specificities of each scale and to the local territorial specificities. At the continental level, Hall (2007) observed that promoting a polycentric development at the European scale could have the consequence of promoting and fostering concentration at the national or regional scale: after some years the predominance of the capital city is seen – as we will discuss below – as a problem in the most peripheral countries of the European Union (e.g., in Greece or Ireland) or in the new members – precisely where the polycentric development should have worked as an equilibrating force.

In general the approach that situated the cities at the center of European economic geography as the engines of territorial development, and recognized the multiple forms of the urban areas (city regions, metropolitan areas, functional urban areas, etc.), has had more implementation in territorial analyses and theoretical discussions than in operational policies.

The elaboration of what has been defined an "urban agenda" since 1997, with the publication of *Towards an Urban Agenda in the European Union*, has been subject of discussion for almost 20 years, with a cyclical debate that periodically approaches the discussion, frequently re-elaborating many of the baseline definitions and concepts, demonstrating that they were far from being consolidated – or that the political agreement was not at all achieved (European Commission 1997). In 2014, probably thanks to the concurring elaboration of the new period for Structural Funds and the recent appointment of the new members to the European Commission, the discussion on the European urban agenda got new energy, starting from the "CITIES, Cities of Tomorrow: Investing in Europe" conference that February. The event was intended to collect a variety of proposals from the European Parliament, the Committee of Regions, Eurocities, and others in order to propose a common strategic document. In July the Commission issued a second report, *The Urban Dimension of EU Policies: Key Features of an EU Urban Agenda*, which was under public consultation until the end of September 2014 (European Commission, 2015a).

This report of the European Commission devotes the first two sections respectively to a brief analysis of the main features of urban development in the EU and then to the state of the art of urban policy. It recognizes that the many national systems are too heterogeneous and articulated to be summarized. Then, it stresses how the European Union has been increasingly working on urban issues, in particular underlining, as we stated above, that initiatives such as the "urban" program have provided local authorities with practical experience of policy-making. The 2014 report refers to this as an "urban *acquis*," referring to the idea of *acquis communautaire*, the set of necessary conditions to be accomplished by a country in order to be part, or to be eligible to become a part, of the European Union. The document recalls that in 2012 the Commission's Directorate General for Regional Policy changed its name to Directorate General for Regional and Urban Policy – but shortly thereafter it is noted that urban issues enter in the spheres of competence of many directorates of the Commission. As to the specifics of the Regional Policy, it is stated that almost half of the European Regional Development Fund will be invested in urban areas in the 2014–2020 period, but we have to underline that these funds are managed at the regional level.

The building blocks for the European model of urban development are presented as based on various fundamental strategy documents (the 2020 Territorial Agenda in particular) and they can be summarized as stating that European cities should be:

- places for advanced social development;
- places for democracy, cultural dialogue and diversity;
- places for greening, ecological, and environmental regeneration;
- attractive poles and engines for economic development.

There are few operational tools suggested in the report up to this point, and the discussion remains quite generic also in the two subsequent sections, where it both summarizes the various requests supporting the need for an urban agenda and presents a brief and quite unsatisfactory section on urban development and the global scale. The reader is really expecting some concrete orientations at this point while approaching the fifth and final section ("Taking the reflections on an EU agenda forward"). The section starts by reporting that the urban agenda should be coherent with the overall EU strategies, the European Union 2020

Strategy, and the principles of subsidiarity. Then it again states that, despite many policies already having an urban dimension, there is a need for more coordination among various levels of government and for an improved attention to urban priorities in the elaboration of policies at the national and European level.

What focus is there then for the "urban agenda"? The report states that the urban agenda could focus on a limited set of general challenges (e.g., sustain-ability, resilience to climate change, demography, etc.) or just on challenges with a precise urban dimension (e.g., urban poverty). This could be achieved with improved participation of the cities in the process of definition of policies at both the national and European level. Finally, the document states the relevance of the availability of data for an informed policy-making, remembering that thanks to the activity of many European research networks this is not a problem but rather a good practice that needs to be continued.

In May 2015 the European Commission published a working document with the results of the public consultation on the document on the key features of an urban agenda that we have just presented (European Commission 2015b). There has been very differentiated participation in the consultation, with a few very active countries (Germany, Italy, France, Spain, Belgium) and many that almost ignored the process, at least according to the replies to the consultation received by the Commission. The comments to the document provide useful insights for improving the definition of the operational area of the urban agenda. The majority supports the idea that "focusing on a limited number of important challenges would make it possible to achieve results" (p. 3), in particular in the priority areas of greening, inclusion, and efficiency of energy and transportation networks. But then the conclusions of the document re-open the discussion, stating that stake-holders and member states need to discuss in the future in order to: (1) identify the "critical urban related issues," (2) map the "urban related Commission initiatives," and (3) identify "the main actors, networks, and platforms."

After many documents and discussions, the latest official document of the Commission is extremely generic and vague and, after almost one year, the con-clusions of the public consultation define a roadmap which, in turn, restarts everything from the beginning (and the Commission proposes, among the other things, to map the urban-related initiatives that the Commission itself promotes!).

In the meantime, the process of the definition of an urban agenda is still far from being completed, despite the fact that, as we will see, it is advocated by many scholars and policy-makers as being essential for the urban and territorial competitiveness of the EU. And what is remarkable is also the approach assumed with regard to the sharing of responsibilities among the levels of government. The expected urban agenda will consider a set of issues related to the cities, but cities are never mentioned as the level in charge of the implementation of pol-icies. This, in our view, is the key obstacle for an "urban agenda." The EU insti-tutions want a policy for the cities but do not want the cities to manage its implementation for themselves. This will be a limitation for the capacity for action of many cities, except for those in a very decentered national system: as we will see in the following section, these are the cities, at least among the second-tier urban areas, that have been more competitive and contributed more to the territorial development of their countries and regions.

These introductory remarks are not intended to outline exhaustively the debate and the elements of urban policies of the European Union. They are a very synthetic and partial excursus that represents more our personal vision as well as the vision proposed by some commenters and scholars. It is now time to focus on how second-tier or small and medium-sized urban areas have been studied and represented in the EU discussion, and how they are being considered by policies. This is the topic of the next section and of the rest of this chapter.

Second-tier and small and medium-sized cities in the EU: discussion

It had been anticipated that, while working on the research for this book, there would be a growing number of occasions on which second-tier cities and, more generally, small and medium-sized cities have been mentioned in the European discussion as a specific point of interest. This is due to the presentation of a few but important research contributions (which we will refer to later), but also to a specific focus chosen by the sixth "trio presidency."[1] In the 18 months between July 2014 and December 2015 the presidency of the Council of the European Union has been held by Italy, Latvia, and Luxembourg. The representatives of the three countries agreed on a common agenda for the 18 months – and among the topics highlighted (although adapted to nation-specific priorities), the role of small cities had a certain relevance. Just to provide an example, during a presentation of the Latvian presidency on June 3, 2015, it was explicitly stated that research tends to focus on larger cities while small and medium ones are underrepresented – with thus the need to draw attention to them in both research and policy.

The assumption behind this attention is itself simple and straightforward:

> small and medium sized cities in Europe have been less explored both in research and in policies ... At the same time, they are the prevailing settlement and a large share (66 percent) of the European urban population lives in urban areas with less than 500,000 inhabitants.
>
> (EUKN 2015, p. 1)

During the Italian term, the priority on this theme was set on small and medium-sized cities and their role in inner areas; during the Latvian presidency, the focus was on the economic growth potential; during the Luxembourg term, attention was centered on the role of small and medium-sized cities in cross-border polycentric metropolitan areas.

As we write this chapter, the latest relevant document, produced in the EU framework on the urban policies, consists of the Riga Declaration "Towards the

EU Urban Agenda," signed during the informal meeting of the ministries responsible for cohesion policy, territorial cohesion, and urban matters on June 10, 2015. The agreement is interesting here both because it is the latest step in the elaboration of an EU "urban agenda" and because it considers the role of small and medium-sized cities. We must underline that, while the broader message proposes the generic idea of the "smaller" cities as those not at the center of large metropolitan areas or large economic and political capitals, the specific statement in the Riga Declaration (and in its preparatory documents) is limited to the cities with a population of 50,000 and below. Nevertheless, it is interesting for our discussion as it is a specific focus on smaller size, officially is referred to in official documents of the EU, and because some of the theses on the advantages and disadvantages of a smaller size are coherent with the hypothesis formulated in this book. The annex of the Riga Declaration devoted to small and medium-sized cities is based on a research report prepared by the Social, Economic and Humanities Research Institute of Vidzeme University of Applied Sciences (HESPI: Latvia) and by the European Urban Knowledge Network (EUKN: The Netherlands) (2015). In their report, great attention is paid to the role of small and medium-sized urban areas as an intermediary level between large metropolitan areas and rural territories, thus contributing to a more balanced territorial development with their role in equilibrating the excessive growth of larger cities and providing, at the same time, services and accessibility to rural areas. Small and medium-sized cities are also considered as outperforming many larger cities in GDP and employment, in particular in countries with a higher average income. They are also seen as performing better in statistics related to poverty and, similarly to our arguments in other sections of this book, as places in which there are better housing conditions and in general an improved quality of life. In the HESPI and EUKN report, smaller cities are seen as facing challenges on many similar aspects to the largest cities: the impacts of demographical challenges and economic transition, and the negative effect of the lack of public funding, especially in the areas of infrastructure and services. Interestingly the report reminds us that many of the positive or negative determinants depend on the specific geographical and functional position of each city in its regional or national context.

The research performed by HESPI and EUKN is not the first presented on the topic at the European level. In this presentation we chose to refer to two specific research projects developed in the ESPON[2] framework: the 2013–2014 TOWN project, *TOWN: Small and Medium Sized Towns in Their Functional Territorial Context* (Servillo *et al.* 2014) and the 2012–2013 SGPTD project, *SGPTD Second Tier Cities and Territorial Development in Europe: Performance, Policies and Prospects* (ESPON *et al.* 2012).

The results of the TOWN project should be analyzed first, as it clearly sets the basis for most of the discussion developed in the above-mentioned report and thus in the definition of the Riga Declaration. The TOWN team developed a methodology for the identification of urban areas, which we will not discuss here, that brings them to dispute the idea of an unavoidable urban shift of the population, after having verified that, at least in Europe, a larger part of the population lives in small cities. The TOWN group performed a detailed analysis which includes the discussion of policies and of a number of case studies in various EU countries (Servillo *et al.* 2014). Comparing the features of smaller and larger cities allows them to underline that European small and medium-sized cities show in general:

- a larger proportion of employment in industrial activities compared with services;
- a higher economic activity rate;
- a larger proportion of population in non-active ages compared with those in active ages, in particular for those with an higher education level;
- a lower proportion of employment in retail;
- a larger proportion of workers who commute to a large city in the same region, compared to those working in the city itself.

This does not mean, according to the study performed by TOWN, that smaller cities necessarily depend on a larger city in their region: this is the case for some cities, but not for the generality of them. As to their economic structure, it is quite common that only above a certain size are cities able to develop a diverse economy, while for smaller cities it is common to have economies relying on a narrower set of activities, frequently "residential," thus making smaller cities less resilient in case of economic fluctuations.

Despite the fact that most of the case studies presented in this book are above the size threshold adopted by TOWN, we will frequently see how the capacity to prevent a crisis in the major local industry has been a key element in the success of certain cities in overcoming the economic transition.

The policy conclusions proposed by the TOWN final report pay attention to the elements of governance and could be summarized in two main aspects: local activism and collaboration. The former refers to the importance, in success stories in particular, of the leadership by a local group of active stakeholders or of an active mayor. The latter refers to the capacity of each individual city to "punch above its weight" not only when in proximity to a larger city (thanks to the "borrowing effect"), but, mostly and more importantly, by developing collaborations at the horizontal level with other cities and at the vertical dimension with other levels of government and the European Union. This allows, in certain cases, the city to overcome the limitations of its size, in particular when looking for resources in order to develop imaginative strategies for the future.

The approach adopted by SGPTD is quite different. They focus on "second-tier" cities and define them as "those cities outside the capital city whose economic and social performance is sufficiently important to affect the potential performance of the national economy" (ESPON *et al.* 2012, p. 1). In this broad definition they are thus able to include very large cities that could eventually be more important economically than the capital city itself (they include, among the others, Munich in Germany and Barcelona in Spain). If the TOWN project considered a set of cities below the size we are considering in this book, the SGPTD project considers case studies that are larger than those we examined – and in fact some of them were included in our previous studies, in which we were not specifically considering a size threshold (Kresl and Ietri 2010, Kresl and Ietri 2012). Another limit, for our current interest, consists in the fact that, being published in 2012, the SGPTD study could access only pre-crisis data (mostly pre-2007 or 2009). For this reason we will not refer here to their quantitative analysis, while we are mostly interested in the general considerations and in the policy suggestions they formulate.

The key message delivered by the SGPTD report is that many second-tier cities contribute in a substantial way to the economic growth of their country – but they could do more if they were properly considered by policies at the regional, national, and EU level. At the national level, one of the key arguments is that decentralization of decision-making and resources will benefit second-tier cities. While emphasizing that national governments are still responsible for delivering resources and distributing powers, at the local level, leadership is also underlined by the SGPTD report, as it was by the TOWN project. Here, leadership is intended rather in a systemic way and the involvement in decision-making of many actors of the city is considered a key for successfully exploiting key local assets. Our experience in the research for this book leads us to underline this aspect that we have been able to verify in many of our case studies.

An effective governance is thus considered a key determinant for success, in particular when it is necessary to define a new trajectory for the development of the city.

According to the case studies examined in the SGPTD project (Barcelona, Cork, Katowice, Leeds, Lyon, Munich, Tampere, Timisoara, Turin), the key determinants for strategic thinking in second-tier cities are identified as being:

- agreeing on common goals and philosophies;
- creating a network of supporting agencies and intermediate actors in public–private partnership (see also Kresl (ed.), 2015);
- fostering inwards investments thanks to the quality of the local environment and opening the city to the activities of potentially successful actors.

These considerations, although hard to disagree with, are less size-specific than what we are looking for in our research. It is also the case for larger cities that effective public–private partnerships, openness, and a set of shared goals could be the key for success: one could consider the Olympic Games in London as a trivial but effective example for this.

What is instead more related to the size-specific aspects we are considering is the discussion developed in SGPTD on the relations between different levels of government and on the diversity of frameworks to be considered in the European territory. One of the key messages in the SGPTD report underlines the importance of decentralization of resources and competences in order to foster the competitive advantage of second-tier cities. But discussing this issue for the

European cities is quite difficult as there are complex and varied situations, with various settings of the levels of government with regard to both the number of sub-national levels and the competences attributed to each of them. Depending on the country, sub-national governments are divided in one, two, or three levels. A first group of countries has one sub-national level: Bulgaria, Cyprus, Estonia, Finland, Lithuania, Luxembourg, Malta, and Slovenia. Another group has three sub-national levels: France, Italy, Poland, Spain, and the United Kingdom. Then there are the federal states: Austria, Belgium, and Germany, and, outside the EU, Switzerland. Another eleven states not mentioned above, which represent the majority in the EU, have two levels of sub-national government.

In general, the first and smallest level of sub-national government corresponds to the municipal, which is constituted by more than 90,000 local authorities in the European Union, 80 percent of which are in five countries (France, Germany, Spain, Italy, and the Czech Republic), which are in fact the countries where more frequently municipalities are very small. In many national systems, the territorial subdivision has been reorganized, usually aggregating small municipalities in larger ones (such as in Denmark), or forcing small municipalities to aggregate services and offices, in order to rationalize public expenditures.

Considering this complex articulation, the SGPTD report has developed some considerations with specific regard to the responsibilities of local levels of government, grouping the EU countries in five clusters:

A   federal states (Austria, Belgium, Germany): this is probably the simplest setting, in which competencies are clearly shared between the federal government and the state;

B   unitary "northern" states (Sweden, Finland, Denmark), in which the local autonomies are strong, with high local revenues;

C   unitary regionalized states (Italy and Spain), where the regional level has the largest set of competences, rather than the local/municipal one;

D and E unitary states in new and old member countries. This is the largest group in the typology by SGPTD: for the new member states it is underlined that the local governments are still fragmented, despite a generalized decentralization of powers. As to the "old" members, some have institutional settings in which local governments have more competences (i.e., France, the Netherlands, United Kingdom), others have less (such as in Greece and Portugal).

It must be noted that changing the institutional setting of the distribution of competences among different levels of government is not only a matter of formal organization of the state. It has impacts, among other things, on the distribution of funds and the way taxes are raised, on the organization of civil servants, on local politics and representation, on autonomies and special statutes – a combination of areas on which citizens in their roles as voters and taxpayers might not be ready to accept changes. For this reason the established distribution of competences among the various levels of government might be per se an advantage for second-tier cities in one country compared with others. At the same time a certain setting could be a motivation for local governments to be more active, while in other cases it could produce the opposite effect.

This is to say, in brief, that there is no surprise in finding out that second-tier cities might have different performances as a mere consequence of a national effect.

Given these differences, the SGPTD study considers whether the individual countries have been implementing policies for second-tier cities or at least for cities in general. The picture is very fragmented and if one had to draw the map of urban policies in Europe it would probably be a very diverse one, with few homogeneities. What is somehow more common is a certain concentration of attention and resources on the national capitals. In the new member countries of Central and Eastern Europe, the predominance of the capital is considered a problem for its consequences on territorial cohesion, thus some of those countries are focusing explicitly on second-tier cities.

When discussing urban policies it is commonly noted that cities (capitals and not) are affected by general national policies, such as infrastructure, research and development, welfare, etc. With a lack of a specific policy for cities, it is likely that the more the individual city has power and resources to plan for itself, the better its government, if effective, will be able to have an impact on the city's urban competitiveness. According to the SGPTD results, "in countries which are less centralized and less economically concentrated, and where cities have greater powers, resources and responsibilities, cities have performed better and helped the national economy more" (ESPON *et al.* 2012, p. 54). That is to say that, in countries dominated politically by the national level and economically by the capital, second-tier cities have less chance to be competitive in the way we see them in our discussion. So every country has its own story. This supports the idea that the second-tier cities in the European Union could not be considered as a single group as we did for the USA. First, on the analysis side, we do not have homogeneous data for many variables. Second, we have virtually as many governance systems as the number of countries we consider in the study.

The consequence for our research is that we will treat the European cities in Chapter 8 in a somewhat different way than the cities in the USA. The implication for the European Union, in agreement with almost all the conclusions we found in all the documents, papers, and research reports we examined, is that an effective European "urban agenda" is indeed urgent and that it will have to consider with great attention the role of second-tier cities and small and medium-sized urban areas.

Notes

1 Each of the 28 member states is in charge for a six-month presidency of the Council of the European Union, according to a rotation.
2 ESPON – European Spatial Planning Observation Network – is a program started in 2006 by the European Commission aimed at "promoting and fostering a European

territorial dimension in development and cooperation by providing evidence, know-ledge transfer and policy learning to public authorities and other policy actors at all levels." In this respect, the program promotes research projects by groups of European researchers according to thematic priorities defined for each seven-year period. www. espon.eu.

7   Small cities and competitiveness in North America

It is true in North America, as elsewhere, that if people all had the same utility function then all would seek to move to the same "best" city or cities. The definition of "best" would have to conform to some universal notions of wellbeing. This would entail city size, and an optimal set of amenities and economic assets, including public safety, access to transportation, congestion, demographic diversity, living standard, and so forth. But many of us seek out other cities – from mega-cities to smaller, more congenial places with idiosyncratic sets of the various amenities, or at least some of them. People choose locations that suit their personal preferences and these vary as wildly as do tastes in, among other things, music or fashion.

In our examination of the experiences of several smaller cities in the United States, Canada, and Mexico, we will present snapshots rather than lengthy elaborations of the experience of each city. The US cities will be presented in short individual treatments of the economic situation of the city and the response to it that has been initiated by local leaders. For the cities of Canada and Mexico we will rely more on work done by local scholars. The context in which each of these cities will be examined is that of its relative competitiveness, that is its economic position over time in relation to other cities with which it ultimately must compete.

The competitiveness of a city can be seen from above or from below. From above, certain specific performance criteria can be chosen: per capita income, growth of economic output, and high-tech production capacity are three that could be chosen. This would explicitly assert that all cities should strive for the same economic outputs or accomplishments. We all prefer more income to less income, don't we? But then, why do residents of Norway work 1,450 hours per year while Americans and Japanese work about 1,950 hours? How can it be that Norwegians would choose to forego the personal income that comes from 500 hours of work? Perhaps it is because the Norwegians are blessed with off-shore oil wealth from which they can derive the equivalent income. But the rest of the European Union work about 1,650 hours, and they do not have streams of income from natural resource wealth. Clearly, not all of us have the same work–leisure trade-off. Many of us prefer more leisure time for recreation, for cultural activities, for vacations, etc., to a better kitchen appliance or automobile, or to a larger and more expensive house. It poses the question – why, then, should we all desire to achieve the same for the city in which we live? Perhaps there are objectives other than per capita income, growth of economic output, and high-tech production capacity.

An alternative way of looking at a city's competitiveness is from below. Here we would ground the strategic plan for competitiveness enhancement on the values that are expressed by the residents of the city. How much social inequality will they accept, how much congestion and pollution will they tolerate, what pace of life do they want, what is their leisure–work trade-off, where are they in the density–sprawl trade-off, are they willing to see their children move to other cities for employment, and so forth? Here the community would have to participate in determining the objectives, structures, and procedures of any economic strategy and its implementation.

Our largest cities are similar to each other in many important ways. They are crowded, they seek to maximize economic output, they tend to have economic strategic plans that are similar to each other, they have a certain undeniable excitement about them, they are well connected, and many individuals tend to be isolated socially. Smaller cities are less similar and more idiosyncratic than are larger cities. While larger cities often have economies that were quite different a century or two ago, over time they have lost their distinctiveness, the way small rocks become river stone after many years in a fast moving stream. Small towns tend to retain their distinctiveness and their accommodation with the demands of a modern economy, with its speed, technology, and extra-regional connectivity, varies dramatically.

When smaller cities design a strategic economic plan, the planners have to immerse themselves in the past, capacities, aspirations, and assets of the city in a way that is not as necessary with larger cities. The vast majority of larger cities plan for high-technology production, research, attracting the "creative class," international connectivity, and attractive cultural and recreational assets. These are usually at the core of large city plans. Smaller cities have a wider range of options for development or creation of an economy that will be more narrowly focused. Some, we shall see, have developed versions of the "eds and meds" (education and health care) that have been so attractive to larger cities, or culture, recreation and tourism, or specialized manufacturing, or specialized business services, or retirement centers – the list goes on.

The options for smaller cities have been greatly expanded due to the numerous advances in telecommunications, production, and transportation technologies. Among other things, this means that firms in small cities can have productive relationships with small/large firms on other continents. One small firm in Lewisburg, Pennsylvania, population 20,000, has working relationships with small firms in Asia and in Europe, all because of the ease of doing collaborative work via telecommunications.

Categories of smaller cities

College/university

Many smaller cities, some with a population of fewer than 30,000, are home to one or more colleges or universities. These are the smaller cities that are most likely to be successful in achieving the economic objectives of their residents, especially in the emerging economy of skill, technology, and connectedness. These institutions of higher learning supply professors/researchers who often begin start-up firms that have positive impacts on the local economy. They also graduate students who, if they can be induced to remain in the community – something that is often very difficult – provide the labor force that is necessary for the new economy; such employees would otherwise have to be recruited to migrate to a city that may not be as immediately attractive as a large city. These institutions also provide a variety of cultural, recreational, sports, and learning assets that make the small city as attractive as a much larger city. This builds on the notion of the economic core of the city, as elaborated in Chapter 4. The experiences of these cities are varied and the cities vary greatly in size, so we will examine their experiences in detail below.

Resource based

These smaller cities may be considered blessed in some way as long as the resource remains available and as long as it is in high demand. However, the landscape is replete with versions of Jerome, Arizona, Madrid, New Mexico, and Centralia, Pennsylvania – once vital settlements that have become ghost towns, once the veins of ore have given out. Madrid declined following a mine explosion in 1932, was for sale for $500,000 for a while – no takers – but is now viable as a funky town of small shops and as an occasional movie location. Centralia's decline was initiated when the coal seam ignited and the town had to be largely abandoned. Jerome survives with a population that has fallen from 10,000 in the 1920s to 450 today as a small center of artists and galleries, wineries, specialty shops, restaurants, and tourism. Others are abandoned because a new interstate highway diverts traffic from the two-lane highway that served them. Glenrio, on the Texas/New Mexico border, and Texola, on the Oklahoma/Texas border, were both lively stops on US 66, but declined when Interstate 40 bypassed them. Now they are abandoned. Terlingua, Texas, is a failed mercury production center that collapsed in the 1940s, but was brought to life as a renowned chili cook-off center. All of these failed resource cities share the same experience of decline and they are either abandoned or hang on through tourism based on their past and on activities that seem to thrive on isolation and low cost, such as artistic centers.

Declining industrial

These cities are less romantic, but much more varied and ultimately more interesting and worthy of study. The textile towns of New England, the steel and manufacturing cities of the industrial heartland, and isolated industrial cities in the South have all suffered this fate of stagnation and ultimate decline. Toward the latter part of the twentieth century firms became increasingly footloose and moved from New England to the South, and from steel and manufacturing cities to locations in Asia and Latin America, where they could take advantage of lower wages and taxes and other costs. Local hydro-electricity to power mills and factories ceased to be an attraction once it was possible to transmit electricity hundreds of miles from the dam. Early industrial production depended upon workers with specific skills, but as production became mass production the need was for unskilled, low-wage labor, often recent immigrants, and plants could be situated almost anywhere. Only in recent years has a premium been paid for highly skilled workers as technology invaded manufacturing. We will see below how some cities have managed to regain their position as manufacturing centers and what the future held for those that could not.

High-tech

When we think of high-tech centers we naturally have Silicon Valley or Austin or Boston in mind. What those larger cities have at hand is a skilled labor force, a set of urban amenities, and one or more research universities. They also have the advanced telecommunications and transportation assets that are vital to a high-tech economy and major universities. However, as has been noted in an earlier chapter, smaller cities can do much with telecommunications that reduce the need for access to a major airport. Many of them also have universities or colleges that bring to the smaller city a sufficient contribution of faculty researchers, skilled students and graduates, and cultural and recreational amenities that make them very viable as high-tech centers, albeit on a small scale. Local firms and entrepreneurs have adequate access to counterparts in other regions or even continents and have little or no need to meet in the same place. If other firms in the same industry are located in the smaller town, some of the necessary face-to-face contact can still take place. We will encounter several smaller cities that have done quite well in this regard in the section below.

Recreation/tourism

While tourism and recreation are something of a lifeline for a sinking resource-based economy, as described above, this has long been a primary activity for many smaller cities that are situated in areas of natural beauty, recreation, and the appropriate urban amenities. Being situated on a body of water is beneficial, as are proximity to mountains and forests, and access to a well-connected airport. In the United States, the Atlantic, Pacific, and Gulf coasts are lined with these cities, as are the mountainous areas of New England, the Appalachian Mountains and the West. Not all specializations in this sector are the same, of course – different age groups, and family constellations, sexual preferences, personal tastes for culture or sport or just relaxing – will find one location or the other to be attractive. Hence, the city that specializes in recreation/tourism must plan carefully what its offerings will be, and this is powerfully determined by the assets at hand. In what follows we will see how some smaller cities have developed into very impressive theater, musical, or artistic centers, often with origins up to a century or more in the past. Others have made their abandoned mining, manufacturing, transportation, or agricultural sites into attractive tourist destinations. Some in the industry are convinced that virtually every town or smaller city has some assets that can be developed into an attractive recreational/tourist destination.

Isolated/peripheral

Throughout the United States, we find many cities of all sizes that are or were sited in isolated and peripheral locations. Many were originally centers of processing or forwarding of the products of natural resource extraction that were linked to the rest of the world by rail or water transportation. This was the case with cities such as Santa Fe, Denver, and Fort Worth. Over time, the wealth that was generated in these activities and the ambition and energy of a sufficient number of individuals with access to it resulted in the development of important urban centers. Santa Fe was an administrative center at the northern end of El Camino Real, originating in Mexico City. Denver processed and forwarded minerals from the Rocky Mountains and then became the principal entrepôt for most of the east face of the mountain range. Fort Worth developed as a junction between cattle drives from the Southwest and the rail connection to eastern markets. Today the three cities remain quite distinct and different from each other – it would be impossible to design one strategic economic plan that would be appropriate for all of them. But when we think of Chicago, Dallas, Philadelphia, and Seattle we would find that they all seek the objectives that were highlighted at the beginning of this chapter: high-tech production, research, attracting the "creative class," international connectivity, and attractive cultural and recreational assets.

Multi-focused

Although some smaller cities are highly focused on one activity, be it furniture-making, recreation, small manufacturing, regional retail, regional transportation, or cultural activities, many others may have had a key single industry abandon the city or have always had a diverse economy. In some small cities, being multi-focused is another way of saying that the city has nothing special that distinguishes it or that gives its economy any particular competitiveness. This can be an indication of a city economy that is in decline following loss of a major firm. For other cities, however, a multi-focused economy can be the result of a purposeful shaping of the local economy so as to make it less vulnerable to a sectoral downturn, perhaps like one that may have cost the city its earlier specialization. While many smaller cities do have one or more universities or colleges and perhaps a regional health care facility, the degree of specialization, one industry or multi-focused, should properly refer to other economic activities, such as, manufacturing, logistics, agriculture, culture, and recreation/tourism. Some of the cities below have managed to do quite well as multi-focused economies.

Some US cases/examples/stories

We have selected 15 US cities with populations of between 14,000 and 488,000 residents. There are five cities in each of three categories: less than 50,000, 50,001–100,000, and 101,000–250,000. The cities were selected with some intention but predominantly by chance; however, sufficient material had to be available online since visits to all of the cities were not practical. The cities were located in all sections of the country. No state capitals were included, since their economies are always distorted by the advantages that attach to this status. We identified each of the cities by the seven descriptions given in the previous section of this chapter: college/university, resource-based, declining industrial, high-tech, recreation/ tourism, isolated/peripheral, and multi-focused.

Our objective in doing this is to get some understanding as to what the capabilities for change are for cities of different small sizes, how they have been able to utilize their capabilities, and how the cities in the three size categories are similar and different as their size increases from small town to "almost large." As was noted above, these will be 15 snapshots rather than intensive examinations. We will gain insights from the totality of the studies.

The Sperlings Best Places site (www.bestplaces.net) calculates a "metro area" for all of the cities in its coverage. For many cities the metro area is double that of the city population but for others it is far greater. Two of the smallest cities show this clearly. Lewisburg has a population of 20,000 but within a circumference of 15 miles there are 44,000 people. Ashland also has a population of about 20,000 but it is only 12 miles from Medford, population 65,000, and in the Medford metro area there are over 200,000. A much larger city, Billings, Montana, with a population of 90,000, four and one-half times that of Ashland, is in a metro area of only 158,000, only a bit over three-fourths that in which Ashland is situated. Hence, it will be impossible to isolate a small city from its metro area population, with the advantages that a larger area brings, since smaller cities may be situated in metro areas that are considerably more populous. Clearly a smaller city may benefit significantly from economic development and planning done by organizations of the larger metro area or administratively by the county in which it is situated. Nonetheless, it remains of interest to examine what actions are or are not taken by smaller city administrations themselves, and how they are able to take advantage of, or to insinuate themselves into, the larger metro area.

In examining these cities there was no attempt to distill a brilliant or preferred strategic response to the need to enhance competitiveness; indeed, not all cities have come to a realization that a strategic planning response is needed. Rather we have a collection of smaller cities that have found themselves in situations that varied from impending disaster to steady progress. We will examine these city experiences by grouping the cities according to population since each size group will be somewhat distinctive in its capacities and assets. Finally, we will base our analysis on the city itself rather than on the metropolitan statistical area (MSA) or some other notion of the urban area. In many instances it is the city rather than its wider region that is faced with the economic challenge that must be met so as to avoid secular decline. However, it is true that as the city gets larger it tends to be a smaller part of its MSA – among the 20 largest MSAs, the principal city is only 24 percent of the total. We found this to be true also for most of the cities with populations of more than 250,000 – for example, Cincinnati, with a population of 297,000 is in an MSA of 2.2 million; for Pittsburgh these figures are 305,000 and 2.4 million, and for St. Louis 319,000 and 2.9 million. So we limited our snapshots of smaller cities to those between 20,000 and 250,000.

Cities with population of fewer than 50,000

Prescott, Arizona

Population: 40,000
Metro area: 5.7 million
City type: Recreation/tourism

Prescott is a city that is situated between Flagstaff and Phoenix in a mountainous and forested area. The Prescott National Forest to the south and west of the city comprises 1.2 million acres, of which about 12 percent is wilderness. Hence, the city gets high marks from hiking and recreation rating services and magazines. Recreation and tourism are then the number one industry for the city's economy with over 1,800 hotel and motel beds. As a concomitant of this, the city is a highly rated place for retirement. Both *Money Magazine* and *Smart Money/Wall Street Journal* rate it among the top five places for retirees (Prescott Chamber of Commerce 2014, p. 8). To enhance its attractiveness to retirees, Prescott has a variety of small city cultural assets – a pops orchestra, theaters, visiting performances by the Phoenix Symphony, and so forth.

Other assets are branch campuses of Northern Arizona University and Yavapai College and, most significantly, a campus of the Embry-Riddle Aeronautical University, with 1,900 students from all over the country and from several foreign countries as well. This, paired with the Prescott Municipal Airport, makes aviation a strength of this small city.

While the city itself is rather small, it is included in the emerging Arizona Sun Corridor mega region, a metro region that now encompasses 5.7 million people in Phoenix, Tucson, Prescott, and Nogales, Mexico; it is anticipated that the region will consist of 7.4 million in 2025. This is a huge region that stretches hundreds of miles through desert. Prescott is at the northern boundary of the region, with Phoenix being 100 miles to the southeast. It cannot be assumed that the city participates in or benefits much from its inclusion in this region. The difficulties of such a region are clearly the intense heat, especially the "urban heat island" phenomenon, and the severe shortage of water. The use of water is heavily contested between agricultural (currently 50 percent of total usage), recreational, industrial, and residential usage. Arizona State University has established the Julie Ann Wrigley Global Institute of Sustainability in perhaps the most challenging area in the United States. Time will tell whether the Arizona Sun Corridor will be indeed find its path to water sustainability. As is well known, the allocation scheme for the Colorado River water was established in the 1920s and 1930s when it was assumed that rain and snow would provide 17.5 million acre feet per year. Those years were extraordinary, and normal supply is only 12–15 million acre feet per year. This has generated schemes for allocation that may mean that the region slowly but increasingly becomes a desert. Prescott is less dependent on agriculture, the heavy user, and industry than is the rest of the Corridor region, but water usage will be a challenge for almost all cities in the Southwest, including Prescott.

In 2008 the city attempted to put itself on a new path of development when it introduced its Strategic Plan for Community and Economic Development, albeit with the rather vague notion that the city "desires to be on the cutting edge of promoting entrepreneurialism and economic development" (*Prescott: A Focused Future II*, 2008). In the years before this, Embry-Riddle Aeronautical University had established a campus in Prescott, the Prescott Film Commission had had some success with film and television production, and there was a new conference center. The Strategic Plan for Community and Economic Development saw Prescott, first, as a regional hub for cultural events, conferences, and government; but given its proximity to Phoenix (100 miles) and Flagstaff (90 miles) there will be stiff competition for this role. Second, was the task of maintaining the natural and recreational assets of the region. Third, was business development that was based on some assets in biomedical/ biosciences and in medical services. Objectively, these assets do not put Prescott in the same frame as several of our other smaller cities. Fourth is a focus on "educational excellence"; however the local assets are hardly competitive, Old Dominion University offered distance learning, Yapapai College had a two-year program, much of it in vocational education, and the Prescott campus of Northern Arizona University offered only a degree in elementary education. Embry-Riddle Aeronautical University is the primary opportunity for the higher-wage jobs the plan envisions. It is difficult to gain an understanding of just what of this plan has been achieved, but it is less promising than are the initiatives of other smaller cities.

Lewisburg, Pennsylvania

Population: 20,000
Metro area: 45,000
City type: University

Lewisburg is a university town, situated on the west shore of the Susquehanna River. Bucknell University has about 3,800 undergraduate and masters' degree students, colleges of arts and sciences, and of engineering, as well as a school of business; it is also the town's largest employer. The university has also established a business incubator center downtown in conjunction with a center supported by the US Small Business Administration. Another strength of the local economy is a robust health care sector with a hospital and a variety of specialist services, many of which are linked with Geisinger Medical Center, 20 miles to the east. Interstate highway 80 is five miles to the north and the town is at the intersection of US 15 and state highway 45. While the town population is 20,000, the metro area, a circumference of 15 miles, captures about 45,000 people. The town has experienced two major economic difficulties in the past quarter century. First, was a weakness in the Market Street retail sector, with a dozen empty storefronts in the five-block business district as late as 1990. Second was the closing of the Pennsylvania House Furniture factory and head office a decade later, when a national furniture firm purchased it and transferred much production to China.

Since the 1970s, one of the principal objectives of the borough council was to maintain the vitality of retail on Market Street. This is in sharp distinction to several other small cities in the area that took a laissez-faire approach to retail vitality – retail was a private matter and it could take care of itself. The local business–community organization, the Downtown Partnership, has worked to restore vitality to Market Street, and for the past several years vacancies have been quickly converted to other shops. The current challenge arises from the fact that a large space is about to be vacated when a CVS pharmacy/drug store relocates a mile to the west, as will the smaller state liquor store. However, these actions are seen by many not as disasters but as opportunities, for example, to induce a food chain to use the CVS space for a small grocery/produce store for residents who prefer to walk to shop for groceries rather than drive a mile or two to one of the two larger grocery stores, a long-established Weis, that had abandoned its downtown location decades ago, and a new Giant that is being located a mile to the west. The local government has become quite active and has been able to keep Market Street retail places fully booked. This too is in contrast with the other smaller towns in the area.

The more significant challenge was the departure of Pennsylvania House and disposal of the very large site it used to occupy. After several years a property development company purchased the site and is currently in the construction phase of the structures that will replace the "chair factory." The CVS pharmacy/drug store and a Giant grocery store are soon to open here, to be followed by two restaurants, the state liquor store, and, probably, a health/fitness center, another restaurant, and some residential structures.

In 2014, the school board decided to move the high school out of the center of town to a peripheral location a couple of miles to the west. Lewisburg then confronted another decision that had to be made about space. Nothing has yet been decided by local officials but three or four options are being considered.

Lewisburg is best described as a small town that has been very active in pursuing its economic development and in maintaining the vitality that has been accomplished. It has risen to the challenges of negative economic decisions by economic actors with intelligence, purpose, and persistence.

Ashland, Oregon

Population: 20,000
Metro area: 203,000
City type: Resort, tourism, multi

As noted above, Ashland benefits from being in the Medford metro area. This may in part be why the city has been so successful in creating a dynamic economy. The town's largest employer, Southern Oregon University, has an enrollment of almost 7,000, with a full complement of masters' degree programs. This creates an educated local labor force which participates in the Shakespeare Festival, about which more will be said shortly. Tourism is the city's largest industry, situated as it is in mountainous and forested southwest Oregon on the California border, roughly between Portland and San Francisco and about five hours from each by car. This, of course, is true for many if not most of the smaller cities in the mountainous West.

But what is distinctive about Ashland is the fact that it has been successful in gaining advantages from its position in the larger Medford metro area and initiatives that emanate from it. Some of the most important are the innovation and invention initiatives in the Rogue River Valley. Recently a consortium of the ScienceWorks Hands-on Museum and the Southern Oregon Historical Society was one of six groups in the US that were selected as "Places of Invention" by the Lemelson Center for the Study of Invention and Innovation of the Smithsonian Institution to inventory and document the "unique combinations of inspiring surroundings, creative people and ready resources that sparked local innovation" (www.insighttoashland.com/rogue-valley-participates-smithsonian-innovation-exhibit). This report has yet to be completed and released. But Ashland does have some strength in this area. There are 54 firms with 544 employees in light manufacturing, and 61 firms with 286 employees in high-tech activity, with half of them in computer systems design and in scientific research and development.

The recognition by *MovieMaker Magazine* of Ashland as the number two city in the US to live and work as a filmmaker was based on a number of factors, including the frequency and quality of filmmaking, the established infrastructure for the industry, community support for filmmaking, and the overall arts scene, cost of living, and quality of life. Filmmakers also get a 20 percent rebate on goods and services purchased and 16.2 percent on labor costs above $1 million. Southern Oregon University students are involved in the Ashland Independent Film Festival, and even the middle school has a film program. The result is that in the past decade, nine feature films and two short films have been made, as well as, in 2013–2014 alone, 15 commercial/corporate shoots (Ashland Chamber of Commerce 2015).

But one of the primary events of the community is its Oregon Shakespeare Festival. This began in 1893 as a Chautauqua event and was then recast as the Shakespeare Festival in 1935 with WPA funds. The festival now brings in an audience of 100,000 annually and has a budget of $32 million; its economic impact on the area is over $85,000,000. Clearly this is the biggest economic activity in a town of 20,000. Southern Oregon University participates significantly in this event. The festival is one of the key elements in the city's success in tourism and recreation.

A final strength of the Ashland economy is the local wine industry. First established in the mid-nineteenth century, the industry fell into decline – perhaps aided by prohibition during the 1920s. The Rogue Valley industry developed again, beginning in 1967 with the planting of a vineyard in some agricultural land belonging to Southern Oregon University. Five years later, a course on viticulture was developed at Rogue Community College. It has not yet achieved the size and significance of the counterpart we are about to encounter in the next city, Walla Walla.

Ashland has achieved a varied economy based on film, recreation/tourism, innovation in light manufacturing, and wine. This has been accomplished with input from the local government, the connections with the Medford metro region, visionary individuals who developed the Shakespeare Festival and other cultural activities, and other individuals who developed its wine industry.

Walla Walla, Washington

Population: 30,000
Metro area: 126,000
City type: University, resources

Walla Walla is a small city that is quite peripheral and isolated in southeast Washington, with two suburbs that bring its population to about 45,000. The city is just over 40 miles from the Kennewick–Pasco–Richland metro area with a population of 126,000, but does not have any strong economic links with this area. Long an agricultural center based on wheat, the Walla Walla sweet onion was developed in the first years of the twentieth century and is so distinctive that it was designated, in 2007, the state's official vegetable! Appropriately, there is a Walla Walla Sweet Onion Festival in July.

More recently, wine production has taken off, with now over 100 wineries in the area, and this has become the city's best-known product. Wine was initially produced by a settler in 1850. A severe frost in the 1880s and prohibition in the 1920s caused the industry to collapse. In the 1970s new growers brought a rebirth of wine production in Walla Walla. The industry was stimulated and put on a more scientific basis when Walla Walla Community College offered a night course taught by two of the first vintners, Gary Figgins of Leonetti Cellar and Rick Small of Woodward Canyon. The course was soon cancelled because some in the community thought it was not appropriate for a college to be teaching about alcoholic drinks. Classes resumed in the 1990s and the college's president, Steven VanAusdle, instituted a center to train students for the growing number of wineries. This time the initiative resulted in the Center for Enology and Viticulture, with substantial funding from the state legislature, the US Department of Agriculture, and private funds (Reddy 2008).

According to an article in the *Wall Street Journal*: "The program and the graduates it produces have helped buoy this struggling eastern Washington city of 30,000, one known for sweet onions and another big employer, Washington State Penitentiary" (Reddy 2008). The Walla Walla economy had just emerged from a period of 25 years of instability and essentially no economic growth. In 2017, the industry is projected to have about 16 percent of all regional jobs, and "Wine production and related industries are thus making indispensable contribution to a more stable regional economy" (EMSI 2007, p. 8).

The story of Walla Walla seems to be a much simpler experience than the other cities in this size category. The reshaping and resurgence of the local economy does not seem to have been the consequence of local government action but rather that of private sector individuals in the wine industry and the local community college and its president who took the initiative to develop this now key industry, in the face of some local opposition.

Ithaca, New York

Population: 30,000
Metro area: 100,000
City type: University, resort, tourism

The home of Cornell University and Ithaca College, Ithaca is a real university/college small city. Cornell is an Ivy League university with over 20,000 students and a full complement of PhD programs. The College of Agriculture and Life Sciences began as a land grant college and later the university was formed. Ithaca College has a full complement of undergraduate degree programs and several at the masters' degree level. Its enrollment is about 6,500. Clearly, the university/college population is almost as high as that of the rest of the town, although the metro region is just over 100,000.

Education employs approximately 55 percent of the local labor force. Cornell's faculty are active researchers and this has helped to generate many smaller high-tech firms in agriculture, medical technology, and all areas of scientific activity. The university has several entities that stimulate job creation and firm start-ups: the Center for Technology Enterprise and Commercialization, the Kevin M. McGovern Family Center for Ventured Development in the Life Sciences, and a business incubator downtown. In addition the university has a Center for Manufacturing Enterprise, and the National Nanofabrication Facility is attached to Cornell. Governor Cuomo was inspired by the experience of Ithaca and Cornell to introduce a program that would allow branches of the State University of New York and some private colleges to offer tax-free zones for new business development in proximity to the campus (McKinley 2013).

While Ithaca has the lowest rate of unemployment in the state, it does have some problems. Over the past decades much of its manufacturing industry, firearms and automobiles, has collapsed or moved elsewhere. Thompson Power Transmission closed its doors in 2010, and there is some concern that the city is overly dependent upon its major industry, higher education (Crandall 2014). The city's two other large employers, Borg-Warner Automotive and Cayuga Medical Center, a regional health care facility, have stable employment, and the medical center is actually expanding. If anything, the local labor force has skills that are in excess of what is required by local firms – the head of the Downtown Ithaca Alliance commented that Ithaca "is the classic place where you have baristas with PhDs" (McKinley 2013).

A powerful contributor to the city's recent success has been the work of the mayor, 26-year-old Svante Myrick, elected in 2011, the youngest African-American mayor ever elected. Mayor Myrick says the city stands out "because our universities have partnered with our private industries," rather than relying on the typical university businesses catering to the needs of students and tourists. He has been "a great friend to the business community and has attracted $200,000 in funds for development in the city, including a multi-million renovation of its central commons" (McKinley 2013).

In short, Ithaca is an example of a success story for smaller cities. It has an enormous advantage with its two institutions of higher learning and the spin-offs they have engendered. So, while it has been dealt a good hand, it has also played it well.

Cities with population of 50,001–100,000

Portland, Maine

Population: 62,000
Metro area: 204,000
City type: Multi, peripheral

Portland is certainly peripheral but, being just over 100 miles from Boston, it cannot be said to be isolated. It has the distinction of being the principal financial center, transportation center, and retail center in a small state. It also has the strongest small business sector of any metropolitan area in the US (www.city-data.com/us-cities/The-Northeast/Portland-Economy.html). Portland benefits from being just 20 miles from Freeport, home to L. L. Bean, the noted retail store that draws about three million visitors each year, many of whom spend time in Portland.

The city was for a long time the ice-free port for Canadian exports, linked by rail to Montreal. Subsequently this function was shifted to Montreal when ice-breakers were developed and when the St. Lawrence Seaway was completed in the 1950s. It remains a major east coast port, with good rail linkages to the interior, and a pipeline feeds crude oil to refineries in Montreal.

During the past decades, manufacturing, fishing, and agriculture have given way as key elements in the Portland economy to finance and services, with several large firms having their head offices in the city. One of the links with the past is Burnham & Morrill Co., maker of the well-known B & M Baked Beans. In accordance with the city's status as a gateway to Maine's coastal and forested recreation and tourist lands, the city is home to 230 restaurants and this is one of the highest restaurant : population ratios of any city in the US.

Portland does not seem to be facing any negative developments in its economy. It has the lowest rate of unemployment in the state and has not suffered the loss of a major company. In spite of this, the Economic Development Department introduced the *Economic Development Vision + Plan*, in August, 2011, but it lacks the clear focus of plans of other cities where the strategy is more pressing. Portland's "vision and plan" highlight three aspects: grow the economy, enrich the creative economy, and support business. The ultimate objective is described as "Creating economic prosperity through growing the City's tax and employment base" (Portland Economic Development Department 2011, pp. 1–2). In the plan, eleven sectors are targeted, virtually every aspect of the city's economy. There are initiatives listed in support of each of the targeted sectors, but no sense that any of them is more important than the others.

Elsewhere the department identified four major development initiatives, of which the two most detailed and important are the Portland Technology Park and biotechnology growth (Portland Economic Development Department 2015). The Technology Park stresses life sciences, including veterinary pharmaceuticals, immunology, and environmental biotechnology, so the two development initiatives blend together into one focus. In discussing both of these, the details of what will be accomplished are not readily discernible. To achieve this, the emphasis is placed on the slower pace of life, avoidance of the inconveniences of commuting, lower space costs, good local cuisine, and access to natural resources for recreation. Lacking is an emphasis on the skills of the labor force and of the contribution of local universities and colleges, curious since the Technology Park, and life sciences, are at the center of its planning.

The impression one gets from examining the Portland economy and plans for it, is that the city and its leaders are rather satisfied with things as they are and have no sense that anything more than marginal modifications are required.

Youngstown, Ohio

Population: 82,000
Metro area: 565,700
City type: Declining industrial

This city was at the center of the collapse of the industrial heartland, following the oil price shocks of the 1970s. "Black Monday," September 19, 1977, is the day that Youngstown Sheet and Tube closed its doors. This is a classic story of a city economy founded on success in an activity, steel production based on access to iron ore and coal, for over 150 years that "had the props knocked out from under it." Almost overnight 40,000 jobs were lost and the city's population dropped from over 165,000 to 65,000 between 1960 and 2010. The loss continued after 2010. The city was additionally burdened by a rather spectacular degree of control by organized crime. This continued until the end of the 1990s when the Federal Bureau of Investigation was able to clean up the city. The economic collapse created over 3,200 vacant industrial and residential properties, 44.8 per 1,000 residents – 20 times the national average (Kenarov 2013). As is usually the case these days, the city tried to pass the vacant lots off as urban gardens, urban farming, and so forth. Sadly, gardens do not pay any taxes to the local government so that in terms of public services nothing is gained, and public transportation remains as poor as it has been, Of the largest 100 cities, Youngstown has the highest percentage living in poverty (Posey 2013). Nonetheless cleaning up the city and some other things have reduced the terrible crime rate by 50 percent from its high a few years ago.

In earlier years, Youngstown was at the heart of a band of steel production that stretched from Cleveland through Youngstown to Pittsburgh. In the years following the industrial heartland collapse of the 1990s and the first years of the twenty-first century, Cleveland and Pittsburgh have been able to create a connection in technology industries, but, sadly, Youngstown has not been able to participate in this new collaboration (Smith 2013). The city did attempt to introduce a strategic economic plan, Youngstown 2010, with "smart shrinkage" as the main approach. The planner soon left for a job elsewhere and for several years no one was hired as a replacement. Hence, city government initiative was not a success.

The recovery that has been slowly gathering strength has had little to do with city planning, but rather to the surge in activity linked to oil and gas fracturing (fracking) that has powerfully stimulated the economy of parts of Pennsylvania and is now slowing moving into the field of hydrocarbons in Ohio. Fracking activity in the Youngstown area provided a stimulus to the Ohio economy from spending on drilling and allied activities. Concern has been raised about the fracking industry since 12 earthquakes of up to 4.0 on the Richter scale have been experienced in a region with no history of seismic activity (Kenarov 2013).

Fortunately there has been a nascent revival of the manufacturing sector, in part linked to oil and gas activity. The French firm, Vallourec, built a $1.1 billion plant to make steel pipes for the industry and a smaller plant to make pipe connectors. Other firms, such as Exterran, have joined in this (Schwartz 2014). The Youngstown Business Incubator, the largest in Ohio, serves as a facility that can assist and promote the formation of new firms in additive manufacturing or products made with 3D printing (Smith 2013). One thing that has worked against this manufacturing revival is residents' lack of confidence that something positive can actually be accomplished in a city that has fallen so far.

In Youngstown we have a city that was described as a "poster child for post-industrial America" (Stanford 2014). It probably fell farther than any other city in the industrial heartland, but has recently seen something of a revival in its manufacturing sector. The recovery, such as it is, is one that has had little help from local government planning, but rather has been generated by private firms seeing opportunities generated by hydrocarbon fracking. This has been facilitated by the highways, rail lines, other infrastructure, and assets that remained from Youngstown's glory days before the collapse of the 1970s.

Duluth, Minnesota

Population: 87,000
Metro area: 279,000
City type: Resources, isolated

Duluth has a population of 87,000; its metropolitan statistical area is 131,000 and it is the single city of any size in the Arrowhead region, essentially all of Minnesota to the north and northeast of the city, with a population of 279,000. The city is the gateway to an enormously popular recreation and resort area of forest and lakes, and another tourist attraction – Lake Superior. The city's economy has always been dominated by this important location. In fact, Duluth and its near neighbor Superior, Wisconsin, have branded themselves as the Twin Ports, evocative of the Twin Cities. The linkage with major rail lines has made this a major inter-modal shipping port, with minerals and grains being paired with shipment of heavy machinery to the Alberta tar sands development.

While minerals, such as iron and taconite, as well as coal and timber, have always been central for the economy of this city in the "iron range," this resource activity began to decline in the post-World War II years. By 1981 the last large enterprise, the US Steel Duluth Works, closed its doors. Soon shipbuilding, heavy manufacturing, and the Duluth Air Force Base also ceased operations. As the rate of unemployment rose to 20 percent in the early 1980s and was still 15 percent in 1990; tourism was then seen to be the key sector for the city. To make itself more attractive in this sector, the downtown was renovated with shops, cafés, restaurants, and hotels, sometimes converted from disused warehouses and other industrial facilities. Duluth has also developed as a regional center of finance, health care, and retail for the Arrowhead region, and for contiguous areas of Wisconsin and Upper Michigan. In 2006, the service sector accounted for approximately 90 percent of total payroll (Duluth Planning Commission 2006, p. 3).

Duluth's history of planning is not a brilliant one. The last plan was in 1927. An attempt was made in 2001 but it was not a success. Finally in 2006 the *City of Duluth Comprehensive Plan* was produced by CR Planning, and the city adopted it. While it is primarily a plan for land use and infrastructure issues, there are bits of it that are of interest from the standpoint of strategic economic planning. The strengths of the economy continue to be medical, educational, and professional services, inter-modal shipping, and tourism. With the exception of firms such as Cirrus Aircraft, small private aircraft, manufacturing does not get much attention. The plan identifies areas for attention – port operations, higher education, affordable housing, integration of industrial with commercial and residential areas, and integrating tourism with other services, industrial activities, and neighborhoods. But there is no focus on new high tech, or small manufacturing, or research activities.

One is left with the sense that Duluth's leadership is fairly pleased with the way the economy has developed in recent years, following the decline in the 1970s and 1980s. Tourism continues to be strong, and the city is secure in its place as a dominant regional health, finance, retail, and education center. One University of Minnesota economist, Jim Skurla, has been quoted as saying that "Duluth has always had this tradition of taking two steps forward, then one step back" (Kraker 2012). There certainly seems to be no rush to create a different, more dynamic economy.

Boulder, Colorado

Population: 95,000
Metro area: 295,000
City type: University, high tech

Boulder began as a gold-mining town and then as a center of support for the industry.

The city is home to a variety of vibrant industry clusters, including the outdoors, natural products, clean tech, bioscience, software, and aerospace industries. The town was incorporated in 1871, and six years later the University of Colorado was established there. The university gradually came to be the principal actor in the economy, especially through the skilled labor force it created and, of at least equal importance, the research activities of its faculty that stimulated the growth of many high-tech firms. In this environment the federal government chose to establish in Boulder 17 major research laboratories and institutions, such as the National Oceanic and Atmospheric Administration, the National Center for Atmospheric Research, the Earth System Research Laboratory, and the National Institute of Standards and Technology.

The majority of high-tech firms are small companies, but over a dozen large firms, such as IBM, Cisco, General Electric, Google, and Lockheed-Martin have established research facilities in Boulder, some as early as the 1950s. The small firms have been stimulated by several programs that support innovation, such as

Promoting Boulder Innovation, Building Innovation Infrastructure, and Advancing Innovative Policy Solutions. The Boulder Chamber of Commerce supports much of this with its Innovation Blueprint 3.0 program (www.bouldereconomiccouncil.org).

These successes in high-tech education, research, and business have all been supported by Boulder's inestimable natural resources that are crucial to its very successful outdoor recreation activities, from skiing and hunting in fall and winter to fishing and hiking in the better part of the year. Not only is Boulder a jumping-off point for these very popular activities, but it has blended this with scores of small businesses producing natural and organic foods, and Celestial Seasonings, one of the world's largest producers of tea. The city hosts a large number of wineries, local craft breweries, and distilleries. *Bon Appetit* named Boulder "America's Foodiest Town" in 2010.

Being a major university town, Boulder has a wide variety of cultural assets and events, including a Shakespeare Festival and a Balloon Festival, among others, one of the nation's oldest Chautauquas, and a host of theaters and galleries.

Boulder's planning has not been done with the objective of survival, rebirth, or refocusing the city's economy. The title of the plan, adopted by the city council on October 29, 2013, was *Economic Sustainability Strategy*. Over the years, the report states, the city's "most important actions were not undertaken to promote economic development" but were, rather, "initiated in response to growth pressures and the sense that the community's unique sense of place and quality of life would otherwise be lost" (City of Boulder 2013, p. 2). Boulder has been involved in growth management and sustainability since the 1970s, when it instituted a height limit for buildings, historic preservation, residential growth-management ordinances, and initiatives to preserve the rural character of lands close to the city. Beginning in 2000, the focus became that of ensuring an adequate supply of affordable housing (City of Boulder and Boulder County 2010, p. 5).

In 2010 the city saw three challenges to its comfortable situation: (1) an aging population, requiring additional services, and the need for affordable housing for lower-income people, (2) the need to improve energy efficiency and to move toward using more renewable energy, and (3) challenges coming from nearby towns and cities as they gain enhanced retail options and experienced job growth, and the need to maintain city revenues to meet demands for more municipal services (City of Boulder and Boulder County 2010, p. 8). In its planning documents, the primary efforts are given to meeting these challenges, but there is no sense that the city should seek to follow another path of economic development.

Boulder is one of the most successful cities in this study. Key to its success is the university and all that attaches to it – high-tech start-ups, major research facilities, a lively cultural scene, and attractive retail aimed at both college and town sectors. The city describes its economy as a "unique mix of a successful and healthy tourist industry, partnerships with universities and federal laboratories, and many arts, cultural, entertainment and retail options" (City of Boulder 2013, p. 5). All this, and it's only 45 minutes from a major internationally connected airport.

Billings, Montana

Population: 100,000
Metro area: 158,000
City type: Resources, isolated

Unlike Duluth, Billings has a history of introducing major strategic economic plans, most recently in both 2003 and 2008. These plans were needed in light of "significant changes in population, growth patterns and economic development" (Billings Planning and Community Services Department 2008). The Billings plan is an excellent one and is a model for other cities. We will examine it after we have developed an understanding of what Billings is and how it has developed.

The city is quite isolated, with the closest city of any size, Bozeman with 25,000 residents, almost 150 miles to the west. The metro area is 158,000, only 75 percent larger than Billings itself, the smallest ratio of any city in this study. The city began as a rail hub that evolved into a regional retail center, as well as a headquarters site for many companies, especially those in the energy sector. Its retail sector is supported by the lack of a sales tax, and this draws costumers from Wyoming and the Dakotas. Billings is in the middle of the nation's largest coal reserves as well as extensive oil and gas fields. It recently established the TransTech Center, an industrial park for high-tech firms. Agriculture, especially sugar beets, has been a mainstay of the economy since its beginnings. The city is rather lacking in higher educational facilities. Montana State University has a campus in Billings with about 5,000 students, with masters' degree programs in business, medicine, and education. Rocky Mountain College is a liberal arts institution with just over 1,000 students. The economy has been strong since the energy sector has been so strong in recent decades. Given its strength in the region, it follows that Billings would also be its health care center as well. The six largest employers in Billings are the federal, state, and city governments, the school district, and two health care facilities; then come two banks, the county, and Better Business Systems, a global business services company.

The plan itself is one that meets the criteria for a good plan that have been set out in a number of sources (Kresl 2007, pp. 27–31). Stating that the plan will be governed by a community vision established "by the people, for the people," the second chapter is an explication of the various mechanisms through which public involvement will be achieved. This will involve both special interest groups representing environmental or business communities, and geographical groups representing neighborhoods. Two hundred residents participated in a survey of the issues and a detailed website was established. The heart of the plan is a set of issues, treating the following elements: land use, economic development, natural resources, esthetics, open space and recreation, transportation, public facilities and services, cultural and historic resources, and community health. For each element, each of up to 15 issues has a goal and a set of two to four objectives for each goal. The result is a comprehensive program treating all of the concerns that the plan is designed to resolve. Given the strength of the local economy, the issues treated are supportive of the general economy with no attempt to chart a course different than the one the city currently enjoys. The city does not have the higher educational facilities that would support development of a major high-tech economy using local skilled labor; the firms that might like to locate here could, of course, bring labor in from other parts of the country.

Billings is a city that has been on a good growth path for a considerable time. Nonetheless, it has engaged the community in a very substantial and serious planning process. The plans primary focus is on growth management, land use, and neighborhood improvement.

Cities with population of 101,000–250,000

Provo, Utah

Population: 113,000
Metro area: 526,000
City type: University, high tech

Provo is another university city with Brigham Young University (BYU), and Utah Valley University (UVU) ten miles away in Orem (population 84,000). Each has about 33,000 students, with BYU having 68 masters' degree programs and 25 programs at the doctorate level. UVU was a vocational college until 1987 when it became a community college, and a university only in 2008. The two institutions are thus dramatically different in their capacity to conduct research, generate start-up firms, and support a high-tech economy.

Normally one would think that a city with such educational assets would have a consistently strong economy, such as cities we have already examined – Lewisburg, Ithaca, and Boulder – but this has not been the history of Provo. In the post-World War II years downtown Provo was doing quite well – retail was bustling. Then in the 1970s the city decided it would not sanction a shopping mall in the city center, and the mall was built instead in nearby Orem. Within five years, vacancies began to appear in downtown Provo as retail succumbed to the convenience of mall shopping. In fact, the mayor took to inviting high school students to display their works of art in vacant shop windows to make them look less a symbol of decline. The two cities tried to work together and even considered, for a short time, combining the two city governments.

The economy of the city turned up in the 1990s when a shopping mall was built in south Provo, and the BYU Academy was converted into the city library and then expanded into the Covey Center for the Arts. At the same time, BYU began to expand its student enrollment and new hotel projects and a city center access ramp to Interstate 15 stimulated downtown vitality. However, early in the 2000s the real estate market collapsed, with prices falling 30 percent (Pugmire 2013).

Provo is only 45 miles from Salt Lake City, with its major airport and the University of Utah, which has a student enrollment of 34,000 and a full array of programs at the doctorate level. Together with BYU this presents a very impressive capacity to do important research that has led to a large number of high-tech start-ups, of which there are more than 400 in Provo alone, and an environment that is very attractive to technology-based firms to establish facilities (www.city-data.com/us-cities/The-West/Provo-Economy.html).

In 2012 the city initiated a strategic economic strategy in which it examined: population demographics, industry growth trends, infrastructure assets, talent availability, education, resources, and quality of life factors (City of Provo 2012, p. 2). These issues must be seen with Provo's proximity to both Orem and Salt Lake City in mind. Being a major university city, Provo firms have access to a stream of educated workers, but given the low income of students the city's retail sector is continually threatened by that of Orem, in particular, and the planners perceived "retail leakage," including some big stores such as Sears and Target. Specific concerns include: that Provo's population growth has been slower than that of either Orem or Salt Lake City; a lack of Class A office space and space for start-ups; an inability to capture spin-offs from BYU faculty; that the business incubator is located in Orem; that the Church of the Latter Day Saints culture may not be inviting to individuals from other parts of the country and cultures; lack of planning for pedestrian-friendly spaces downtown; and, due to no history of strategic planning, there is no master plan for the city.

The planners do not see Provo as being in a state of crisis, but they do see the city not being able to achieve what should be its potential. In addition to its being on the southern periphery of the Salt Lake–Orem–Provo metro region, the city is also penned in by mountains on the east and the lake on the west. Hence, the concerns about space for business growth. If the city had more space in all directions, its problems might be less significant and the growth in high-tech and retail activities more easy to achieve.

Shreveport, Louisiana

Population: 200,000
Metro area: 441,000
City type: Multi, recreation, tourism

Shreveport is in the northwestern corner of Louisiana, at least 200 miles from other larger cities, such as Dallas and New Orleans. Bossier City is a sister city on the other side of the Red River and has a population of 63,000; Barksdale Air Force Base is situated in Bossier City. Shreveport was, for decades, a major city in the oil and gas industry, but in the 1980s its major firms merged with larger companies and the Shreveport operations deteriorated dramatically. The negative situation was exaggerated by the fact that the city had the highest property taxes in Louisiana, resulting in residents moving to areas outside the city, such as Bossier City. Lower-income residents were exempt from this tax and consequently the city was strapped for funds and could do little to respond to the loss of residents and retail and to the needs of lower-income residents for public services. The economy has recovered a bit due to development of the casino and riverboat gambling industries. More recently, in 2012 General Motors closed a major production facility, and weakness in gas prices in the US has put a damper on the Haynesville shale development. Shreveport was recently identified as the "fastest shrinking economy in the nation," for the second year in a row. Municipal output declined 12 percent in 2012 and another 5 percent in 2013 (Hess *et al.* 2014).

Local officials attribute this to the closing of the GM plant and the loss of 3,000 jobs and point to other new industrial investments. However, these investments and the economic vitality that exists are attributed to what is happening across the river in Bossier City rather than in Shreveport (*KSLA News* 2014).

The educational assets of Shreveport do not serve it well. The nearest major university is Louisiana Technological University (LTU), in Ruston, 70 miles to the east. LTU has 11,000 students of which 1,700 are in a handful of graduate programs.

Louisiana State University (LSU) at Shreveport is not considered a significant asset to the economy. It has 3,200 undergraduates and 870 graduate students in 12 masters' programs and one doctorate in education. LSU has established the LSU Health Science Center that, in addition to being a regional health care institution, conducts research into a variety of medical and health issues. A regional business incubator center has been established, but across the river in Bossier City.

Although the two cities are just across the Red River from each other, we were not able to discover any joint economic planning. The planning for Shreveport tends to be done through the Shreveport–Caddo Parrish under the Metropolitan Planning Commission, or through a northwest Louisiana structure. The first document we will examine is *Great Expectations Shreveport–Caddo 2030 Master Plan*, adopted in 2010. The document begins by noting that the previous plan was adopted 50 years ago, in 1957, in response to the disruptions of the post-World War II period. The 2010 document was adopted in the heady years of the Haynesville shale development. The picture was rather rosy, before the deterioration of a couple of years later, and local officials had high expectations about the future writing that: "Shreveport is the creative and flourishing powerhouse of the ArkLaTex region" (Shreveport Metropolitan Planning Commission, 2010, p. 1.2). In this spirit, the document paints a picture of an ideal future in 2030. The future is seen as pretty much more of the same, with marginal improvements in infrastructure and education, as well as the ongoing struggle to make the city maximally business friendly. The key sectors are oil and gas, defense, health care, tourism, biomedical, film and digital media (Shreveport Metropolitan Planning Commission, 2010, pp. 7, 12). The other document, the *2013–2017 Northwest Louisiana Comprehensive Economic Development Strategy* (Shreveport Coordinating and Development Corporation 2014), is a plan for the ten counties of northwest Louisiana and is not specifically designed to speak to Shreveport's situation and needs. This being the case, it is not of use to examine the details of the strategy. But it is of interest to note that Shreveport has not done the sort of strategic-economic planning that would speak to the situation and needs of its own local economy. Coordination with its natural partner, Bossier City, seems to be underdeveloped and it is hard to see how the city will be successful in charting a course for its future development.

Eugene, Oregon

Population: 156,000
Metro area: 351,000
City type: University, multi

Eugene is home to the University of Oregon (UO), with 25,000 students and a full array of masters and PhD degree programs. During the past decade, state funding was cut from 40 to 13 percent of the university's budget. The university has had to push for private benefactors and recently raised $850 million. In fact, there was some discussion of privatizing the university, and also the University of Oregon and Portland State University (Wang 2013). The concern of many citizens of the state is that this will mean increased payment by students, whether rich or poor. Whatever its status, UO is the key element in the city's economic strength. In 2006 construction began on a new research center for the Oregon Nanoscience and Microtechnologies Institute, as well as many other research institutes.

In addition to the university, Eugene is the base of Land Community College. Its situation has become somewhat difficult in the recent recession, with enrollment falling and the need to increase tuition. Much of the program is two-year certificates, with many courses that prepare students for vocational employment. It has currently about 14,000 full-time equivalent students. Together with UO it helps to assure that Eugene has the skilled services workforce that it will need.

Other sectors of importance are timber and agricultural production. Eugene is at the southern boundary of the Willamette wine district, so this industry has not been as important as it has to Walla Walla and even to Ashland; research and teaching in the sector are done at Oregon State University. Eugene is where the running shoe company, Nike, was founded, and it has long had an association with running, cycling, outdoor activity, recreation goods manufacturing, organic food, and green economy activities. As a university town it has a full array of cultural assets, including several choral and orchestral groups. Summer events include the Bach Festival and the Festival of American Music.

With the university and local health care institutions at the heart of its economy, Eugene has not experienced any sort of economic crisis since the timber industry had a downturn in activity in the early 1980s, from which the industry rebounded quickly. Spin-offs from the university have created an economic strength in software, biomedical, innovative manufacturing, clean technology, and renewable energy – including solar panels.

The economic plan that was adopted in 2010, the *Regional Prosperity Economic Development Plan* (Eugene Joint Elected Officials 2010), was the product of the cities of Eugene and Springfield (bordering Eugene on the east), and Lane County. The core of the strategy is focused on three sectoral clusters that are to be developed as the continuing core of the local economy: manufacturing machinery, education-technology, and food and beverages. These three sectors are the most rapidly growing areas of the economy. Manufacturing, overall, is not seen as a sector that will grow; the objective is to restructure this activity toward higher-skill and higher-wage aspects of "advanced" manufacturing. This is made necessary by the competition from production in low-wage countries and by the lowering cost of using robots in place of human labor; clearly, this is a powerful threat for older workers (Livability Lane 2010a, p. 1). The education-technology industry consists, in Eugene, of video games, social science research, and computer science. This is a rapidly changing sector and both the university and Lane Community College are revising their curricula so they and their graduates can continue to be competitive (Livability Lane 2010a, p. 1). The last of the three sectors that will be privileged is food and beverages. Agriculture has been a key sector for the entire history of Eugene due to the fertility of the soil and the mildness of the climate. What is required for the future is an effort at branding or identity, job creation, and development of infrastructure. The wine industry has become very important for the Pacific coast, and Oregon has carved out a specific place for itself (Livability Lane 2010c, p. 1).

The strategic economic planning that has been done by Eugene and Lane County does not argue for any significant change in direction. The assets in terms of soil and weather, research capability, and skill of the workforce are supportive of the existing competitive strengths of the regional economy. The planning was done with substantial input from the residents and appears to have been done in a very competent and well-focused manner.

San Bernardino, California

Population: 214,000
Metro area: 4,000,000
City type: Multi

The recent economy has not been kind to San Bernardino, the birthplace of McDonalds fast food restaurants, in 1940. The city is a bit smaller than Riverside (population 316,000) with which it serves as center of the "inland empire," between Los Angeles and the Mojave Desert. Two fires destroyed almost 1,300 homes in 1980 and 2003, Norton Air Base was closed in 1994, to become the municipal airport, and the city suffered three recessions during the last years of the twentieth century. In July 2012 the city declared Chapter 9 bankruptcy, the largest city to do so until Detroit followed suit one year later. About 35 percent of residents were below the poverty line, the highest of any city in California; with a population of 200,000, 36 percent earn below $25,000 per year – in a state with 88 billionaires. Thousands of San Bernardino residents lost their homes in the real estate loan crisis that began in 2007. The situation was exacerbated when the city, under increasing fiscal pressure, had to lay off municipal workers and cut expenditures (Romero 2011).

In February before the bankruptcy, Governor Brown's proposal that all redevelopment agencies in the state be eliminated was enacted. The City of San Bernardino then took over the activities of the city's Redevelopment Agency (City of San Bernardino 2015). As yet the city does not appear to have done much with its new mandate in the way of strategic economic planning. What has been done has been focused on downtown revitalization that consists of a series of infrastructure projects, a housing project, and revitalization of Theatre Square, and "around-the-clock entertainment district" that will become a "hotspot of Downtown" (www.downtownsanbernardino.org).

An earlier plan, adopted in 2005, had as its economic objectives some general notions of transportation advantages, capturing growing markets, revitalizing retail, partnering with local institutions, invigorating investment, and enhancing the city's image as a gateway to the mountains and desert. But there was nothing specific as to sectors or industries that would be promoted. The problem was that San Bernardino had been an economically distressed community for the previous two decades due to the closure of Norton Air Force Base and a number of other important employers (City of San Bernadino 2005, p. 4.1). So for about 30 years the primary objective of the city has been avoiding collapse of its economy.

The current situation has been worsened by what two journalists referred to as "a noxious political atmosphere that has paralyzed City Hall throughout the economic crisis" and that may "lead to criminal charges" (Willon and Sewell 2012). In September 2014, a new director of economic development, Bill Manis, was appointed. He began by noting that "the development function of the city was dormant for a period of time" – an understatement if anything (Hagen 2014). Among the suggestions he offered, such as a better webpage for the city, working on long-term property management, seeking outside funding, and working with other offices, Manis highlighted the need for an economic development strategic plan. This has not yet been decided or completed. The city does need to do something dramatic.

San Bernardino is one of the less successful of our smaller cities. It has been buffeted by loss of employers, inept government, and a lack of specific economic development planning. It provides a cautionary note to other city leaders as to how things can deteriorate and the extent to which this deterioration can become a quagmire from which the city will have great difficulty in extricating itself.

Lubbock, Texas

Population: 239,000
Metro area: 301,000
City type: University, isolated

Lubbock is a city that is dramatically different from San Bernardino. Its economy is based on agriculture – principally cotton – education and health care.

Local officials are concerned that cotton is grown using water from the Ogallala aquifer, a vast body of underground water that brings water from the northern plains down to Texas. This aquifer is threatened by recent shortages of rainfall and by the gradual diminution of water availability. The industry has also depended heavily on subsidies from the federal government. Sooner or later cotton will be a less reliable part of the local economy than it has been in the past.

Texas Tech University is perhaps the primary asset of the city. The principal university in the west two-thirds of Texas, having 34,000 students and an array of graduate programs, Texas Tech supports 60 research centers and institutes. It established its Research and Technology Park at the end of 2014 and has just signed up its first tenant, Chromatin – an agbiotech firm based in Chicago. Its first task is to work on reducing the demand for water from growing sorghum, and other aspects of agriculture in low-water environments (Michael 2015). This is obviously an initiative that is directly linked to the needs of the local economy.

The university has done a study of the impacts of Texas Tech on the local economy, in terms of employment, household income, and output (Ewing 2010). The categories of activities studied were: (1) operations, employees and research, (2) student spending, (3) non-football visitors, and (4) football game fans. Employment was increased by these activities by (1) 9,740, (2) 3,261, (3) 1,162, and (4) 576, for a total of 14,739. Household income increased by over $612 million and output rose by $1.2 trillion. In addition, of course, the university greatly increased the attractiveness of Lubbock to firms looking for a locale for a research facility in agriculture or oil and gas. So from a macro-economic approach, the university was a primary, if not the primary, actor in the local economy.

Lubbock is not a center of traditional culture – dance, theater, classical music, and art. These are often popular in cities with substantial liberal residents; Lubbock was found, in 2005, to be the second most conservative city in the US, behind only Provo (American City and County 2014). The university has a College of Visual and Performing Arts, with a typical university schedule of events, although it is not possible to ascertain how many of the local residents attend these. Lubbock's free-time activity institutions and programs are focused on ranching, on the music of favorite son Buddy Holly, and on sports. This is often a deterrent to companies that are looking for a city in which their highly educated and skilled employees can find the sort of environment they insist on, at least for their children. One of this book's authors remembers doing a research project on off-shore oil in Norway and Eastern Canada. When discussing the future with the senior executive for Mobil Oil (Canada) in Halifax, he asked whether the head office would be moved to St. John's since that was where the big deposits were located. The executive responded, "No, of course not. I could not have my children grown up on a city without theater, music, dance and art." As the report to be discussed in the next paragraph put it: "one person's 'good place to raise a family' might translate into another's 'there's nothing to do in this town'" (LEDA 2015, p. 16).

The Lubbock Economic Development Alliance (LEDA), formed in 2004 after a decision by Lubbock voters, issued its Economic Development Strategic Plan in March, 2015. The plan sets out key strategies for three goal areas: business development, talent management, and entrepreneurship and innovation (LEDA 2015, pp. 2–4). The guiding principles of the plan are: (1) forward-thinking, (2) talent-driven, and (3) collaborative. The rest of the document lays out strategies and actions for each of the three goal areas. The authors of this book have rarely seen a plan that was so focused on the assets and capacities of one institution – in this case Texas Tech University. Almost all of the strategies and actions are simply enhancement of what already exists as the strength of the local economy and the strengths of the university. There do not seem to be new directions that are identified – the city economy goes where the university goes, for whatever reasons.

In Lubbock we see a city that seeks to move increasingly into high-techy activities, based on the capacities and intentions of Texas Tech University. The contributions of the city tend to be in general supportive of these activities, but one sees competition from other university cities that Lubbock may find to be very challenging.

The smallest cities

While we did not include cities of fewer than 20,000 population in our study, in 2006–2007 a team of researchers from the School of Government of the University of North Carolina conducted a study of 50 of the smallest towns in the US, half of which were in North Carolina, all with a population of fewer than 10,000, including some with just a few hundred. A sub-set of 30 of these towns was published by UN-Habitat in 2012 (UN-Habitat 2012, pp. 81–82). The towns were grouped in four categories (UNC School of Government 2008):

- recreation or retirement destinations or near to an abundance of natural assets;
- historic downtowns or cultural or heritage assets;
- adjacent to a college campus;
- adjacent to a metropolitan area or an interstate highway.

They distilled the following seven lessons, or conclusions, with regard to things that were found to be of importance from this study that can be applied to small towns and cities in general (UNC School of Government 2008):

- community development is economic development;
- success is linked with being proactive and future-oriented and accepting of change and assumption of risk;
- successful strategies are guided by broadly held local vision;
- defining assets and opportunities broadly allows the city to capitalize on its competitive advantage;

- innovative local governance, partnerships, and organizations are crucial;
- a comprehensive package of strategies and tools is preferable to a piecemeal approach;
- for long-term community development to be achieved, it is necessary to identify, measure, and celebrate short-term successes.

These 30 very small cities were characterized as taking one or more of four approaches to development: entrepreneurship and small enterprise incubation-based, place-based, human capital-based, and industry or manufacturing-based.

What have we learned?

In general, smaller cities do have access to the resources, assets, and skilled professionals that are required for effective management of their local economy. This is probably due to the fact that in smaller towns the talents and qualities, positive as well as negative, of most residents are known due to social contact over many years. High-quality strategic economic plans have been designed and implemented by Boulder and Billings and other cities have planned in ways that were appropriate to their needs. Usually, a plan does not have to try to effect a major restructuring of the local economy. In some cases, such as Youngstown, San Bernardino, Shreveport, and Lewisburg, a major employer has left and the city has had to attempt, sometimes successfully but not always, to refocus the economy.

Facilitating the effectiveness of smaller town planning is the fact that in many of them during the past several decades the dominance of local politics and decision-making by prominent "founding" families and social clubs, such as the XX City Club or the Lions or the Rotary, has given way to often voluntary associations of local businessmen, university presidents and faculty, and representatives of women's, social, labor, and other local organizations. These individuals come with new and diverse ideas and suggestions and with new energy and talent. They tend to be more future oriented, less risk averse, and more connected with the world outside their smaller city or town, than the traditional decision-making individuals. We have seen this in several of the 15 cities we have just examined. This in itself has dealt with several of the accepted weaknesses or disadvantages of smaller cities, as elaborated earlier in Chapter 3.

One of the most powerful conclusions that emerges from our study of these smaller cities is the importance of the combination of one or more universities/colleges and a regional health care facility. Among the advantages this brings are: stability of employment over the business cycle (no "boom and bust" cycle); the employment of a relatively educated, skilled, and well-paid workforce; what this does to make the city attractive for high-tech start-ups; and the availability of cultural and adult learning opportunities for the educated workers and for retirees looking for a stimulating place to live. Cities as diverse as Lewisburg, Boulder, and Provo have demonstrated this to be true; conversely, Prescott, Youngstown, and Shreveport have lacked these assets and the vitality that accompanies them.

It is also clear from these snapshots that smaller cities can, indeed, comprehend their competitive situation, design a strategy to deal with it, and mobilize the resources required to achieve the end they desire. Billings is probably the best example of this, but Ithaca, Portland, and Duluth show how city leaders can manage a steady path with no major crisis. Smaller city leaders have generally done what was necessary, while others, such as Youngstown and Lubbock, have benefited from what private and public sector actors have done independently of action by the city.

It may very well be that these cities would have been able to take advantage of their local assets if they had had access to agglomeration economies. But it is clear that most of these cities have been able to create the degree of economic competitiveness they need to meet their objectives in the absence of proximity to a major hub airport, one or more large industrial clusters, major research facilities, or an array of professional services. But, as was emphasized in Chapter 3, these deficiencies can be overcome by modern telecommunications and production technologies. Smaller cities have been successful in adapting to the situation in which they find themselves.

As should be clear from the discussion above, the lessons gained from the UN report on the smallest cities are generally in accordance with what we found to be true for the larger small cities in our study. Most of the seven "lessons" were mentioned in the discussion of strategic economic planning in Chapter 3. Of the four categories, the one that was most striking for our 15 cities was the importance of not just a university or college but the combination of this and a regional health care structure. Cities that are weak in these assets tend not to have economic experiences that are as satisfying. Access to a major highway, for example an Interstate highway, benefits cities of all sizes; loss of that access has turned many smaller cities into mere shells of what they used to be; firms and then residents drift away until the town is little more than a ghost town that has experienced the playing out of a mineral vein or, as we are seeing now in the West, loss of access to water.

As a McKinsey study pointed out, "there is no single path to economic success" (McKinsey 2012, p. 24). We have shown here that smaller cities have indeed followed dramatically individual approaches to enhancing their economic competitiveness and vitality. There is no single end to this process and some cities have chosen path-dependent approaches while others have struck out on new trajectories. Some have concentrated on "eds and meds," while others have developed cultural or natural resource or local talent options. Clearly, it is necessary to undertake a unique and individual study of the city's relative strengths and weaknesses.

It is also the case that societies throughout the industrial world – Europe, Japan, and North America – are also aging. This demographic phenomenon has not been welcomed, but it does create a cohort of the population that has disposable income, free time, and mobility. Not all seniors fit into these categories, of course, but many do. Smaller cities and towns are particularly attractive to this population and, as noted as the first of the four categories above, cities that can make themselves attractive to this group can develop this stream of spending into a strong element in the local economy.

Finally, while transfers of additional resources from national and state governments would have facilitated matters and allowed for even more competitiveness enhancement, smaller cities have been rather creative in accommodating themselves to this recently developed situation.

8   Small cities and competitiveness in Europe

Introduction

The presentation of the European case studies will be organized in a different way from what we presented for the USA. This is mainly due to the fact that the topic – as anticipated in Chapter 6 – is the focus of interest in this specific period, in particular thanks to two specific aspects: first, the evidence that European small and second-tier cities have been more resilient to the economic crisis than larger cities and rural territories; second, as the focus chosen by the EU presidencies of Latvia, Italy, and Luxembourg, that put the smaller cities at the center of their agenda, from mid-2014 to the end of 2015. In Europe we thus had the opportunity to consider some specific case studies, but also to review recent research reports and studies performed by others.

In the first part of this chapter we will present what we have learnt from the literature on the role of the second-tier cities during the economic crisis – a topic that we already introduced in Chapter 6. Then we will follow what was proposed at the very beginning of the Luxembourg presidency: that attention be focused on the second-tier cities in cross-border regions. This is clearly a peculiarity of the European case and, standing on the recent research performed on the subject, we decided to include the topic and discuss it as a specific category of cities.

With this relevant exception, many of the European small cities we considered in this study are representative of the same categories we have seen for the USA group. There are some differences, that we will highlight when presenting the categories later in this chapter. The case study cities we selected for the European group do not all pretend to be exhaustive of every category, representative of every territory, size, country, etc. They have been selected primarily according to the availability of documents, information, data, and local institutions that could devote time for meeting and interviews to us. We have tried ideally to represent some of the macro-regions of Europe: we have cities in the Scandinavian countries, in the European core (many of those studied being in the cross-border group), in the Alpine area, and in the northern Mediterranean. We are aware of the fact that we are not representing in this study the cities of the most external periphery of the European Union (southern Mediterranean, Atlantic, eastern border): but it was not our aim to represent every European macro-regional context and this would require a research project quite different from the one we have imagined for this book.

Nevertheless we have been studying cities in at least 14 European countries, covering both very large regionalized states and small countries, federal stated and centralized ones, very new and very old members of the European Union – and the Swiss case too. We thus hope that our sample, which still is not exhaustive, will however provide an interesting overview of the European context.

The territorial impact of the economic crisis in Europe

In this section we propose an outline of the impact of economic recession in the European regions since 2006. This topic is interesting from our point of view because, as we already anticipated in Chapter 6, the European cities reacted to the economic shock differently according to their size, and the small towns and second-tier cities have been crucial for their contribution to the economic recovery and growth of many countries. We are interested in cities and territories, so our discussion needs to be based on territorial evidence – facts and figures referred to the adequate territorial scale and comparable among many European countries. In this respect we affirm that we selected a specific source and that we followed it for this illustration. This source is the ESPON program (see Chapter 6, note 2) and its project reports, in particular the Third ESPON Synthesis Report published in October 2014 (ESPON 2014), summarizing the results of 66 recent trans-national projects.

In Europe the economic crisis began in 2007 and by 2011–2012 the most evident signs of its impact were the growing share of population at risk of poverty and social exclusion (25 percent in 2012) and the loss of jobs. However, an attentive observation of the territorial data shows a great diversity among European regions. Regarding the decline of employment in 2007, only some regions were affected, in particular the peripheral areas of Romania, Bulgaria, Hungary, Italy, Portugal, and the UK and then in 2008 of France, Spain, Poland, Ireland, and Latvia. Only in 2009 were entire national systems in almost every part of the continent in recession, except Switzerland, Belgium, Luxembourg and the Netherlands, the western part of Germany, and some regions of France, Austria, Poland, and the UK. But in 2011–2012 these same regions contributed to the recovery and many others were already out of recession, such as Austria, Denmark, the south of Sweden and Norway. In this heterogeneous situation, the ability of regions to react to the crisis has been described with the word "resilience": regions were not expected to recover to the pre-crisis levels of GDP and employment, but they are instead considered according to whether they are more or less vulnerable to a macro-economic shock. In fact, it has been noted that those regions that specialized in a wider number of industries have been less vulnerable than those relying on only a few sectors or larger firms. It has also been noted that a flexible and effective structure of local governance and innovative policy-making helped the most resilient regions. But what is relevant for our study is that "the presence of an urban center, in particular second-tier centers, is positively associated with resilience of a region" (ESPON 2014, p. 25).

The ESPON report devotes considerable discussion to the role of cities for economic growth, emphasizing the articulation of the European urban structure and providing separate illustrations for (1) global and capital cities, (2) second-tier cities, and (3) small and medium-sized towns.

1 Global and capital cities

During the economic crisis the economies of agglomeration and the diversity of industries helped the global and capital cities to avoid the negative effects and recover more rapidly. But there are vulnerabilities too. One aspect is related with the age structure of the population living in the capital cities. Larger cities attract the largest part of the young population – but they have also been the most vulnerable in times of crisis; at the same time it has been noted that older citizens left many European larger cities looking for better urban life in smaller cities. Another aspect is social cohesion: larger cities are more likely to be affected by social exclusion (they have larger peripheral areas; but they also attract and tend to segregate minority groups) and by social polarization. Finally, as to the policies, the report underlines that capitals are supported more than other cities by public policies and the presence of institutions. When the economic slowdown imposes less public spending, this might have a stronger negative impact on capitals than on other cities that rely less on public spending.

2 Second-tier cities

In the years between 2007 and 2011 "in 15 out of 27 countries one or more second-tier city region outperformed its capitals in term of either higher real annual GDP growth rates or smaller real annual falls" (ESPON 2014, p. 44). This is for example the case of cities in a group of very heterogeneous countries, such as Norway, Switzerland, and Italy. While, according to the ESPON data, second-tier cities accounted for a 29.9 percent of GDP growth in 2007–2011 vs. 30.2 percent for capitals, in Germany, Italy, Spain, Switzerland, Poland, the Netherlands, and Norway they had a share of GDP growth higher than capitals. The 30 vs. 30 percent average share of national growth between capitals and second-tier cities varied to a certain degree among the European countries. In a group, capitals are largely more relevant than second-tier cities: this is the case of the former socialist countries (with the exception of Poland, Slovakia, and Romania) and of many unitary countries in the north (Denmark, Finland), the west (Portugal, Ireland), and the south (Greece and Cyprus, with Malta being an obvious exception). In another group of countries, capital cities are more relevant, but second-tier cities remain around or above the 30 percent, as smaller cities are poorly contributing to the economic growth: this is the case of France, Lithuania, and the Czech Republic. Finally, in general, in the regionalized (Spain, Italy) and the federal states, the capital cities are less relevant and show the lowest share of contribution to the GDP growth, with the extremes of Switzerland (12.3 percent for the federal capital Bern) and Germany (5 percent).

In many of these countries the GDP growth is due to the performance of second-tier cities, but also to small and medium-sized towns.

3 Small and medium-sized towns

We have already discussed the geography of small and medium-sized towns in Europe in Chapter 6. As to their reaction to the crisis, the ESPON report outlines four categories, describing both a positive and a negative situation, according to the demographic trends: (1) population growth; (2) positive migration, but aging; (3) labor exporting; (4) declining. It is hard to summarize a common policy approach for those cities, but it is possible to state that the regional/national context is influencing the performance of smaller cities more than any other of the above-mentioned categories. Being located in a remote area – as it is the case for many smaller European cities – might be an advantage or a disadvantage depending on factors such as:

• being in a cross-border area and thus benefiting from the position between international networks (such as in some examples described below);
• being in a remote area where national policies support the local services, e.g., to preserve the natural heritage or improve the tourism industry (this is the case of some coastal or mountain areas);
• being more attractive than other areas thanks to the beauty or popularity of the landscape or the presence of strong social networks (this is the case for example of cities in inner areas of Tuscany, in Italy);
• benefiting from special autonomies thanks to linguistic or territorial peculiarities (as many self-autonomous regions of the Alps, or many islands);
• being close to or effectively connected with one or more major urban poles (like some smaller cities in southern Sweden or in Switzerland).

These are only a few examples of factors improving the resilience of small cities. There are also factors related to their economy: smaller cities are more likely to be based on manufacturing industries – more vulnerable to the crisis – but also at the same time more resilient as they rely on a residential economy mostly dependent on local demand. But there are exceptions too. For example many cities specializing in tourism have both a local and an international demand, and those that have been able to develop a top-class world market rarely suffer from the economic recession (this is the case of cities such as St. Moritz or Davos in Switzerland). Cities like Struer, in Denmark, are a similar exception: a city of 10,000 residents in a less densely populated area of northern Jutland, but home of the Bang & Olufsen headquarters, the world-renowned manufacturer of designer music appliances. The Italian headquarters of Ferrero (which resembles several brands in the food industry including Nutella) in Alba, a 32,000 population city in Piedmont, is another example.

The European Union has been developing research on its future scenarios, including those related to the development of regions and cities. The ESPON ET2050 project (www.et2050.eu) has compared three scenarios for the development of the European territory in the next 35 years:

- a Europe of metropoles, following the Europe 2020 strategy of promoting the global competitiveness of the European Union by promoting the development of the largest metropolitan areas with global importance;
- a Europe of cities, following the priorities of the European Spatial Development Perspective and the 2007 and 2011 Territorial Agendas, for a balanced polycentric territorial development based on secondary urban poles;[1]
- a Europe of regions, with a shift of paradigm toward an effective response to climate changes and scarcity of resources, promoting small cities and medium-sized cities as centers for the development of resilient regional economies.

The ET2050 project underlines the role of smaller cities in two out of three scenarios, emphasizing that the "Europe of cities" scenario appears as the most expansive in terms of GDP, in particular for countries and regions in southern Europe (those most affected by the economic crisis). In these areas, fostering a balanced territorial development strategy, where smaller cities and their regions will take advantage of spill-over effects from larger metropolitan areas and development will take place where small and medium enterprises and clusters are located and/or promoted.

These are mainly general features referred to the European territory, with its heterogeneous reality. In the following pages we will enter into more detail, discussing the categories of small cities and then the case studies we selected and examined individually.

Small and medium-sized cities in cross-border regions

As we anticipated, this category of cities and this insight is specific for the European case. The European Union has been developing for decades cross-border and international cooperation between member states, funding specific programs and including it also as a priority for European structural funds. Non-member states have also been involved, participating in cross-border programs such as Switzerland in the Alps with the Interreg program, just to cite an example (www.alpine-space.eu). The international cooperation of the European Union includes also the programs devoted to candidate countries, the Mediterranean, etc.

In North America this cross-border relationship rarely exists. Along the Canada–US border only Detroit and Windsor have the necessary proximity; with the only other possibility, Seattle and Vancouver, the cities are just a bit too far from each other to allow for such an interaction. Along the Mexico–US border there are several candidates for cross-border interaction but concerns for corruption, crime, and illegal migration, as well as substantial differences in incomes and economic activities have left cross-border interaction under-developed.

Many cities in EU cross-border regions have taken part in projects, but considering the general features of management and organization of programs the most active territorial scale has always been the regional one. Each cross-border cooperation area included a certain number of regions with actors eligible for cooperation projects – including cities.

Thanks to the progress in European integration, to the above-mentioned programs, to the adoption of a common currency, and to the advances in the free circulation of citizens, many of the border territories of the EU have overcome their former economic isolation. As to the political and cultural aspect, many border territories suffered also from their proximity to "potentially hostile" countries – despite having deep cultural similarities, as in the case of many areas along the pre-2004 eastern border of the EU, or along the borders between new members.

In many regions of the older members, European integration improved or re-established a cultural and linguistic homogeneity that has characterized these areas for centuries, despite the geopolitical changes: this is the case of many regions in the Alps or in the Belgium–France–Luxemburg–Germany areas in the north. Finally, in other cases, integration has been improved thanks to the construction of ambitious infrastructures, such as the Øresund bridge between Sweden and Denmark.

Many of the border regions are far from the political and economic capitals, but instead many economically relevant second-tier cities are located there (e.g., Geneva, Basel, Trieste, Strasbourg, Maastricht, Lille) or vital small and medium-sized cities, such as in the Alps.

Also some capital cities are located in cross-border regions and they also have benefited from territorial integration: probably the most relevant case is represented by the twin cities Vienna and Bratislava, but also Copenhagen on the Øresund. Luxembourg City is another city that has been able to "punch above" its small size thanks to its geographical location.

In 2015 the Ministry of Sustainable Development and Infrastructure in Luxembourg promoted a study on small cities in cross-border areas that was presented and discussed at the very beginning of the Luxembourg presidency of the European Union. The study, performed by the Luxembourg Institute of Socio-Economic Research (LISER) provides relevant information for our topic. The report discusses both policy considerations and case studies. As to the policies, the authors argue that small and medium-sized cities in cross-border areas have the opportunity to be competitive through three main groups of factors and strategies: pooling of resources, developing common territorial strategies, and strengthening the image. Cities can pool their respective resources to achieve a mass that enables them to be competitive: they can join forces, they can share their competences, and search for complementarities. As to joining forces, this is useful when a group of cities needs to finance and operate infrastructures that could not be supported by a single city alone: this is the case of the Øresund bridge, and of many others, infrastructure projects, despite the fact that one should not underestimate the role of national and sub-national governments in defining infrastructural strategies and funding their operation. As to sharing competences, the LISER report argues that small and medium-sized cities in cross-border areas could work together in universities, research centers, innovation poles, clusters, science parks, etc. in order to promote and exploit the benefits of "cross-fertilization" of competences. While this is undoubtedly an important aspect, it is not very convincing from our point of view, as it is not specific for small and medium-sized cities and cross-border areas: the experience in the EU framework instead shows that cooperation in research, education, business innovation, etc. has been successful in very heterogeneous networks, including those with actors participating from very far territories and very different urban contexts. These features of innovation networks have been discussed more than a decade ago, e.g., in a special issue of *Regional Studies* edited by Gernot Grabher (2002) or in quantitative analyses such as those performed by Maggioni *et al.* (2007).

What we find very convincing is when small cities engage in cross-border cooperation to "search for critical mass," exploiting complementarities: one example is cooperation in health care, such as the cross-border hospital in Cerdagne on the French–Spanish border, funded by the European Regional Development Fund, France, and Cataluña (www.hcerdanya.eu). Other examples are the cross-border employment agencies on the Franco-German border and in the area between the Irish Republic and Northern Ireland, and projects for environmental protection, such as cross-border filtering plants or the prevention of flood risk along rivers (Decoville *et al.* 2015).

Small cities in cross-border areas also have the opportunity to foster their competitiveness, thanks to the elaboration of common development strategies with their neighboring regions. According to the LISER report, cities could develop "coopetition," an opportunistic collaboration on strengthening complementarities while keeping active the competition for attracting residents, investments, etc., in each respective territory. Among the most effective aspects of collaboration, other than environmental protection and risk prevention, are the common strategies for promoting the international image of the cross-border area. We have already noted that one of the weaknesses typical of small cities is the fact that they can hardly be found in the global map. Cities in proximity could develop shared strategies in this respect, to develop a common stronger image and thus overcome the limitations of their size. Moreover, a cross-border region could have some attractive factors per se: it could be more interesting for investors by being a multi-lingual area, thus being more open and more international; it could also be considered as a bridge for international trade. These factors could provide a small city in a cross-border area a competitive capacity well beyond what it would otherwise have according to its size. In the Alps a very appropriate example is probably the city of Bolzano/Bozen in the semi-autonomous province Alto Adige/Südtirol in Italy. This city of 100,000 residents is strategically located on the Brenner highway, connecting some of the most economically active areas of northern Italy with Austria and southern Germany. The city and its territory have been granted some degrees of autonomy for being on the border, in the Alpine area, and for the linguistic and ethnic mix, with German-speaking residents making up more than 25 percent in the city to more than 60 percent in the province. Being a multilingual area, despite some political tensions, has fostered the role of the city as a bridge between the German-speaking and the Italian-speaking areas of the Alps: the local university, for example, presents itself as "trilingual and intercultural," with 16 percent of students of international origin (the national average is around 3 percent) and more than one third of the tenured research and teaching staff of international origin (www.unibz.it). The city hosts also a couple of innovation parks, with business incubators and clusters in the environment industry and "alpine technologies" (building, sports, risk management, etc.) and the BLS – Business Location Südtirol – a marketing agency for attracting businesses with a particular specialization in the film industry (the agency started a film fund in 2010 and since then more than 100 films have been shot in the area, including several very successful international productions).

The strategies we mention in this section depend on the geographical situation of the cooperation area and on the effectiveness of the structures of governance. As to the geographical aspects, the openness of the border (and the length of time the border has been open) is crucial, so is the distance between cities and the extent of their respective metropolitan or functional areas. As to governance, its efficiency depends on the legal background allowing a common structure of governance, the commitment of policy-makers, and the involvement of local stakeholders in the process. Also the feeling of belonging to a cross-border area by citizens is important, and this depends also on cultural and historical aspects.

We will see how these various elements emerge in a few cases, some of which are presented by the LISER report. A last remark should be made before these summary presentations. What we discussed here with regard to the small and medium-sized cities in a cross-border area might be relevant not only in the case of the existence of an international border. Many countries in Europe have relevant internal borders, between regions, states, etc. It is thus notable from our point of view to consider the advantages of cooperation among small cities in a wider set of scenarios, in which the cross-border context is only one of the many possible situations in which small cities could benefit from building networks and joining forces. In the European Union, side by side with the cross-border cooperation programs, the trans-national programs have supported the creation of networks of cities. In recent years, while the European urban policy has been constantly an object of discussion, as we described in Chapter 6, the URBACT program gave energy and scope to the ambitions of many second-tier and smaller cities to cooperate with other territories. As Knox and Mayer underline, the URBACT program allowed the creation of networks of European cities gathering around thematic projects and common issues (Knox and Mayer 2012). The authors cite the Creative Clusters Network, established among cities aiming to exploit creativity as a lever for economic development, or the HERO ("Heritage as Opportunity") network, aimed at developing solutions for the management of urban heritage and monument sites. Also during our in-the-field research we encountered several networks of cities, some of which originated during an URBACT partnership. One of the most remarkable for the thesis developed in our study is the EUniverCities network started in 2012 and now involving 14 cities with their respective university institutions, in 12 countries of the European Union plus Norway (eunivercitiesnetwork.com). The purpose of the network is to exchange experiences and best practice between medium-sized cities where the university is a relevant actor and where there are practices or objectives in the areas of city–university cooperation: local economy, internationalization, science, student life, and attractiveness.

Categories of small cities

We repeat in this section some of the categories we used to group the US cases, with some modifications, and a couple of different categories. This is intended to provide the reader with an autonomous section for each group of cities and at the same time allow more comparison options when the categories are replicated.

University

Many smaller cities, some with a population of fewer than 30,000, are home to one or more colleges or universities. At first sight, universities in Europe tend to have been founded earlier than in the USA, preferably in larger cities; but there are also relevant old universities in small cities and there has also been a recent tendency to have education facilities in smaller cities and in less central areas, precisely as levers for local development. Many of these smaller cities are most likely to be successful in achieving the economic objectives of their residents, especially in the emerging economy of skill, technology, and connectedness. The institutions of higher learning supply professors/researchers who often begin start-up firms that have positive impacts on the local economy. They also graduate students who, if they can be induced to remain in the community – something that is often very difficult – provide the labor force that is necessary for the new economy, a workforce which would otherwise have to be recruited to migrate to a city that may not be as immediately attractive as a large city. Finally, education institutions frequently provide a variety of cultural, recreational, sports, and learning assets that make the small city as attractive as a much larger city; or even if this is not the case, the population of students and researchers/professors provides a stable audience for cultural activities. This builds on the notion of the economic core of the city, as it was elaborated in Chapter 4.

Industrial

The crisis of manufacturing industries has been affecting cities throughout the whole of Europe, with similar issues despite their size: unemployment, out-migration and shrinkage, pollution, abandoned industrial areas, decline in real estate prices, etc. Both large and small cities, facing the transition of their local traditional industries, have been facing the necessity to react and elaborate one or many strategies to stop the otherwise unavoidable decline. We will see below how some small cities have managed to keep or regain their position as manufacturing centers and what the future held for those that could not. Many small cities have been able to create a new path for their economy, relying on alternative local resources; we will see how they have also been regenerating their old industrial areas in imaginative ways, even creating a new urban landscape and a renewed attractive external image for the city.

High-tech

When we think of high-tech centers we naturally think of larger cities, which have at hand a skilled labor force, a set of urban amenities, and one or more research universities. They also have the advanced telecommunications and transportation assets that are vital to a high-tech economy and major universities. However, as has been noted in an earlier chapter, smaller cities can do much with telecommunications that reduces the need for access to a major airport. Many of them also have universities or colleges that bring to the smaller city a sufficient contribution of faculty researchers, skilled students and graduates, and cultural and recreational amenities that make them very viable as high-tech centers, albeit on a small scale. Local firms and entrepreneurs have adequate access to counterparts in other regions or even continents and have little or no need to meet in the same place. If other firms in the same industry are located in the smaller town, some of the necessary face-to-face contact can still take place. We will encounter several smaller cities that have done quite well in this regard in the section below.

Recreation/tourism

While tourism and recreation are something of a lifeline for some former industrial economies, this has long been a primary activity for many smaller cities that are situated in areas of natural beauty, recreation, and have the appropriate urban amenities. Being situated on a body of water is beneficial, as are proximity to mountains and forests, and access to a well-connected airport. In Europe, the Mediterranean coasts are lined with these cities, as are the mountainous areas of the Alps; the Scandinavian coasts and the furthest Nordic islands also have their touristic charm, as do the many lake districts and mountains in Central and Eastern Europe, such as the Tatras. Not all specializations in this sector are the same, of course – different age groups, and family constellations, sexual preferences, personal tastes for culture or sport, or just relaxing will find one location or the other to be attractive. Hence, the city that specializes in recreation/tourism must plan carefully what its offerings will be, and this is powerfully determined by the assets at hand. Moreover, much depends on the proximity or the accessibility to a sufficiently large pool of potential visitors – in this respect tourism in small Alpine cities can always rely on the large urban areas of Italy, France, and

Germany. In what follows we will see some smaller cities that, despite being located in a prominently touristic region, have developed a local economy supported by an heterogeneous set of industries.

Multi-focused

Although some smaller cities are highly focused on one activity, be it furniture-making, recreation, small manufacturing, regional retail, regional transportation, or cultural activities, many others may have had a key industry abandon the city or have always had a diverse economy. In some small cities, being multi-focused is another way of saying that the city has nothing special that distinguishes it or that gives its economy any particular competitiveness. This can be an indication of a city economy that is in decline following loss of a major firm. For other cities, however, a multi-focused economy can be the result of a purposeful shaping of the local economy so as to make it less vulnerable to a sectoral downturn, perhaps like one that may have cost the city its earlier specialization. While many smaller cities do have tourism amenities, universities or colleges, and perhaps a regional health care facility, the degree of specialization, one industry or multi-focused, should properly refer to other economic activities, such as manufacturing, logistics, agriculture, culture, and recreation/tourism. Some of the cities below have managed to do quite well as multi-focused economies.

Regional capitals

Regional capital status is a way to address small cities that are isolated in a marginal or peripheral region, far from the larger metropolitan areas. Many regions in Europe are characterized by the absence of a large metropolitan area in close proximity; some countries themselves do not have one or more large metro(s). In what follows we selected cases of "regional capitals" with these features; in addition we chose those which, despite not even being an administrative/political center for their region, are the only urban pole in a sometimes very vast region; they might have their economy fostered by the benefits of being central (as the only city in the region) despite their small size. As they are providing urban services to many smaller towns in their region, they sometimes display an inverse borrowing size effect, as their borrowed size is originated by smaller towns rather than by a larger one.

Cross-border/network

We have presented this category above. These are the cities that are located along a border and – after the progress in European integration – have a growing set of opportunities to exploit thanks to collaboration with their neighboring cities. In the following examples we include in this category also the cities that have been developing strong inter-city collaboration without necessarily having a border (or a former border) between them. We thus consider in general the cities that have been developing networks with their neighbors in order to overcome their size or function limitations, up to the point of creating together metropolitan areas of a notable size.

Some European examples

We have selected 17 cities (eight of which are grouped in three networks) in Europe, with populations of between 10,000 and 460,000 residents. The cities were selected according to whether sufficient material was available or when city executives or members of the local government were available for visits and interviews. The cities are located in 13 European countries and can be arbitrarily grouped into five geographical areas: the Scandinavian/Baltic area (Aalborg, Lund, Gdansk–Gdynia–Sopot), the European core (or "blue banana" as it has been referred to in many documents in the past: Leiden, Basel–Lorrach–Saint-Louis, Esch-sur-Alzette–Villerupt), the Alpine area (Lausanne and Salzburg), the Iberian peninsula (Aviles and Covilhã), and finally northern Italy and the northern Adriatic (Udine and Rijeka). No state capitals were included, since their economies are always distorted by the advantages that attach to this status; while some of the cities are regional capitals, many of them are not the seat of any administrative power, except for their own municipality. We identified each of the cities by the descriptions given in the previous section of this chapter: college/university, declining industrial, high-tech, recreation/tourism, isolated/peripheral, multi-focused, regional capitals, and cross-border/networks.

As with the US examples, our objective in doing this is to get some understanding as to what the capabilities for change are for cities of different small sizes, how they have been able to utilize their capabilities. These will be 12 snapshots, with different levels of detail in the examination, depending on the availability of documents or the possibility of doing study visits in the city and meeting policy-makers and other stakeholders.

Following several different sources, we try to provide for each city the estimation of its "metro area." For many cities the metro area is double that of the city population but for others it is far greater. Hence, it is impossible to isolate a small city from its metro area population, with the advantages that a larger area brings, since smaller cities may be situated in metro areas that are considerably more populous. Clearly a smaller city may benefit significantly from economic development and planning done by organizations of the larger metro area or administratively by the county in which it is situated. Nonetheless, it remains of interest to examine what actions are or are not taken by smaller city administrations themselves, and how they are able to take advantage of, or to insinuate themselves into, the larger metro area.

In examining these cities there was no attempt to distill a brilliant or preferred strategic response to the need to enhance competitiveness; indeed, not all cities have come to a realization that a strategic planning response is needed. Rather we have a collection of smaller cities that have found themselves in situations that varied from impending disaster to steady progress. We will base our analysis on the city itself rather than on the metropolitan statistical area or some other notion of the urban area. In many instances it is the city rather than its wider region that is faced with the economic challenge that must be met so as to avoid secular decline.

Esch-sur-Alzette, Luxembourg

Population: 33,000
Metro area: 91,000
City type: Cross-border/network

Villerupt, France

Population: 10,000
Metro area: 91,000
City type: Cross-border/network

We anticipated that a remarkable feature of small and second-tier cities in Europe is urban areas that are situated across a national border and are progressively creating (or have the potential for creating) a cross-border integrated metropolitan area (https://portal.cor.europa.eu/egtc/about/Pages/menu.aspx).

There are many such cases along the French–Belgian and French–German border and the interaction (commuting in particular) is even more intense in the Luxembourg area, where the small Grand Duchy (the richest country in the European Union according to many figures, including GDP per capita) lies between Belgium, Germany, and France. This is a very densely populated, built, industrialized infrastructure area, where we find many cities of small size within a limited distance of 80 or 100 kilometers. As an example, Luxembourg City (103,000 residents) is 40 km from Arlon (30,000) in Belgium toward the west, and 47 km from Trier (105,000) in Germany toward the east. There are intense interactions between the main localities, with sometimes also an impressive impact on traffic and congestion. The economic and political role of Luxembourg and European integration have fostered cross-border relations.

Luxembourg City itself is a very interesting case of a city small in size but operating and providing functions well beyond its size: but we will not discuss it among our cases as we decided not to include capital cities.

We will refer instead to the urban area formed by the city of Esch-sur-Alzette in the south of Luxembourg (33,300 residents) and the neighboring city of Villerupt (9,300) in France. With the municipalities of Sanem (Luxembourg) and Audun-le-Tiche (France), they have formed, since 2013, a European Grouping for Territorial Cooperation[2] of 92,000 residents in 170 sq km. The European Grouping for Territorial Cooperation (EGTC or GECT) is the first European cooperation structure with a legal personality defined by European law. It was established in 2006 to facilitate cooperation among local authorities in cross-border, transnational, and inter-regional activities.

The history of the cross-border region is tied to the development of the steel industry. Lying on a land rich in resources, in the late nineteenth century this area developed as the *Metropole du Fer* (the steel metropolis), with the development of mining and then of the steel plants, that – with the interruption of World War II – prospered until the 1970s and attracted workers and residents from the neighboring regions and from every part of Europe. The crisis of the 1970s had a dramatic impact on the area: the last operating mine was closed in the 1980s; there are still a few plants operating nowadays.

A large area of 120 hectares close to the city of Esch-sur-Alzette, right on the French border, was converted in the first decade of the twentieth century to a site for steel industry. The site grew with several modernizations and improvement until the early 1980s: since then the plants have been progressively dismantled or abandoned. This opened the discussion on the destination of the area. Given the economic conditions of the Grand Duchy of Luxembourg, the urban growth of the area and the value of the land, the government has been able to create a partnership with a private group (ArcelorMittal) in order to start an ambitious reconversion of the entire area, that started in 2001 with a masterplan. The new area, whose construction and conversion has been ongoing for the last decade and is still in progress, aims at creating a new town – Belval – for 30,000 people, with multiple functions:

- residential, with the first new residents entering their apartments in 2009;
- research, with the almost complete relocation of all the facilities of the University of Luxembourg, buildings for research centers in technology and social sciences, and schools for pupils of different ages;
- commerce and recreation, with commercial areas, parks and the new Rockhal, the largest concert hall in Luxembourg, opened in 2006.

This set of functions is complemented by some office buildings, intended for hosting high-level international businesses, hotels, and a train station with connections to the capital and the surrounding cities.

Belval is an impressive transformation project – the reconversion of such a large brownfield site has several risks – but the investors clearly have considered the advantages of being in a cross-border area and the need for residential and office options in a region where the pressure of commuting, prices, and congestion is very high.

Interestingly the capital city is relocating to Belval one of its most valuable assets, the university. This reciprocity between the two cities is certainly possible thanks to the small size of the country, but it is also likely that the new location of the campus will attract students from many neighboring areas in France and Belgium.

The smaller cities in the agglomeration should plan their strategies in order to maximize the advantages of the new town, which in a negative scenario could also enlarge even more the gap in the average income across the border.

Basel, Switzerland

Population: 173,000
Metro area: 830,000
City type: Cross-border/network

Lorrach, Germany

Population: 48,000
Metro area: 830,000
City type: Cross-border/network

Saint-Louis, France

Population: 20,000
Metro area: 830,000
City type: Cross-border/network

The region around Basel includes cities in a cross-border area in Switzerland, France, and Germany. The largest city is Basel (173,000), the most relevant economic pole of a cross-border region that has already several decades of political history. This is an economically strong region at the center of Europe and with the area of Geneva and Lugano–Mendrisio is where the integration between Switzerland and the European Union has been taking place for workers and functions before and beyond any political agreement.

The cross-border region, Regio Basiliensis, promotes itself as a "pocket-size cosmopolitan city," with the transnational atmosphere of the border region and the international profile of the residents, attracted by one of the most active and diversified urban economies of Switzerland. Cross-border commuting in the area amounts to more than 30,000 commuters, mostly from Germany and France to Switzerland. Among the strengths of the region, with also a symbolic role, the EuroAirport Basel–Mulhouse–Freiburg, a unique infrastructure serving as hub for three countries, the metropolitan area, and the nearby French city of Mulhouse and German city of Freiburg.

Among the distinctive features of the cross-border region, one of the most interesting and developed, is the structure of governance that allows the cooperation in the area between the group of medium and small cities and the levels of government of each country. The "Transnational Eurodistrict Basel" is the largest level and involves representatives from 85 local authorities in an association in charge of developing a common transportation and planning policy for the region and promoting projects in the areas of culture and education to foster exchange and mutual knowledge among citizens.

According to the Swiss territorial organization, Basel has also a "metropolitan conference," a structure of governance for the metropolitan area that integrates four Swiss cantons and the French and German counterparts. The metropolitan conference promotes the political focus on the river port on the Rhine, on the chemical and pharmaceutical industry, on the education sector, and on the construction of the cross-border RER (fast tramway line) connecting the international region, including the EuroAirport. This project is certainly strategic, given the level of congestion in the area caused by commuters, but also by the transportation of goods and by the fact that Basel is on the strategic node connecting the highways of Switzerland with those of France and Germany – thus, in another scale, connecting the central Alpine area with Germany and the north.

The governance and cooperation among cities and the different levels of government, overcoming international barriers, are clearly providing to the cities of the area a critical mass in developing projects and functions with ambitions comparable with many large cities in Europe.

An interesting set of good practices in the area are related also to the creation of a common labor market. There is a growing recognition of the specificities of a cross-border labor market vis-à-vis an international labor market. Several projects are being promoted in the Basel area in this respect in order to overcome the administrative and legal differences and also to improve socio-cultural relations. The Infobest office is the cross-border contact point and information center on regulations, tax and social security systems, education, and living and employment conditions for the workers in the cross-border area. It also provides support and practical information for workers and families who decide to move to/from one of the countries of the region. On the French-German side, the local office of EURES (European Employment Service) is one of the 11 cross-border employment services partnerships in the European Union.

Gdansk, Poland

Population: 460,000
Metro area: 1.2 million
City type: Cross-border/network

Gdynia, Poland

Population: 248,000
Metro area: 1.2 million
City type: Cross-border/network

Sopot, Poland

Population: 38,000
Metro area: 1.2 million
City type: Cross-border/network

In the north of Poland, the cities of Gdansk, Gdynia, and Sopot, with their metropolitan area, form an agglomeration of 1.2 million inhabitants – the Troj-miasto

(Three Cities) region. The Three Cities area is located in a north–south segment about 25 km long, with Gdansk and Gdynia as the southern and northern extremes and Sopot in the middle, in a strategic position on the southern part of the Baltic Sea onto which face nine countries of the European Union, and Russia. Gdansk and Gdynia have been specializing, beginning in the 1970s in particular, in the shipbuilding sector and in activities related to their ports. Sopot has conversely developed a cultural and leisure vocation, coherent with its relatively small population. The hard factors in the urban economies of the Three Cities declined in the post-industrial era, as is the case for many other industrial cities, and the effects have been even more severe as a consequence of the collapse of the national Polish industrial system. It is important to remember that Gdansk gave birth to the Solidarność (Solidarity) trade union in 1980, which history has firmly tied with the processes that led Poland in 1989 to its first free elections.

In contrast to other cases, the transition of the Three Cities has been accompanied by a rapid opening of international markets and by the positive effects of plans issued at national level, with major recourse to EU funds, in the last decade. This support facilitated a development strategy started by Gdansk in 1998 with EU pre-accession funds and then, after 2004, with the implementation of EU regional policy. The strategic position in the Baltic area, the availability of infrastructures in the framework of the TEN (Trans-European Networks), the establishment of a special economic zone in the region, and the regeneration of the waterfront, made Gdansk, in particular, very attractive for smaller firms in several high-technology industries (ICT, pharmaceuticals, etc.) and for the conversion of traditional sectors (Scoppetta 2011). There is quite efficient infrastructural and functional integration in the region, and integration is also effectively operational on the side of businesses and institutes, which "are not limited at all by the municipal borders of the three cities when doing business" (Meijers, *et al.* 2012). Cultural events are listed in a common regional calendar. On the institutional side, however, collaboration at the level of the metropolitan area is still characterized by many weaknesses, due in part to the fact that there are no legal frameworks of inter-urban collaboration and also because local competitiveness between the two largest cities unfortunately still exists.

Salzburg, Austria

Population: 145,000
Metro area: 220,000
City type: Tourism

Salzburg is located on the western part of Austria and has a peculiar position right on the international border with Germany. It is the capital city of the Land, the administrative unit into which the federal republic of Austria is divided. This is one of the richest regions of Europe, with a GDP per capita of approximately €41,000 in 2011, well above the average for Austria. While the region has manufacturing activities and still some rural tradition, the economy of Salzburg is almost exclusively based on tourism. The city is the hub for access to the surrounding Alpine area, but it is mainly a tourist destination per se, with its historical center and its architecture (it is a UNESCO World Heritage site), and for being the birthplace of Wolfgang Amadeus Mozart. In 2014 Salzburg registered 1,501,078 arrivals and 2,634,694 nights spent in the city (www.stadt-salzburg.at/pdf/der_tourismus_im_jahr_2014__broschuere_.pdf). The city attracts tourism from all over the world, with a growing number of arrivals from the USA, China, Taiwan, and South Korea, and a constant frequency of Japanese and South American visitors. It is remarkable that almost half of the visitors choose one of the four-star hotels in the city: in general the facilities are very high quality and there are many options also for luxury accommodation, dining, and recreation. Given these figures, it is obvious that the largest number of jobs in the city are in the services sector related to hotels, restaurants, and commerce. Moreover, in order to encounter the demand of tourists, the city has an all-year cultural program, of music in particular.

In order to have a growing number of visitors from every region of the world, with no seasonality, a nice downtown and an illustrious citizen are not enough. There are at least three policy options that have been constantly promoted in the city that have contributed to its success in tourism:

- The preservation of the old town. After having been only marginally damaged during World War II, the old town has been protected by the first protection law in Austria; moreover, the restoration of old buildings has been constantly subsidized, in order to maintain the particular urban landscape and atmosphere.
- Three decades ago the city government established a "green wall," in order to protect a vast green area within the city boundaries.
- Initiatives in arts and culture. These contribute to the ambience of the city and to the vitality of its cultural industry. The summer music festival is probably the best known on the international stage.

In 2011, out of 108,000 jobs in the city of Salzburg, more than 90 percent were in the service economy, notably in trade and commerce (almost 20,000), accommodation and restaurants (more than 7,200), and arts and recreation (2,300), all prominently tourism sectors (www.statistik.at). The economy of the city is also characterized by relevant education institutions: Salzburg University, with four faculties, 2,800 employees and 18,000 students, the University of Applied Sciences (Fachhochschule), with 2,600 students and 291 employees, and the Mozarteum University, the academy of music established in 1841. The Fachhochschule is located in the Salzburg region, but both the university and the Mozarteum have excellent locations in the city center, with some remarkably attractive buildings for facilities and departments. Finally, the health care and social sector represents approximately 10 percent of the jobs in the urban economy; given the presence of health care facilities and the growing number of senior residents in the city, it is likely that this sector will be a growing one.

Salzburg is clearly an attractive small city, rich, with a vibrant economy and with relevant assets in culture and education. But also in this excellent situation there are relevant challenges for the local government – and these are particularly interesting for us.

The first and most evident challenge for the city is commuting. With 108,000 jobs in a city of 140,000 residents, commuters represent a large share of employees – a rough estimate is that 50,000 commuters travel to the city on a daily basis. This is evident in the congestion that occurs on the main roads connecting the suburbs with the city center, despite the strategic central location of the train station and the availability of three park and ride facilities on the periphery.

The pressure of traffic and commuting is an obvious consequence of the very limited residential options in the city. This is due to the poor availability of areas for developing residences. The city has a limited area (65 sq km), and several restraints due to the commitment to protect the green areas and the historical buildings. Additionally, a remarkable part of the urban area is used by the railway facilities and by the airport – very close to the center and crucial for tourist accessibility to the city. As a result, housing prices are extremely high and frequently hardly accessible, in particular for younger residents or medium- and low-income households.

This challenge might have a possible solution in cooperation with the neighboring towns, but this is not very developed, as there is no governance at the metropolitan level and planning at the regional level is quite ineffective. Some opportunities might be offered by cross-border cooperation with Germany. The national frontier (which coincides in part with the city boundary) has been neglected for a while in the policy discourse, but cross-border commuting and cooperation in the areas of transportation and mobility have been growing in recent years, and also in some economic development projects. As the closest German city (Munich) is farther than Salzburg for many towns and, thanks to the common language, the city is providing urban functions in a cross-border area. Cooperation with the Austrian towns in the metropolitan area should be made easier by the fact that municipalities in Austria receive transfers from the federal government according to the number of residents and employees of the local businesses, which in turn are what Salzburg would need to locate in the metropolitan area. But at the same time the level of income is so high in the region that the smaller towns are not really pushed to cooperate and preferably opt for a very conservative approach.

Probably the most important challenge for Salzburg is instead in the core engine of its wealth: the predominant tourism sector and the fact that the city relies on it. It is a sort of "one-industry town" and in the unlucky (and not probable, it must be underlined) situation of a drastic slowdown in tourism, the city would be in severe trouble. Thus, the diversification of the local economy is certainly a key objective for a probable future strategy of the city, given that education and health care facilities are already contributing in this respect.

While in the process of assessing and reorienting the planning strategy started in 2007, Salzburg adopted a wide and ambitious smart city masterplan for 2025, with several objectives in the areas of energy, mobility, climate change, etc. The smart city masterplan in Salzburg has got significant support from the city council and has the opportunity to foster the development of the (under-represented) areas of science and technology in the local economy, in cooperation with local small and medium-sized enterprises and the university (also with the availability of attractive locations for technological businesses) in the framework of the "Science: City: Salzburg" project (www.stadt-salzburg.at). Given the strengths of the attractive features of the city, a sustained effort in this direction has the potential to put Salzburg on the map of the best smart cities in Europe.

Rijeka, Croatia

Population: 129,000
Metro area: 220,000
City type: Industrial

In the northwestern part of Croatia, the city of Rijeka is situated on the Adriatic Sea, on the most northern part of Kvarner Bay, bounded by the Istrian peninsula on the west. It is a port city, and it has been the theater of many geopolitical changes: formerly part of the Austro-Hungarian empire, it developed as the port city of Hungary, while Trieste – 80 kilometers away – was the port city of Austria. Since the end of World War I, the city has been disputed between Italy and Yugoslavia, has been independent for a short period and then became part of Italy for more than two decades, with the name Fiume. After suffering heavy damages during World War II, the city became part of Yugoslavia. In the early 1990s the federation of Yugoslavia collapsed with a devastating conflict that also led to the independence of Croatia from 1991. In 2013 the Republic of Croatia became a member of the European Union and Rijeka, its third city according to size, being only a few kilometers from Slovenia and Italy, became central in a cross-border Alpine–Adriatic area. If one considers only the twentieth century, the city has been doomed (or blessed?) by history periodically to undertake a new start: when it became part of Italy, then after World War II, after the collapse of Yugoslavia, and finally more recently with accession to the European Union. Clearly these events have been dramatic for many aspects, but they have also forced the city to reinvent itself, despite the fact that the presence of the port is a constant in its history.

In a very large number of cities, the last decades of the twentieth century have been characterized by the transition from an economy based on traditional sectors: in Rijeka this has also been accompanied by geopolitical change and the end of a state-led economy. Thus it is no surprise that the city has seen many years of stagnation; its population fell from more than 162,000 in 1991 to 128,000 in 2011.

The current mayor, Vojko Obersnel, took office in 2000 when his predecessor became deputy prime minister of Croatia, and he has been re-elected five times so far. With his staff, he has been able to elaborate and implement a comprehensive strategy for the city, organized in four-year plans, with the last one covering the extended period from 2014 to 2020, according to the programming framework of the European Union.

The transition in Rijeka has its visible physical evidence in the buildings lying along the very long waterfront, which includes the port area and many industrial facilities – in particular the shipyards that characterized the urban economy for decades and that are still active after transformations and privatizations (the shipyards nowadays specialize in building chemical tankers, car carriers, and other specialized vessels). Industrial buildings are also spread through other areas of the city and were used for the paper industry, tobacco manufacture, engines, chemicals, and refineries. The regeneration of several former industrial areas has been a constant and visible element of the transformation of the city in the last years and such projects are still ongoing: we will briefly refer to the most important transformations later while commenting on the strategies of the city.

A few words on the geographical position of the city. Being in a gulf, surrounded by hills and mountains, the city has several physical constraints and also administrative ones given the fact that the municipality per se has only and area of 44 sq km. The river Rijecina and its long canyon run across the urban area and used to be a border in the past; the river creates a delta, which is the only part of the waterfront which has not been filled with industrial buildings and port facilities: in the past it hosted several timber warehouses, as the wind flowing from the river canyon would be of particular benefit for the conservation of the wood. The city center, which includes several amenities, the pedestrian main road (the Korzo), and the vibrant and colorful city market, lies right on the seashore but the water is almost never accessible from the Riva, except for the Molo longo, the old harbor wall of the central port which was opened to the public in 2009 and offers now an attractive 2 km promenade in front of the city. Here, as in other port/industrial cities, access to the waterfront is absolutely crucial for the improvement of the urban quality of life and for the identity of the residents, as they rediscover this formerly inaccessible part of the city turning it into a new identity for the whole urban area. The opening of the Molo longo was part of the transformation put in place in the last decade, that included also the improvement of the university, which has been endowed with new facilities, including a science park and business incubator. Facilities for research and innovation, that have become a key element of the city's strategies, have been located in several areas of the municipality, many of them former industrial areas.

This introduces one of the three strategic goals for the city in the 2014–2020 period, the development of a competitive economy based on the knowledge society. In this respect the concept of the triple helix is developed,[3] based on the available university assets and on the positive experience of Start-up Inkubator Rijeka, which in 2014–2015 had already hosted 63 businesses and involved more than 1,000 people. More than the physical space for new enterprises, the incubator offers a network of 26 mentors who provide free consultancy and support to the new entrepreneurs. The city fully supports the operation of Start-up and of the two other facilities located in former industrial areas via the Rijeka Development Agency, which is 100 percent owned by the municipality. While Start-up is reserved for entrepreneurs with no previous experience, the other facilities are open to businesses in ICT and manufacture and have already hosted 166 businesses with an average incubation of three years.

With regard to economic strategy, the city is working on the ambitious project of creating three centers of competences specializing in:

- biotechnologies, based on the well-established presence of a specialized department at the university and a large private pharmaceutical laboratory;
- shipyard technologies, based on the local traditional industries;
- smart cities, which aims at creating a new path, operating with private partners and SMEs and developing specialization in niche industries (such as the 3D-printing technologies, in which the city hosts some leading international actors).

The local university supplies graduates in technical subjects, but there is also a strong presence of arts and humanities. In these sectors there might be fewer opportunities for young graduates. One of the reasons could be found in an apparently very positive factor: the cultural sector is steadily funded by the city and the national government: Rijeka has a vibrant cultural scene that includes programs for different age groups and for the many linguistic and national minorities living in the city. Among the various options, we highlight the excellent work done by Art Kino in a beautiful old cinema in the city center, with more than 1,200 events per year (www.art-kino.org). Nevertheless there is not really adequate space for private initiatives in the cultural sector, given the large availability of publicly funded activities. In this respect some difference could be made by the Creative Startup project, which supports the elaboration of business plans starting from innovative ideas in the fields of culture and education.

Knowledge and innovation are one of the three goals for the Development Strategy for the City of Rijeka 2014–2020. Another main pillar is related to the global positioning of the city and the development of the Rijeka traffic routes. We mentioned that in the past the port was the city's main lever for development, in combination with its strategic position on the Adriatic Sea, supported by rail connections to the cities of Vienna and Budapest. Nowadays the city has still this unique position, but with less advanced infrastructures than are necessary for competing in the global economy. Thus improvement of the port facilities and in particular of the rail connections with nearby cities in Italy and Slovenia and with the rest of Croatia is crucial. The improvements to be performed at the regional and national scale are complemented by projects at the urban level to improve local connections, e.g., between the port and the highway networks. These interventions, together with an international marketing effort performed in cooperation with the nearby cities of Koper in Slovenia and Trieste in Italy, aim to reposition the city on the global map, based on its traditional vocation.

The third complementary goal of the development strategy focuses on a mix of physical and functional tasks in the areas of urban regeneration, quality of life, and social inclusion. The most evident upcoming activities will change many areas of the city. On the waterfront, the delta area will be transformed into a park and host a new district with residences, commercial areas, and cultural venues. The Bencic area (that in the past hosted the tobacco industry and engine manufacturing), a large brownfield site in the city center, will be transformed into the city library and museums as the flagship project for the candidature of Rijeka as European Capital of Culture in 2020. The interventions made in the past decades to clean the waters in the city area from industrial pollution now offer residents and tourists "thematic beaches" close to the city center, and a 20 km walkable waterfront promenade is projected, from Rijeka to the neighboring city of Opatija, a charming town on Kvarner Bay that has been a tourist destination since the Austro-Hungarian empire.

Many of the above-mentioned projects are the continuation of activities started in the past, supported by the municipality and by funds from national and European agencies. There is nevertheless also a growing need for private investments (developers, businesses, etc.) that might be more uncertain after the current economic slowdown. Some projects may be implemented later or others might be downsized, but it seems anyway positive that the municipal authority has a clear and systematic path for the future.

One of the possible solutions is the project of urban agglomeration that the city is creating with nine close municipalities, that will give birth to an agglomeration of 188,000 residents in 414 sq km. The objective of the project, fostered by the opportunity of being eligible for specific European funds, is to focus on some large urban projects, located in the various participating cities, able to produce positive impacts and provide urban functions at the level of the entire agglomeration. The projects include the Bencic area in Rijeka, and the regeneration of ex-industrial and ex-military areas, that will be transformed into areas for research facilities and for tourism and recreation. The success of these projects depends much on the capacity of the municipalities to integrate and demonstrate a common effort in promoting a strategy at the level of the agglomeration.

There are two specific aspects that make the case of Rijeka interesting in comparison with the other case studies we are presenting. First, given the constraints of its size – in particular the limited area of the municipality – the city is systematically pursuing collaboration with the neighboring towns with an approach that might benefit all. Rijeka, the largest city of the agglomeration, has the financial and organizational capacity to promote new urban functions and projects, but has no space for them within its boundaries. The smaller towns have free areas but lack resources. While keeping many value-added functions still in the city center, the decentralization of some of the new functions allows Rijeka to improve its attractiveness, expanding its potential area to a metropolitan region of more than 180,000 residents. In this case the "borrowing size" effect has some reciprocity, in the exchange between functions, resources, and available areas. Despite the fact that in Rijeka the creation of coordination at the level of the metropolitan area is a task that needs significant political and administrative effort, the results already achieved are very promising and represent a model for other cities that are facing the same issues.

The second aspect specific for Rijeka as a second-tier city is how its unique geographical position has led its development path but also allowed it to host functions and attract investments well over its size. The position of the port and its connection with Vienna and Budapest have been the trigger for its first development, and probably its unique position could be again the most important factor in improving its competitiveness in the economic and infrastructural integration of the Alpine–Adriatic area. For this reason the local government, while pursuing the strategies for completing the ongoing transition, is also concerned with positioning the city on the global scale with new infrastructural investment. Clearly the main uncertainty is still the macro-economic trend that will have a large impact on the probability of attracting new investments that will eventually speed up or slow down the projects of the city.

Aviles, Spain

Population: 83,000
Metro area: 120,000
City type: Industrial

After the pervasive transformations that affected the economies of many cities starting from the late 1970s, many urban areas lost industries and population, with outmigration of active and young residents, deterioration of local services, poverty, and decline of the built environment. This phenomenon has been labeled "shrinkage" and there have been several studies on the issue of shrinking cities. In Europe, when referring to this phenomenon, usually reference is made to cities in England, in eastern Germany, or in the former socialist countries, or even more frequently to the industrial heartland of Europe.

In Asturias, on the northern Atlantic coast of Spain, the city of Aviles is an example of a small city that has been facing the challenges of shrinking after losing its main industry. The economic development of the city is related to mining and the steel industry. In the nineteenth century, the exploitation of the mines in Castrillón began. The city already had some port facilities, thanks to its strategic location on the estuary of the Aviles river, and the port was thus developed for the needs of the mining industry. After World War II, the city was identified by the national government as the ideal location for the steel and iron industries and the public company ENSIDESA (Empresa Nacional Siderúrgica Sociedad Anónima) established a large plant in the area. In the 1950s the city had 21,000 residents and in the following decades it became the destination for a large number of migrants, up to a population of 85,000 in 1975, when the immigration was then stabilized (Sánchez-Moral *et al.* 2015). As was the case for many cities with such a rapid growth, the new population needed housing and services, that were built in new peripheral neighborhoods around the city, with a planning scheme of a strict separation of the new district from the city center; this created a situation of segregation. The historical city was progressively surrounded by port and industrial facilities along the river shore and by new residential neighborhoods – impressive rows of tall anonymous buildings with the ground floor reserved for commerce and services. Then, the main part of the steel industry was built right across the river in front of the city center in an area extending for several kilometers, following the last curve of the river before the estuary.

In the medium term, the worst consequence of industrialization in Aviles has been the environmental impact of industries: after the analysis of the levels of polluting substances, the city was declared in 1981 *zona de atmosfera contaminada* (zone with contaminated atmosphere) putting the city on the unenviable list of the most polluted cities in Europe.

In the 1970s the crisis of large manufacturing plants was already occurring throughout Europe, and the industries in Aviles were restructured, privatized, and largely downsized. According to Sánchez-Moral *et al.* (2015), deindustrialization was only the initial cause of the crisis that affected Aviles. They argue that the city suffered from the loss of more than 6,000 jobs from 1990 to 2000, by outmigration and aging of the population, especially in the working-class neighborhoods, accompanied by discouragement and various social ills such as poverty, segregation, unemployment, etc. Moreover, the crisis in manufacturing was worsened by a general obsolescence of the production facilities, with waste and ruins, that complicated the environmental situation along the river shores in particular.

Starting in the first years of the 2000s, the city undertook a process of regeneration, that has been fueled by the availability of significant amounts of funds from the European Union and by the formation of a strong local coalition of actors and stakeholders, including the local and regional government, several public companies. and the international holding owning the still active parts of the industrial facilities. This latter aspect is considered to be very important, as it contributed to containing the depopulation and maintaining the industrial basis that is still part of the identity of the city. In this respect, a major effort in physical transformation has been done in modernizing and the expanding of the port and the railway and road infrastructures, thanks to the combination of funds from different levels of government.

The strategies for the city have been declared in the recent years with two documents – *Aviles Avanza* (2008–2011) and *Aviles Acuerda* (2012–2015) – outlining the strategies for employment and economic development, signed by the mayor of Aviles and by the representatives of businesses associations and trade unions (Ayuntamento de Aviles 2009, 2014).

The development of new businesses and the diversification of the local economic base have been promoted with the creation of a business park (Parque Empresarial Principado de Asturias) in the area that formerly hosted the steel industry. On the other side of the river, a large investment of several million euros has been devoted to the regeneration of the historic center and also of the working-class neighborhoods in the periphery.

The area formerly used by the steel industry and now used by the business park on the east and the historic center and the Aviles river on the west delimit a large area that has been identified as the new focus for the city, with the science park Isla de la Innovacion (Innovation Island) meant to launch the city as a location for innovation, research, and business development. The flagship project for the area is the Centro Niemeyer, a modern multi-purpose building designed by the Brazilian architect for the northern area of the "island" and opened in 2011. The building, as in many other cases, has the symbolic function of representing the resurgence of the city, and includes an auditorium, an exhibition building, shops and cafés, and an outdoor area. It hosts a rich agenda of cultural events (theater, dance, music, cinema, conferences) and exhibitions: the activities are supported by the Asturias government, by the city, and by the Port Authority of Aviles. The municipalities and their partners are committed to completing the Isla de la Innovacion project to welcome new businesses to the city and offer new areas for the expansion of the existing ones, collaborating also with the academic institutions of the centers of Oviedo and Gijon.

The city has certainly been able to attract and exploit resources from different levels of government and from the European Union, and to form a local coalition able to sustain the transition. Nevertheless, the latest available data (for 2012; Ayuntamento de Aviles, 2014) show that the positive economic and demographic trend that the city was experiencing before 2008 was halted by the economic crisis and turned into a negative trend in the last years. As it is still affected by macro-economic shocks, the limited critical mass and economic differentiation of the city could still be a threat for its uncertain future.

Covilhã, Portugal

Population: 36,000
Metro area: 52,000
City type: University

Covilhã is a city in the central region of Portugal and is the hub or main city in the mountain region of Serra de Estrela, the highest mountain range in Portugal. The city is situated in a valley and, thanks to the rivers Carpinteira and Goldra, it was the center of the wool industry for centuries. The city was thus strongly dependent on its traditional manufacture and when it entered a period of crisis in the 1960s and 1970s the consequences were severe both for the city and for the surrounding communities. The city's geographical position turned it into a relatively isolated "industrialized enclave" in an area with a mainly rural vocation. It faced the economic downturn with the weaknesses of being based on a mono-industry specialization.

In this context, the Working Group for the Regional Planning of Cova da Beira started promoting the idea of a higher education institution that then developed in a few years from the Instituto Politecnico da Covilhã (Polytechnic School of Covilhã), founded in 1973, to the University of Beira Interior in 1986 (www.ubi.pt). The university, a public institution, was decisive for the economic and physical transition of the city. It has been growing since 1986 to a structure with five faculties, almost 7,000 students, and 700 professors. Given the size of the city, the economic impact of such a large population of young students and researchers is obviously relevant for many areas of the urban economy, from commerce, cafés, and restaurants, to the wider array of urban amenities in culture and recreation, that in turn improve the quality of life for all the residents of the city. The geographical position of Covilhã gives to the university a unique location in a very large region that otherwise would not host any higher education institution. The closest public universities are in Coimbra and Vila Real, while the Universidade Catolica Portuguesa has a campus in the city of Viseu. Covilhã can actually be considered a European example of a university town.

As to the physical impact of the university on the city, it must be underlined that the seats of the campus have been established in the city in regenerated former industrial buildings. This benefited the city with the restoration of buildings of historical and architectural importance that also contribute to the identity of the city. In this process a museum of the wool industry (Museu do Lanificio) was established. The university has now four sites with an available space of 134,000 square meters (www.ubi.pt).

In a paper by Martins Vaza and Matos (2015), the transition of Covilhã is seen in relation to the development of other cities in the region, in particular those where the institutions of higher education and health care facilities are located. In fact,

> the creation in 2000 of the Health Sciences Faculty with the medicine course in the UBI, promoted the articulation of the hospitals of the region (Guarda, Covilhã, Castelo Branco), that took advantage of the association with the faculty and of a stronger connection among them.
>
> (Martins Vaza and Matos 2015, p. 391)

The future of Covilhã and its region seems to depend also on developing a polycentric urban network with strong connections among the cities. This should allow the region to develop economic and urban functions without putting pressure on the environment, in particular on the natural landscape of the mountain region that has also some potential for diversifying the economy with new businesses in the tourism industry.

Leiden, The Netherlands

Population: 121,000
Metro area: 259,000
City type: High-tech

Leiden is situated in the Randstad, the Dutch metropolitan network of more than seven million residents that extends for several kilometers from the cities of

Amsterdam and Utrecht in the north to the delta area in the south, where the cities of Rotterdam and The Hague lie. Leiden is almost halfway between The Hague/Rotterdam and Amsterdam. It is part of an economically vital area, with infrastructure and relevant assets in terms of urban functions and amenities. But in this context, the presence of a multi-polar network of very close cities puts some competitive pressure toward a certain degree of autonomy and specialization. Consider, for example, the research and education institutions: the University of Leiden is 25 km from Delft with its Technical University, 35 km from Rotterdam, with the Erasmus University, and only 21 km from The Hague University of Applied Sciences. Car commuting in the Netherlands can be a dramatic experience in rush hours, but the efficient railway system allows rapid movements among the many cities. To sum up, the city of Leiden had to find a way to develop a distinctive path compared to other small cities and to the very close larger one.

One asset in the recent development of the city is the Leiden Bio Science Park. As many other industrial cities, Leiden faced deindustrialization and unemployment in the 1970s and 1980s. The northwestern part of the city – outside the historic center and across from the train station – has been progressively allocated to buildings hosting the university, research centers, and health care facilities. The "eds and meds" strategy has been fostered by the establishment in 1984 of the science park that hosted, 30 years later in 2014, 173 organizations (of which 130 are companies) and almost 17,000 employees. The focus on research and education in life science and health care has been possible thanks to the university, that enrolled more than 5,000 students on the park facilities in 2013/2014 (http://leidenbiosciencepark.nl). A document by the Leiden Bio Science Park Foundation, The Hague Chamber of Commerce, the Association of Leiden Bio Science Park Companies, and the Confederation of Netherlands Industry and Employers (2010) estimated a multiplier of two for the size of indirect employment on the region (12,000 direct employees in the Science Park and 24,000 indirect in 2010). In 2013, 36 more hectares were announced for development, to host laboratories, offices, university buildings and apartments, hotels, and other facilities (Leiden Bio Science Park 2013). Moreover, the park is part of the Medical Delta consortium, that promotes synergies and the creation of a cluster in life sciences in the area of Delft, Rotterdam, and Leiden.

Leiden obviously pays specific attention to attracting international students and workers to the city. The range of job and educational opportunities and of facilities is complemented by the well-preserved historic center of the city (where are still located many university buildings and where it is common to experience the atmosphere of an old university town) and by an Expatcentre that helps the expats and their families to relocate and settle in the Netherlands. Events and venues are organized to facilitate the integration of new residents and their socialization.

Leiden is an interesting case of a city bidding on a recognizable specialization in an innovative industry and working on its development as an economic engine with a potential impact going well beyond its size and administrative status.

Lund, Sweden

Population: 83,000
Metro area: 116,000
City type: University

We decided to include Lund in this presentation of case studies as we wanted to have at least a couple of European examples for the university-town category: small cities where the local higher education institution is the principal activity for the urban economy.

Lund is located in the southern part of Sweden in the Skåne region. It is a countryside town, but it is only a few kilometers from the sea and a few minutes by car or train from the city of Malmö. From there the network of cities in Skåne is connected with the large cross-border Øresund region and the eastern part of Denmark (Sjælland). We put this aspect of Lund at the forefront as it is certainly relevant that this small city has access to a large international region of almost four million inhabitants, which includes, among the other things, a national capital (Copenhagen) and an intercontinental airport that can be reached in a train ride of 30–45 minutes.

When visiting Lund (or just examining a map) the presence of the university is very evident. The University of Lund was established at the end of the seventeenth century and it is one of the oldest academic institutions in northern Europe. It has been ranked among the top 100 or 150 in several global university rankings (www.lunduniversity.lu.se). The University of Lund has 42,000 students in eight faculties; one student in seven is an international student, and 3,200 are research students. A large area of the city of Lund, in particular in the northeastern quadrant including part of the city center, is occupied by university departments and student houses. Some university locations are also in the central historic part of the city, facing the park and the 1,000 year-old cathedral.

Lund is an example of small university town but also of the features of the small cities that we summarized in the previous chapter on the concept of optimal work–life balance or "a good place to raise children." The city has scored third in 2014 and second in 2015 in "The Best City to Live In," a ranking of 290 Swedish cities by the *Fokus* magazine (www.fokus.se/bastattbo). The ranking considers 43 variables compiled with the Jönköping International Business School and is updated yearly: Lund has seen its position constantly improving and is now second only to Stockholm, the capital city ten times larger in demographic size.

The population of Lund has been growing in the past years and so too has the number of commuters. Of the 60,000 people who work in Lund every day, 50 percent are commuting from other municipalities, while 15,000 of the local workforce work in other municipalities. A new masterplan for the city is being adopted for the years after the 2010 plan, articulated around a vision of Lund for 2025 as a "city of ideas." The vision stresses the integration of the city in the region, the adoption of sustainable practices in mobility and energy efficiency, and a balanced development between the city center and the hinterland. The quality of life and openness of the city are seen as levers for attracting businesses and researchers and thus in turn for making the city an international reference for entrepreneurship and research (Lunds Kommun 2010). The 2010 masterplan, which considers the larger territory of the municipality, including Lund and nine towns in the same administrative unit, foresees an increase of more than 30,000 residents in a 20- to 40-year period, half of them as the result of densification and new expansion areas in central Lund. The combination of densification and the development of new areas close to the existing towns should allow the natural features of the countryside that are an important asset for the quality of life of the city to be preserved.

Udine, Italy

Population: 100,000
Metro area: 540,000
City type: Regional capital

We include Udine in our study because it represents a category of city per se. It is a city without any status of capital even at the regional level: it is located in Friuli–Venezia Giulia, the most northeastern region of Italy, where the regional administrative capital is Trieste. Udine has an administrative status for the provincial level, but this has been progressively emptied of any actual political power after recent reforms of Italian local administration. But for economic, cultural, and historical reasons Udine is considered – and as a matter of fact has the role of – a "capital city" of a large heterogeneous territory that extends for more than 120 kilometers from the Alps to the Adriatic Sea. But we should first examine the city profile.

In the last 20 years the city has had a relatively positive demographic dynamic, with now a population of almost 100,000 residents. As is the case in every Italian city, the population in Udine is aging, but a growing number of foreign immigrants (the total foreign population was 14,500 in 2013) works as a compensating force against the otherwise unavoidable demographic decline. The municipality has an area of 57 square kilometers out of which 26 are urbanized, six are available for new development, five are natural areas, and 20 have an agricultural use: this is a specific feature of the city, a strong relation with the primary sector which in turn is one of the distinctive and competitive industries of the urban and regional economy.

During the economic crisis that started in 2008 and in the years until 2014, the city showed a strong resilience: despite the loss of jobs, the number of businesses in the metro area has been reduced by only 0.68 percent vs. an average for the region of 4 percent.[4] There are many possible explanations. One simple reason is the richness of the city and the region. The average bank asset per capita was €97,000 pre-crisis; that became €75,000 after the crisis. Thus consumers have been able to use their savings in order to maintain, at least partially, their lifestyle. Then there is the role of the city in its large region, for which it provides urban services to the citizens but also to the large number of small firms that compose the industrial fabric of the region. Thus, from the Alps to the Adriatic shore, when in need of specific goods or services, citizens and businesses will refer to Udine. In this sense the city is a unique "regional capital": the city – despite its limited size – is the only urban pole in a large area to which it provides services and thus is able to operate its urban economy and functions at a level that is beyond its own size. This is very evident when considering the traffic and congestion, problems that are inducing several local stakeholders to propose the construction of a light rail service to connect the city center with its hinterland and thus moderate the pressure at least for the metropolitan area.

The role of the city at the regional level is also evident in the structure emerging from its cultural policy, with a calendar of events both for a local audience and for a regional one.

In general, in different areas and sectors, the city maintains a prominent role both for the region and for its metropolitan area, for which there is an ongoing process of rationalization of services that should bring an aggregation of offices among several municipalities of the metropolitan area.

There is something very distinctive in the economic profile of the city with regard to its "triple helix" strategy. First, as to the research and education part of the helix, Udine has a university (established by a bottom-up initiative after the earthquake that caused heavy devastation and losses in the region in 1976), but the emphasis is put on many different levels of research and education, and in particular on vocational training, which has been a competitive asset of the city for decades. This is coherent with the industries that define the local specialization and that are considered to be the key levers for the future: the production of goods and services for domestic well-being (furniture and appliances, also wine, food, and their preparation) have been a common thread that has characterized the regional economy for decades.

This is connected with a worldwide trend that the local administration has been able to grasp with the effort of the mayor Furio Honsell and his staff: the concept of well-being and the "healthy city." The city has been participating in the World Health Organization's "Healthy Cities" project since 1995. Several initiatives in this area, some with a certain visibility in the media, allowed Udine to develop a specialization in this area of policy-making and also to be more visible on the "global map" with some possible developments for "eds and meds" in the future.

There are certainly some challenges for the future of Udine. One is to overcome the general sentiment of "declinism" (using the words of the mayor) that has been pervading the local community in the last years, probably more from a perceived uncertainty about the future than, as the figures show, from a truly negative situation. The second challenge is related to the decisions to be made on several brownfield sites in the urban area: in particular, as Friuli–Venezia Giulia was a border region, there are many abandoned former military sites in the region to be converted (an estimated 102 sq km in the region, out of which at least one is in the center of Udine). Related to this is the possible relocation of the railway lines that actually cut the city in two parts with quite a strong physical separation.

The third challenge is related to the geographical position of the city, close to the border with Austria and Slovenia and thus with the central and eastern economic area of the European Union. Although the road infrastructure is developed and being improved, the railway connections are poorly developed and the city lacks connections with close cities such as Ljubljana. Many of the necessary policy options depend on the availability of public funds that will not be abundant in the near future. Udine will probably have more opportunities from the ability of its local small firms to individuate the future economic trends, and from the development of public–private partnerships for which there are some recent good practices for the regeneration of the stadium and for the modernization of the central bus station.

Lausanne, Switzerland

Population: 138,000
Metro area: 278,000
City type: Multi

Lausanne is a city of a limited size in its core area but is situated in a large metropolitan area that extends from west to east along the northern arc of Lac Leman, from Geneva to Montreux. Lausanne is situated in the central part of the arc.

Its demographic size is not proportional with the array and level of functions that are located in the city. It hosts the headquarters of several corporations, seats of international organizations (in sports in particular, notably the International Olympic Committee), museums, and cultural institutions in several areas of the arts. The city also hosts one of the two polytechnic universities in Switzerland (EPFL, École Polytechnique Fédérale de Lausanne), the University of Lausanne, and several businesses and professional schools. The EPFL and the university together enroll more than 20,000 students and some 3,000 faculty and researchers, and have prominent positions in the international rankings. They are located in the western part of Lausanne metropolitan area, in a large campus close to the lake shore, with a growing number of modern and attractive buildings that include the Rolex Learning Center that hosts the EPFL library, an auditorium, a cafeteria and restaurant, beautiful spaces for students and researchers, and the most recent Géopolis that hosts the faculties of political science, and geography and environment. In the city center, the Centre Hospitalier Universitaire de Lausanne (CHUV) is the university hospital, an excellent health care facility, with almost 10,000 employees and collaborators of 113 nationalities (www. chuv.ch). The city also has a science park of 80,000 square meters on the northern periphery of the city, connected with the city center and the railway station via the subway. This array of functions is completed by the attractive site of the city, on the shores of the lake surrounded by the Alpine landscape and by small villages and vineyards, and with a well-preserved historic center.

It is in no way surprising that the city provides more than 90,000 jobs and that the number of residents has been growing from 124,000 in 1995 to 138,000 in 2012, with the share of foreign residents growing from 33 percent to 41 percent. The effect on the other municipalities of the region (in large part much smaller than Lausanne in size) has been obvious: every town experienced a relative growth of the population larger than Lausanne. From 2002 to 2010 the residents in the city grew by 9.4 percent while in many towns the rate was higher than 20 percent or even 30 percent (Ville de Lausanne 2014). Moreover, between 2005 and 2012 the price of renting an apartment in the city rose by 20–30 percent.

Facing such a growth would be impossible without metropolitan governance: in 2007 the Agglomération Lausanne-Morges was created, including 27 municipalities and 278,000 residents.

The development of urban policies in Lausanne is promoted at the level of the Agglomération and at the city level (and there is also the Vaud canton and the federal government). We will refer to the agglomeration level first and then provide some details for the city level. The PALM project (Projet d'Agglomération Lausanne-Morges), currently in its second generation as a plan, approaches the growth of the metropolitan area by planning for 40,000 new residents and 30,000 new jobs in a 2020 perspective. The city of Lausanne engages with the municipalities of the agglomeration to host 30,000 new residents in its territory. The agglomeration plan focuses on three areas: urbanization, green issues, and mobility. Given the features of the territory of the agglomeration (slopes, the lake, natural environments, traditional agriculture, etc.) the expected urbanization pattern will be densification and compact growth, developing in the internal areas and preserving the green areas. Mobility in the region is a crucial challenge. Inter-regional and international mobility is provided by the railway system connected with the rest of Switzerland, with the European (French in particular) high-speed lines and with the international airport of Geneva (40 minutes from Lausanne). At the agglomeration level, the growing number of commuters will be managed with the expansion of existing lines and the creation of new ones, with the target of increasing the number of users by 45 percent.

The plan for the agglomeration has its corresponding effects in the municipal plan (*plan directeur communal*) (Ville de Lausanne 2014). Here, the areas that will host the new residents are identified in particular in the northeast and northwest of the city and in two corridors to the west, in the area close to the municipality of Renens, not far from the university campus. In the short term, these areas will be interested in the "Metamorphose" plan, a participative project of transformation in five areas of the city, with the construction of two ecological neighborhoods and sport facilities (Olympic pool, athletics stadium, and a large sports park). The facilities and the new residences are expected to be ready between 2017 and 2019.

The central part of the city is less involved in the transformations because of the presence of the station and many historical buildings. A remarkable transformation occurred in the Flon neighborhood, a river valley right in the city center, formerly used as a freight deposit and then regenerated in the last decade to host administrative, commercial, and recreation functions. Another project in the city center is "Beaulieu 2020," the modernization of the central 1920s conference center, in order to relaunch it without altering its original function.

It is clear that the strategic choice for the future of Lausanne is growth – and this choice is justified by the dynamism of the local economy and by the area's capacity to attract people and resources on a global scale. Interestingly, the municipal plan underlines a possible conflict and incoherence between the attractive international functions and the preservation of areas of the economy (and, by extension, of the society) with a more local vocation. The openness of the city is also an effect of a good balance between a cosmopolitan attitude and local identity. A substantial percentage of the citizens of Lausanne and of the region are from families who have been living there for centuries, preserving their cultural and physical heritage, such as the vineyards that characterize the landscape just outside Lausanne on the south, or the local community associations and activities related to the presence of the lake. The city will probably be even more successful if it can preserve its identity in local communities and neighborhoods which maintains the quality of life in Lausanne at the level that one expects in a "small city."

Aalborg, Denmark

Population: 130,000
Metro area: 203,000
City type: Multi

The case of Aalborg is relevant for many aspects related to our discussion on small and second-tier cities but also, more generally, with the discussion on urban competitiveness. In these pages we have space only for the illustration of some of the features, transformations, and policy choices of this city that has been able to completely transform its economy and be visible at both the national and the global scale.

The metropolitan area of Aalborg extends on both sides of the Limfjord, where heavy industries and shipyards prospered until the 1970s. Then the city faced the usual transformation of the traditional industries, and for some years the center, which is situated on the south shore of the fjord, was still separated from the water by a long line of abandoned industrial buildings. At that time, the then mayor Jensen started the project of regenerating the waterfront area, starting from a section in the northwest of the center. Despite the large economic effort for the city and the fact that the area was probably too densely built and without commercial spaces, the operation was successful. The municipality was then able to progressively buy and regenerate the waterfront line for a large area of the south shore of the Limfjord, right to the north of the historical center. The continuation of the city toward the water was a great discovery for the citizens of

Aalborg: they found a new identity for the city and a new landscape in an area that was previously abandoned and unpleasant. The regeneration continued on the southern shore with the progressive involvement of private local investors, and on the north, where the municipality transformed a former industrial area in order to relocate some of its departments.

There are several aspects that distinguish the regeneration in Aalborg from other cities. First, the municipality has always been the first mover, promoting more than the initial stages of redevelopment in order to make the transformation visible and the effort reliable; and then the private investors entered in the process. The south shore of the Limfjord offers a visible illustration: the western part of the regeneration was supported only by the municipality, the central part was public–private, and now the eastern part is private investors only. Second, the private developers involved in the transformations in Aalborg are local: no international speculation, no global real estate companies. Third, the policy option for the city of Aalborg is its attraction for university students. Thus, many of the best buildings and best waterfront locations are reserved for student housing (and for public areas and cultural venues). There is a growing urbanization trend in Denmark and also in the Northern Jutland region where Aalborg is located and is the only real urban pole in a large rural area. Nevertheless, the explicit focus of the city is to attract young students to its university. Founded in 1974 after a bottom-up initiative to promote problem-oriented research and teaching in Aalborg, the university is now a very relevant actor for the local economy, community, and governance.

Collaboration is the key feature in every policy area of the city. In cultural policy, for example, many initiatives are designed with the departments of the university or are intended to involve the students in the creation of "their" cultural city. The city provides a little financial support for many events promoted by students, provided that they will be open to local residents and will use several spaces in the city. The small size of the community allows the executives in charge to assess how resources are spent. At the same time the city has regenerated or built some iconic buildings to host cultural activities (the Musikkens Hus (House of Music) on the waterfront, the Nordkraft cultural center, located in a former power plant), and large-scale events such as the Tall Ships Race or the yearly Aalborg carnival, the largest and most popular event in the city, intended to allow every person in Aalborg to express herself or himself in every form of art and expression.

Aalborg is recognized for the Aalborg Charter (1994), one of the fundamental steps toward the European-wide commitment to sustainability at least at the urban scale. The charter, more than "branding" the city, fostered a general commitment by local stakeholders toward sustainability that has been put in practice for two decades by the local government with the involvement of the university, private businesses, and the citizens. This has allowed, among other things, the development of the biggest facility in Europe for the production of windpower generators and also the conversion of local traditional large and small businesses (including shops) to more sustainable practices and processes.

The challenges of the city for the future could be summarized in three areas: First, the "Smart Aalborg" project, strongly supported by the city council, which aims to transform Aalborg into a CO^2-neutral city before 2050 and to develop a technological and productive specialization in the area of the Internet of things.

Second, a light rail project, that will run across the urban area from the airport (northwest) to the university campus and future regional hospital (southeast). Again, in this project the municipality will be the first mover, with a large participation of the national government that still needs to be secured. This is a very expensive and ambitious project, larger than the size of the city, but according to its promoters it will be a lever for developing and regenerating many areas of the city far from the waterfront, where the attention has been constantly focused in the last decades.

Third, the development of the Business Region North Denmark, that is intended to join the forces of 11 municipalities and the regional authority in the northern part of Jutland in order to influence the agenda of the national government and promote joint projects for economic growth in the Jutland "corridor" that runs from Aalborg and the close municipalities southwards to the Hamburg area, with the perspective of a progressive cross-border integration with Germany.

Websites

www.art-kino.org
www.chuv.cheunivercitiesnetwork.com
www.interreg-italiasvizzera.it
www.hcerdanya.eu
www.lunduniversity.lu.se
https://portal.cor.europa.eu/egtc/about/Pages/menu.aspx
www.statistik.at
www.ubi.pt
www.unibz.it/it/public/press/Documents/Dati%20e%20fatti/2015-08-10_Zahlen_
   Daten_Fakten_unibz_online_it.pdf

Notes

1 See Committee on Spatial Development (1999), "Territorial Agenda of the European Union. Towards a More Competitive and Sustainable Europe of Diverse Regions," agreed on the occasion of the Informal Ministerial Meeting on Urban Development and Territorial Cohesion in Leipzig on May 24–25, 2007; "The Territorial State and Perspectives of the European Union. 2011 update. Background document for the Territorial Agenda of the European Union 2020," presented at the Informal Meeting of Ministers responsible for Spatial Planning and Territorial Development, May 19, 2011, Gödöllő, Hungary. These documents and other references are available at http://ec.europa.eu/regional_policy/en/policy/what/territorial-cohesion.

2 The European Grouping for Territorial Cooperation (EGTC or GECT) is the first European cooperation structure with a legal personality defined by European law. It was established in 2006 to facilitate cooperation among local authorities in cross-border, transnational, and interregional activities (https://portal.cor.europa.eu/egtc/about/Pages/menu.aspx).

3 The "triple-helix" refers to the fruitful cooperation among universities, businesses, and the government in order to foster innovation and territorial development. The literature on the subject is very rich and we propose here only Etzkowitz and Leydesdorff (2000).

4 The source for the figures presented in this section is Comune di Udine and Camera di Commercio di Udine (2014).

9 Summing it up
Options for smaller cities

The issue we explored in this book is whether smaller cities have much of a place or a role to play in the contemporary global economy. We noted that the literature and the news sources are replete with references to, if not celebrations of, mega-cities, global cities, world cities, and global urban regions. The biggest are certainly the most noticeable, but are they the most competitive or the most attractive to the workers who are most valued in contemporary firms and production processes? The largest of our cities benefit from economies of agglomeration, reputation, linkages, connectivity, full complements of skilled professionals, and, usually, privileged relations with their national government and its agencies. This is a formidable set of assets and advantages that at first glance would appear to give the game, so to speak, to these nodes of economic power and decision-making, and relegate smaller cities to distinctly subordinate places. However, we discovered that not all is well with our largest cities. Many of them are beset with problems that are generated by the very size some of us celebrate. The most common of these are congestion, social isolation, pollution, income inequality, slums, difficulty in making connections, long commutes, harried lives, deficient public security, and so forth. Furthermore, research tells us that much of the vaunted higher incomes that are to be found in large cities is eaten away by higher housing and other living costs, thus reducing further the advantages large cities are alleged to have over smaller cities. Many of the giants do indeed have feet of clay. This suggests that there is a place for smaller cities, as we have found in this project.

This understanding raises the question: exactly how can and do smaller cities participate effectively, productively, and lastingly in the global economy? Certainly smaller cities cannot go "toe to toe" with the big boys in economic activity. But perhaps their agility, social cohesiveness, common commitment to an objective, sufficient concentration of relevant labor and other assets, and the ability to network with other similar cities will be sufficient for them to create a space for themselves in this larger world. In this book, we have discovered and elaborated many reasons for this to be possible and, indeed, many examples where this has been done.

Some smaller cities have had success because of their proximity to a larger city, with all of the advantages that come from this. There can be some natural spill-over from the big to the small, but smaller cities also have the capability to "borrow size" through a conscious effort to selectively strengthen some linkages with the large city. In some countries, such as France and the UK, there is essentially one large city, typically the national capital, and very few smaller cities have the opportunity to benefit in this way. However, in the US, Canada, and Germany there are several or many large cities and many more smaller cities can work to derive benefits from this positioning.

Advances in the technologies of transportation, production, and communication have dramatically altered the competitiveness and the situation for smaller cities. We argued how this would work and then illustrated how it has in fact been realized in a set of quasi randomly selected smaller cities. The removal of distance as an obstacle to economic interactions among cities works powerfully to the advantage of smaller cities. At the same time, these new technologies reduce the effect of the obvious disadvantages of these cities. Not only can economic actors have closer and more productive interaction with colleagues throughout the national or even global space, but the smaller cities can develop beneficial networks with distant cities in similar situations that are pursuing similar objectives. Small cities are thought to be risk averse and to have a preference for doing what they have always done economically. Participation in a network can show them alternatives to narrowly path-dependent thinking; if other similar cities have developed new ways of thinking and of imagining their future, so too can the individual city in question.

We encountered researchers who have found that both social capital formation and city identity-branding initiatives are more easily done in smaller cities than in their larger counterparts. This has important consequences for their capacity to engage in effective strategic economic planning. One of the key elements in doing this is the benefit that comes from hosting one or more universities/colleges. We examined the several advantages this brought to a smaller city, in terms of the impact on supporting research and development, in generating start-up firms, and in the array of cultural and recreational assets and activities that attach naturally to an institution of higher learning. Having a university/college seems to be close to a *sine qua non* for developing a successful and competitive economy for a smaller city. It does very much enhance the lifestyle aspects of the city that are so attractive to a desired labor force and to firms that are in advanced and higher-wage sectors of the economy. What we discovered with regard to cities as small as 20,000 or 30,000 has been corroborated for cities of between 250,000 and one million, specifically for the cities that are home to the Universities of Wisconsin, North Carolina, Kentucky, Michigan, and Colorado State, with the rubric "university city" being applied (Shapiro 2015). It is clear that for cities of all sizes of population, the presence of one or more universities and/or colleges is a powerful contributor to a strong and competitive economy.

Supporting this notion of the potential of smaller cities is the endorsement, in Chapter 3, by both UN-Habitat and the consultancy McKinsey that, beyond the competitiveness of the individual smaller city, these cities are essential to the resolution of problems of rural depopulation and the exacerbation of the negative aspects of larger cities; they also exhibit the true vigor of the US urban economy, and arguably those of other nations. In the discussion of the experiences of smaller cities in the US and in the EU, we showed exactly how many smaller cities have been able to succeed in these roles.

In the US, for example, cities between 20,000 and 500,000 were found to be successful in creating competitive economies that met the demands imposed by their residents for urban amenities, good employment, quality of life, and whatever else they felt was desirable. We also found cities that had either been "asleep at the wheel" or inept at charting a course for the economy and achieving success with it. The successful cities tended to have one or more universities/ colleges, good bottom-up participation by the citizenry, effective government and governance, and good social relations among the various groups in the city. They differed dramatically in their basic situation. Some were resources based, or declining industrial, or high technology, or recreational and tourism, or isolated or peripheral, or multi-focused. Each had a situation that was largely unique, and posed different challenges and different opportunities than were available to other cities. Success was not tied to being larger or smaller in population.

When Pittsburgh suffered its collapse, it lost 29 productive entities in the steel industry in a short time in the early 1980s – it lost an entire industry. For smaller cities, it is often the departure or failure of just one large employer. The keys to recovery for the smaller city are leaders in the public and private sectors who know their community – its strengths and its people. This group then has the insight to discover how a successful recovery strategy could be composed. They also have the support of the city when it comes to implementing the strategy. Indeed, in instances when local government was inept or inactive, individuals and firms in the business sector have taken the initiative by themselves. Smallness, as has been noted above, can be advantageous in this situation.

In the European Union we selected a set of cities larger in average size compared with the USA group. This is mainly due to the fact that, while we were researching this project, there has been growing attention paid by the European institutions to the role of second-tier cities. There is evidence supporting the idea that second-tier and smaller cities have contributed in a substantial way to the economic growth in Europe during the years of the crisis – and the scenarios proposed for the future underline that this will be the case also in the years to come. Considering the different ways in which powers are attributed to different levels of government, we have noted that the greater the autonomy a city has, the more likely it is to be effective in strategic planning. And, as a matter of fact, second-tier cities have been able to develop strategies to a large extent comparable with those performed by their larger fellows: they have regenerated their waterfronts, launched research centers and business incubators, developed relevant education institutions, participated in the building and operation of infrastructure, approached the challenges of an aging population, international migration, the financial crisis, etc. with a mix of success and failures, as is obvious, but frequently overcoming in a creative way the limitations of their scale and "punching above their weight." In these challenges the role of local government and of local leadership has been crucial in developing the basis for the participation of citizens and for the creation of public–private partnerships. And also the negotiation with other levels of government has had a crucial role – as we will discuss later.

Another finding is that there is no such thing as an optimal size for a city. Economists argue that there is a broad range of city sizes that can be considered optimal depending on what indicator is used. Analogous to this is the notion of the economic core of a city. The sector(s) that give the city its competitiveness may have a labor force of X thousand workers. If the city population is 10X, the population above X thousand is either support or totally irrelevant. If the city population is 20X, then, would this make the city any more competitive? It is hard to argue that the additional 10X thousand beauticians, auto repair specialists, convenience store staff, plumbers and carpenters, landscapers, and so on have a positive impact on the competitive sector(s). The city is certainly larger but the added population is superfluous and irrelevant to the competitiveness of the city's economy. So being a large city in total population may have little or nothing to do with urban competitiveness.

An increasingly important issue today is the level of financial support the city can gain from superior levels of government. Given the climate of fiscal austerity that has gripped governments in both the US and, especially, the EU, the capability of smaller city governments to find the resources needed for measures to enhance competitiveness is most likely to be reduced in the coming years. This is more crucial for cities in the EU because while US cities get little aid from the national government, this is not true for their European counterparts. The addition of hundreds of thousands of refugees from Africa and the Middle East can only add more strains to intergovernmental fiscal transfers. We may, in fact, be confronting a decline in the capacity of superior levels of government to participate actively in programs at the level of the city that meet the traditional functions of local government. But some cities we studied for this project have demonstrated an ability to find alternative financial sources to support their strategies, from effective public–private partnerships to project financing or cross-border partnerships.

An important asset for the attractiveness of smaller cities is quality of life and of social relationships, the livability of public spaces, and all the urban amenities, among which cultural venues and events clearly have an important role. In a smaller city, cultural institutions have the challenge of less financial resources compared to large metropolises. But they have advantages too. First, they have the opportunity to build an international identity thanks to a well-recognized cultural event or venue: everybody knows Montreux Jazz, the Spoleto Festival, the Banff Mountain Film Festival, just to cite a few examples. Second, thanks to their size, these cities frequently have the capacity to effectively involve the local community as an audience and in the organization too – thus favoring the sense of belonging and socialization. Third, the cultural venues and events also provide a multiple role of the city at the various scales in which it is involved. It can be "seen on the map" with a large specialized event, it can provide a set of cultural amenities for its residents, and it can provide cultural opportunities for the region, thus involving a larger audience than the city's size and providing this urban function which would otherwise not be performed at all, especially in the regions that are very far from a large metropolitan area.

All of this suggests that a certain energy is flowing down to smaller cities from second-tier cities with populations of 100,000 to 150,000 to the cities as small as 20,000 or 30,000 in our study, and that their leaders now understand that a variety of things have changed, from various technologies to the locational strategies of large firms, that give them new potential and capacity for enhancing the economic vitality and competitiveness of their smaller city. Large cities will, of course, continue to have certain advantages, but many of them have lost their way due to poor decisions, structural changes in the economy, and simple inaction. Not all large cities will be sufficiently nimble and far-sighted to retain their position at the top of the pile. The deindustrialization of the 1980s has shown how many previously prominent large cities, both in North America and in Europe, have suffered economic stagnation and even decline. Other large cities have restructured their economies and have moved back into positions of economic strength.

Nothing is, of course, certain for smaller cities, but in this study we have demonstrated that they do potentially have the assets, capacity, and energy to become sufficiently competitive to create the economic futures to which their residents aspire. We have offered several examples of smaller cities that have done just this.

Bibliography

Alonso, W., 1971, "The economics of urban size," *Regional Science Association Papers*, vol. 26, no. 1, pp. 67–83.

Alonso, W., 1975, "Urban zero population growth," in Mancur Olson and Hans H. Landsburg (eds), *The No Growth Society*, Abingdon: Frank Cass, pp. 191–206.

American City and County, 2014, "2005 study rankings on liberal and conservative cities," October 27. www.americancityandcounty.com.

Andersen, Kristina Vaarst, Markus M. Bugge, Högni Kalsö Hansen, Arne Isaksen, and Mika Raunio, 2014, "One size fits all?" In Charlotta Mellander, Richard Florida, Bjørn T. Asheim, and Meric Gertler (eds), *The Creative Class Goes Global*, Abingdon: Routledge, pp. 117–137.

Ashland Chamber of Commerce, 2015, *Ashland Business Resources*, Issue 2. Ashland, OR: Ashland Chamber of Commerce. www.ashlandbusinessresource.com.

Ashworth, Gregory, 2010, "Personality association as an instrument of place branding: possibilities and pitfalls," in Gregory Ashworth and Mihalis Kavaratzis (eds), *Towards Effective Place Brand Management*, Cheltenham: Edward Elgar Publishers, pp. 222–233.

Atkinson, Rob, 2001, "The emerging 'urban agenda' and the European spatial development perspective: Towards an EU urban policy?" *European Planning Studies*, vol. 9, no. 3, pp. 385–406.

Atkinson, Rob, 2007, "EU urban policy, European urban policies and the neighbourhood: An overview of concepts, programmes and strategies," European Urban Research Association (EURA): 10th Anniversary Conference, University of Glasgow, Scotland, September 12–14, 2007.

Ayuntamento de Aviles, 2009, *Aviles Avanza*, Edicion Excmo. Ayuntamento de Aviles.

Ayuntamento de Aviles, 2014, *Aviles Acuerda*, Edicion Excmo. Ayuntamento de Aviles.

Bairoch, Paul, 1988, *Cities and Economic Development*, Chicago: University of Chicago Press.

Balchin, Paul N., David Isaac, and Jean Chen, 2000, *Urban Economics*, London: Palgrave.

Baum-Snow, Nathaniel, and Ronni Pavan, 2013, "Inequality and city size," *Review of Economics and Statistics*, vol. 95, no. 5, pp. 1535–1548.

Begović, B., 1991, "The economic approach to optimal city size," *Progress in Planning*, vol. 36, no. 2, pp. 94–161.

Billings Planning and Community Services Department, 2008, *Yellowstone County and City of Billings 2008 Growth Policy Update*. Billings: Planning and Community Services Department.

Borja, Jordi, and Manuel Castells, 1997, *Local and Global*, London: Earthscan Publications.

Boyle, Matthew, 2013, "Aging boomers befuddle marketers aching for $15 trillion prize," *Bloomberg News*, September 17. www.bloomberg.com/news/articles/2013-09-17/aging-boomers-befuddle-marketers-eying-15-trillion-prize.

Bradford, Neil, 2004, *Creative Cities: Structured Policy Dialogue Report*, Ottawa: Canadian Policy Research Networks.

Brennan-Horley, Christopher R., 2010, "Creative city mapping: Experimental applications of GIS for cultural planning and auditing," Doctor of Philosophy thesis, School of Earth and Environmental Sciences, University of Wollongong. http://ro.uow.edu.au/theses/3235.

Brookings Institution, 2003, *Back to Prosperity: A Competitive Agenda for Renewing Pennsylvania*, Washington, DC: Brookings Institution. www.brookings.edu/research/reports/2003/12/metropolitanpolicy-pennsylvania.

Broxterman, Daniel A., and Anthony M. Yezer, 2014, "City size and skill intensity: Is it all housing cost?" George Washington University, Working Papers, March 12.

Camagni, Roberto, Roberta Capello, and Andrea Caragliu, 2015, "The rise of second-rank cities: What role for agglomeration economies?" *European Planning Studies*, vol. 23, no. 6, pp. 1069–1089.

Cheshire, Paul, 2005, "Resurgent cities, urban myths and policy hubris: What we need to know," *Urban Studies*, vol. 43, no. 8, pp. 1231–1246.

Christaller, Walter, 1966, *Central Places in Southern Germany*, trans. Carlisle W. Baskin, Englewood Cliffs, NJ: Prentice Hall. (Originally published 1933, *Die Zentrallen Orte in Suddeutschland*.)

City of Boulder and Boulder County, 2010, *Boulder Valley Comprehensive Plan 2010*, Boulder, CO: City of Boulder and Boulder County. www.boulder-valley-comprehensive-plan-2010-1-201410091122.pdf.

City of Boulder, 2013, *Economic Sustainability Strategy*, Boulder: City Council, October 29.

City of Provo, 2012, *Citywide Economic Development Strategy*, Provo: City of Provo, October 25, 2012.

City of San Bernardino, 2005, *General Plan*, San Bernardino, CA: City of San Bernardino, November 1.

City of San Bernardino, 2015, "Successor agency to the former redevelopment agency," April 11. www.sbcity.org.

Columbus Area Visitors Center, 2012, *Columbus, Indiana: A Look at Modern Architecture and Art*, 8th edition, Columbus, IN: Columbus Area Visitors Center.

Commission of the European Communities, 2005, *Confronting Demographic Change: a New Solidarity Between the Generations* (Green Paper), Brussels: Commission of the European Communities, March 16.

Committee on Spatial Development, 1999, *ESDP European Spatial Development Perspective Towards Balanced and Sustainable Development of the Territory of the European Union*, Luxembourg: Office for Official Publications of the European Communities.

Comune di Udine, Camera di Commercio di Udine, 2014, "Agenda del futuro: Udine 2024," Udine: Camera di Commercio di Udine.

Congressional Budget Office, 2010, *Fiscal Stress Faced by Local Governments*, Economic and Budget Issue Brief, Washington, DC: Congressional Budget Office, December.

Crandall, Brian, 2014, "Ithaca's economy, unemployment rate: Everything you need to know," *The Ithaca Voice*, June 14. http//ithacavoice.com/2014.06.

Cronen, William, 1991, *Nature's Metropolis: Chicago and the Great West*, New York: W. W. Norton.

Cuadrado-Roura, Juan R., 2009, "Towards new European peripheries?" in Charlie Karlsson, Börje Johansson, and Roger R. Stough (eds), *Innovation, Agglomeration and Regional Competition*, Cheltenham: Edward Elgar Publishers, pp. 170–197.

David, Quentin, Didier Peeter, Gilles Van Hamme, and Christian Vandermotten, 2013, "Is bigger better? Economic performances of European cities, 1960–2009," *Cities*, 35, pp. 237–254.

Davis, Mike, 2004, "Planet of slums," *New Left Review*, no. 26, March–April (electronic edition).

Decoville, Antoine, Frédéric Durand, and Valérie Feltgen, 2015, *Opportunities of Cross-border Cooperation between Small and Medium Cities in Europe*, Luxembourg: LISER.

Denis-Jacob, Jonathan, 2012, "Cultural industries in small-sized Canadian cities: Dream or reality," *Urban Studies*, vol. 49, no. 1, pp. 97–114.

Dijkstra, Lewis, Enrique Garcilazo, and Philip McCann, 2013, "The economic performance of European cities and city regions: Myths and realities," *European Planning Studies*, vol. 21, no. 3, pp. 334–354.

Dresden Wirtschaft und kommunale Amt, 2003, *Economic Report 2003*, Dresden: Wirtschaft und kommunale Amt.

Dukes, Thea, 2008, "The URBAN programme and the European urban policy discourse: Successful instruments to Europeanize the urban level?" *GeoJournal*, vol. 72, pp. 105–119.

Duluth Planning Commission, 2006, *City of Duluth Comprehensive Plan*, Duluth: Planning Commission.

Duranton, Gilles, and Diego Puga, 2005, "From sectoral to functional urban specialization," *Journal of Urban Economics*, vol. 57, pp. 343–370.

Economist Intelligence Unit, 2013, *Hot Spots 2025: Benchmarking the Future Competitiveness of Cities*, London: The Economist Intelligence Unit.

Elvery, Joel A., 2010, "City size and skill intensity," *Regional Science and Urban Economics*, vol. 40, pp. 367–379.

EMSI, 2007, *Economic Analysis of the Walla Walla Wine Cluster: Past, Present, and Future*, Moscow, ID: Economic Modeling Specialists Inc.

Erickcek, George A., and Hannah J. McKinney, 2004, *Small Cities Blues: Looking for Growth Factors in Small and Medium-Sized Cities*, Working Paper no. 04–100, Kalamazoo: Upjohn Institute.

ESPON (European Spatial Planning Observation Network) and European Institute of Urban Affairs, Liverpool John Moores University, 2012, *SGPTD Second Tier Cities and Territorial Development in Europe: Performance, Policies and Prospects*, Luxembourg: ESPON.

ESPON (European Spatial Planning Observation Network), 2014, *Third ESPON Synthesis Report. Territories Finding a New Momentum: Evidence for Policy Development, Growth and Investment*, Luxembourg: ESPON.

Eterno, John, Arvind Verma, and Eli Silverman, 2014, "Police manipulations of crime reporting: Insiders' revelations," *Justice Quarterly*, online, November 17.

Etzkowitz, Henry, and Loet Leydesdorff, 2000, "The dynamics of innovation: From national systems and 'Mode 2' to a triple helix of university–industry–government relations," *Research Policy*, vol. 29, no. 2, pp. 109–123.

Eugene Joint Elected Officials, 2010, *Regional Prosperity Economic Development Plan*, February 26, Eugene, OR: Joint Elected Officials.

EUKN (European Urban Knowledge Network) and Grand-Duché de Luxembourg, 2015, "The trio presidency theme of small and medium-sized cities: Contributions of the Italian and Latvian presidencies," materials for the workshop "The Potential of Small and Medium Cities in Cross-border Polycentric Regions," Luxembourg City, 30 June.

European Commission, 1997, *Towards an Urban Agenda in the European Union*, Luxembourg: Publications Office of the European Union.

European Commission, 2013, *Quality of Life in Cities*, Luxembourg: Publications Office of the European Union.

European Commission, 2014, *Sixth Report on Economic, Social and Territorial Cohesion*, Luxembourg: Publications Office of the European Union.

European Commission, 2015a, *The Urban Dimension of EU Policies – Key Features of an EU Urban Agenda*, Communication from the Commission to the European Parliament, the Council, the European Economic and Social Committee and the Committee of the Regions, Brussels: European Commission.

European Commission, 2015b, *Results of the Public Consultation on the Key Features of an EU Urban Agenda*, Commission Staff Working Document, Brussels: European Commission.

Evans, Richard, 2015, "Harnessing the economic potential of 'second-tier' European cities: Lessons from four different state/urban systems," *Environment and Planning C: Government and Policy*, vol. 33, pp. 163–183.

Ewing, Bradley T., 2010, *The Economic Impacts of Texas Tech University*, Lubbock, TX: Texas Tech University.

Florida, Richard, 2002, *The Rise of the Creative Class*, New York: Basic Books.

Friedman, Avi, 2014, *Planning Small and Mid-sized Towns: Designing and Retrofitting for Sustainability*, Abingdon: Routledge.

Friedmann, John, 1995, "The world city hypothesis," in Paul L. Knox and Peter J. Taylor (eds), *World Cities in a World-system*, Cambridge: Cambridge University Press, pp. 317–331. Originally published in *Development and Change*, vol. 17, no. 1, pp. 69–84.

Fugita, Masahita, Paul Krugman, and Anthony J. Venables, 2001, *The Spatial Economy: Cities, Regions, and International Trade*, Cambridge, MA: MIT Press.

Gabaix, Xavier, 1999, "Zipf's Law for cities: An explanation," *Quarterly Journal of Economics*, August, pp. 739–767.

Garreau, Joel, 1992, *Edge Cities*, New York: Anchor Books.

Glaeser, Edward, 2011, *The Triumph of the City*, New York: Penguin Press.

Glaeser, Edward, and Joshua D. Gottlieb, 2006, "Urban resurgence and the consumer city," *Urban Studies*, vol. 43, no. 8, pp. 1275–1299.

Glaeser, Edward, Joshua D. Gottlieb, and Orin Ziv, 2014, *Unhappy Cities*, Working Paper 20291, Cambridge, MA: National Bureau of Economic Research.

Goodyear, Sarah, 2014, "The NYPD's biggest problem might actually be an overreliance on numbers," *Citylab* (website), January 8. www.citylab.com/crime/2015/01/the-nypds-biggest-problem-might-actually-be-an-overreliance-on-numbers/384284.

Government Accountability Office, 2010, *State and Local Governments' Fiscal Outlook: March 2010 Update*, Washington, DC: Government Accountability Office.

Grabher, Gernot, 2002, "Cool projects, boring institutions: Temporary collaboration in social context," *Regional Studies*, vol. 36, no. 3, pp. 205–214.

Gray, H. Peter, and John H. Dunning, 2000, "Towards a theory of regional policy," in

John H. Dunning (ed.), *Regions, Globalization, and the Knowledge-Based Economy*, Oxford: Oxford University Press, pp. 409–434.

Hagen, Ryan, 2014, "San Bernardino development director Bill Manis has a plan for the city," *The Sun*, December 26.

Hall, Peter, 2001, *Cities in Civilization*, New York: Fromm International.

Hall, Peter, 2007, "Europe's multi-centered urban future," in *Cities and Regions Facing up to Change*, Bollschweil: Hagbarth, pp. 24–26.

Hall, Peter, 2009, "Looking backward, looking forward: The city region of the mid-21st century," *Regional Studies*, vol. 43, no. 6, pp. 803–817.

Henning, C. Randall, and Martin Kessler, 2012, *Fiscal Federalism: US History for Architects of Europe's Fiscal Union*, Working Paper Series, WP 12–1, Washington, DC: Peterson Institute for International Economics.

Hess, Alexander E. M., Michael B. Sauter, and Thomas C. Frohlich, 2014, *America's Fastest Growing (and Shrinking) Economies*, 24/7 Wall St. http://247wallst.com/special-report/2014/01/31/americas-fastest-growing-and-shrinking-economies/5/.

Holzer, Marc, John Fry, Etienne Charbonneau, Gregg Van Ryzin, and Eileen Burnash, 2009, *Literature Review and Analysis Related to Optimal City Size and Efficiency*, New Brunswick: Rutgers University School of Public Affairs and Administration, May 6.

Ingram, Gregory K., and Yu-Hung Hong, 2010, "Municipal revenue options in a time of financial crisis," in Gregory K. Ingram and Yu-Hung Hong (eds), *Municipal Revenues and Land Policies*, Cambridge, MA: Lincoln Institute of Land Policy.

Islam, Frank, and Ed Crego, 2013, "Braking bad: The critical need to end Congressional gridlock," *Huffington Post*, October 28. www.huffingtonpost.com/frank-islam/braking-bad-the-critical-_b_4167947.html.

Jackson, Maria Rosario, Florence Kabwasa-Green, and Joaquín Herranz, 2006, *Cultural Vitality in Communities: Interpretation and Indicators*, Washington, DC: The Urban Institute.

Jacobs, Jane, 1992, *The Death and Life of Great American Cities*, New York: Vintage Books.

Johansson, Börje, and John M. Quigley, 2004, "Agglomeration and networks in spatial economies," *Papers in Regional Science*, vol. 83, pp. 165–176.

Johnson, David A., 1993, "World city/capital city: New York in the changing global system," in John Taylor, Jean G. Lengellé, and Caroline Andrew (eds), *Capital Cities/ Les Capitales*, Ottawa: Carleton University Press, pp. 377–398.

Katz, Bruce, and Jennifer Bradley, 2013, *The Metropolitan Revolution*, Washington, DC: Brookings Institution Press.

Kenarov, Dimiter, 2013, "Here in Youngstown: The promise and curse of shale gas," *Shale Reporter*, January 16. www.shalereporter.com.

Kenyon, Daphne A., 2003, "The federal government's impact on state and local government finances," in David L. Sjoquist (ed.), *State and Local Finances under Pressure*, Cheltenham: Edward Elgar, pp. 163–178.

Knox, Paul, and Helke Mayer, 2012, "Europe's internal periphery: Small towns in the context of reflexive polycentricity," in Anne Lorentzen and Bas van Heur (eds), *Cultural Political Economy of Small Cities*, London: Routledge, pp. 142–158.

Kotkin, Joel, 1990, *The New Geography*, New York: Random House.

Kotkin, Joel, 2014, *Size Is Not the Answer: The Changing Face of the Global City*, Singapore: Singapore Civil Service College.

Kraker, Dan, 2012, "Duluth showing signs of economic revival," *MPRnews*, November 27. www.mprnews.org/listen?

Krätke, Stefan, 2011, *The Creative Capital of Cities*, Oxford: Wiley-Blackwell.

Kresl, Peter Karl, 2007, *Planning Cities for the Future*, Cheltenham: Edward Elgar.

Kresl, Peter Karl (ed.), 2015, *Cities and Partnerships for Sustainable Development*, Cheltenham: Edward Elgar.

Kresl, Peter Karl, and Balwant Singh, 2012, "Urban competitiveness and US metropolitan centres," *Urban Studies*, vol. 49, no. 2, pp. 239–254.

Kresl, Peter Karl, and Daniele Ietri, 2010, *The Aging Population and the Competitiveness of Cities: Benefits to the Urban Economy*, Cheltenham: Edward Elgar.

Kresl, Peter Karl, and Daniele Ietri (eds), 2012, *European Cities and Global Competitiveness: Strategies for Improving Performance*, Cheltenham: Edward Elgar.

Kruse, Kevin, 2015, *One Nation under God*, New York: Basic Books.

KSLA News, 2014, "Shreveport-Bossier fastest shrinking economy in nation?" *KSLA News*, February 4. www.ksla.com/story/24627192/shreveport-bossier-fastest-shrinking-economy-in-nation.

Landry, Charles, 2000, *The Creative City: A Toolkit for Urban Innovators*, London: Earthscan.

Landry, Charles, 2011, "A roadmap for the creative city," in David Emanuel Andersson, Åke E. Andersson, and Charlotta Mellander (eds), *Handbook of Creative Cities*, Cheltenham: Edward Elgar Publishers, pp. 517–536.

Laquian, Aprodicio, 2005, *Beyond Metropolis: The Planning and Governance of Asia's Mega-urban Regions*, Baltimore: Johns Hopkins University Press.

Leachman, Michael, Richard Kogan, Vincent Palacios, and Kelsey Merrick, 2012, *Ryan Budget Cuts to State and Local Services Would Be Far Deeper than Cuts under Sequestration*, Washington, DC: Center on Budget and Policy Priorities, December 5.

LEDA, 2015, *Economic Development Strategic Plan*, Lubbock, TX: Lubbock Economic Development Alliance.

Leiden Bio Science Park, 2013, *Fact Sheet, 2013*, Leiden: Leiden Bio Science Park.

Leiden Bio Science Park Foundation, The Hague Chamber of Commerce, the Association of Leiden Bio Science Park Companies and the Confederation of Netherlands Industry and Employers, 2010, *The Economic Impact of the Leiden Bio Science Park*, Leiden: Leiden Bio Science Park.

Lewis, Nathaniel M., and Betsy Donald, 2010, "A new rubric for 'creative city' potential in Canada's smaller cities," *Urban Studies*, vol. 47, no. 1, pp. 29–54.

Leyden, Dennis P., and Albert N. Link, 2013, "Collective entrepreneurship: The strategy management of Research Triangle Park," in David B. Audretsch and Mary Lindenstein Walshok (eds), *Creating Competitiveness*, Cheltenham: Edward Elgar Publishers, pp. 176–185.

Liptak, Adam, 2013, "Smaller states find outsize clout growing in Senate," *New York Times*, March 11. www.nytimes.com/interactive/2013/03/11/us/politics/democracy-tested.html#/#smallstate.

Livability Lane, 2010a, *Economic Cluster Reports: Educational Technologies*. www.livabilitylane.org/files/Cluster-EduTech.pdf.

Livability Lane, 2010b, *Cluster Economic Cluster Reports: Manufacturing*. www.livabilitylane.org/files/Cluster_Manufacturing.pdf.

Livability Lane, 2010c, *Food and Beverage Cluster Report: Key Findings and Recommendations*. www.livabilitylane.org/toolkit/economic-prosperity_food-beverage-cluster-report.html.

Lizza, Ryan, 2012, "Fussbudget: How Paul Ryan captured the GOP," *New Yorker*, August 6. www.newyorkermagizine.com/magazine/2012/08/06/fussbudget.

Lorentzen, Anne, and Bas van Heur (eds), 2012, *Cultural Political Economy of Small Cities*, London: Routledge.

Lunds Kommun, 2010, "Översiktsplan för Lunds kommun ÖP 2010," Lund.

Maggioni, Mario A., Mario Nosvelli, and Teodora Erika Uberti, 2007, "Space versus networks in the geography of innovation: A European analysis," *Papers in Regional Science*, vol. 86, issue 3, pp. 471–493.

Markusen, Ann, and Greg Schrock, 2006, "The distinctive city: Divergent patterns in growth, hierarchy and specialization," *Urban Studies*, vol. 43, no. 8, pp. 1301–1323.

Martin Prosperity Institute, 2015, *Creative and Diverse: Ranking Global Cities*, Toronto: Martin Prosperity Institute.

Martins Vaza, Domingos, and Maria João Matos, 2015, "Regional polycentrism in a mountainous territory: The Case of Covilhã (Portugal) and alpine cities," *European Planning Studies*, vol. 23, no. 2, pp. 379–397.

McDermott, Gerald A., 2013, "The strategic recombination of regional innovative capacities: Public–private institutions as knowledge bridges," in David B. Audretsch and Mary Lindenstein Walshok (eds), *Creating Competitiveness*, Cheltenham: Edward Elgar Publishers, pp. 54–87.

McGranahan, David A., Timothy R. Wojan, and Dayton M. Lambert, 2001, "The rural growth trifecta: Outdoor amenities, creative class and entrepreneurial context," *Journal of Economic Geography*, vol. 11, pp. 529–557.

McKenzie, Brian, 2013, *Out-of-State and Long-Commutes: 2011*, Washington, DC: Department of Commerce.

McKinley, Jesse, 2013, "Colleges help Ithaca thrive in a region of struggles," *New York Times*, August 4. http://nyti.ms/148IYU6.

McKinsey Global Institute, 2012, *Urban America: US Cities in the Global Economy*, New York: McKinsey Global Institute.

Meijers, Evert, Koen Hollander, and Marloes Hoogerbrugge, 2012, *Case study: Tri-City Region*, The Hague: European Metropolitan Network Institute.

Michael, Karen, 2015, "Texas Tech announces Chromatin as first tenant in Research and Technology Park," *Lubbock Avalanche-Journal*, February 11. http://lubbockonline.com/local-news/2015-02-11/texas-tech-announces-chromatin-first-tenant-research-and-technology-park.

Modares, Ali, 2014, "Life as a second city," Newgeography.com, February 11.

Musgrave, Richard, 1959, *The Theory of Public Finance*, New York: McGraw-Hill.

National League of Cities, 2013, *City Fiscal Conditions in 2012: Tax Revenues*, Washington, DC: National League of Cities.

National League of Cities, 2014, *Cities and State Fiscal Structure, 2015*, Washington, DC: National League of Cities.

National League of Cities, 2015, *Cities and State Fiscal Structure*, Washington, DC: National League of Cities.

Neffke, Frank, Martin Henning, and Ron Boschma, 2011, "How do regions diversify over time: Industry relatedness and the development of new growth paths in regions," *Economic Geography*, vol. 87, no. 3, pp. 237–265.

Ni Pengfei, Peter Karl Kresl, and Li Xiaojiang, 2014, "China urban competitiveness in industrialization," *Urban Studies*, vol. 51, no. 13, pp. 2787–2805.

Nivola, Pietro S., 2003, *Fiscal Millstones on the Cities: Revisiting the Problem of Federal Mandates*, Brookings Policy Brief Series, #122, Washington, DC: Brookings Institution.

Nomninos, Nicholas, 2013, *The Age of Intelligent Cities: Smart Environments and Innovation for All Strategies*, London: Routledge.

OECD (Organization for Economic Cooperation and Development), 2006, *Competitive Cities in the Global Economy*, Territorial Reviews, Paris: OECD.

OECD (Organization for Economic Cooperation and Development), 2009, *How Regions Grow*, Policy Brief, Paris: OECD.

Packalen, Mikko, and Jay Bhattacharya, 2015, *Cities and Ideas*, Working Paper 20921, Cambridge, MA: National Bureau of Economic Research.

Pagano, Michael A., and Richard J. T. Moore, 1985, *Cities and Fiscal Choices: A New Model of Urban Public Investment*, Durham, NC: Duke University Press.

Parkinson, Michael (ed.), 2005, *European Metropolitan Governance: Cities in Europe – Europe in the Cities*, Vienna: Node Research.

Parkinson, Michael, Richard Meegan, and Jay Karecha, 2015, "City size and economic performance: Is bigger better, small more beautiful or middling marvellous?" *European Planning Studies*, vol. 23, no. 6, pp. 1054–1068.

Piketty, Thomas, 2014, *Capital in the Twenty-First Century*, Cambridge, MA: Harvard University Press.

Portland Economic Development Department, 2011, *Economic Development Vision + Plan*, Portland, OR: Economic Development Department of the City of Portland.

Portland Economic Development Department, 2015, *Economic Development*, Portland, OR: Economic Development Department. www.portlandmaine.gov.

Posey, Sean, 2013, "America's fastest shrinking city: The story of Youngstown, Ohio," Clifton Park, NY: Hampton Institute, June 18. www.hamptoninstitution.org/youngstown.html#.VqKtMq-kqK0.

Prescott: A Focused Future II, 2008, Phoenix: APS.

Prescott Chamber of Commerce, *Prescott Arizona*, 2014, Prescott: Prescott Chamber of Commerce. www.prescott.org.

Pugmire, Gennell, 2013, "Downtown Provo: 30 years of economic growth," *Daily Herald*, November 3. www.heraldextra.com.

Putnam, Robert, 2002, *Making Democracy Work: Civic Traditions in Modern Italy*, Princeton: Princeton University Press.

Rapoport, Amos, 1993, "On the nature of capitals and their physical expression," in John Taylor, Jean G. Lengellé, and Caroline Andrew (eds), *Capital Cities/Les Capitales*, Ottawa: Carleton University Press, pp. 31–67.

Reddy, Sudeep, 2008, "How a college's budding vintners helped Walla Walla create a buzz," *Wall Street Journal*, January 4. www.wsj.com/articles/SB11994166295 2867073.

Romero, Dennis, 2011, "America's second poorest big city is right here in Southern California: San Bernardino," *LA Weekly*, October 17. www.laweekly.com/news/americas-second-poorest-big-city-is-right-here-in-southern-california-san-bernardino-2393508.

Sánchez-Moral, Simón, Ricardo Méndez, and José Prada-Trigo, 2015, "Resurgent cities: local strategies and institutional networks to counteract shrinkage in Avilés (Spain)," *European Planning Studies*, vol. 23, no 1, pp. 33–52.

Sassen, Saskia, 1991, *The Global City*, Princeton: Princeton University Press.

Satow, Julie, 2015, "Why the doorman is lonely," *New York Times*, Sunday Business, January 9, p. 8.

Saxenian, AnnaLee, 1994, *Regional Advantage: Culture and Competition in Silicon Valley and Route 128*, Cambridge, MA: Harvard University Press.

Schlichtman, John Joe, 2009, "The niche city idea: How a declining manufacturing center exploited the opportunities of globalization," *International Journal of Urban and Regional Research*, vol. 33, no. 1, pp. 105–125.

Schwartz, Nelson D., 2014, "Boom in energy spurs industry in the Rust Belt," *New York Times*, September 8. http://nyti.ms/1qHn6ZI.

Scoppetta, Cecilia, 2011, "The Polish seaport-city of Gdansk: A gateway for the Baltic Sea EU macro region," *Portus plus*, vol. 2. http://retedigital.com/portus_plus/portus-plus-2-2011.

Scott, Allen J., 2010, "Space–time variations of human capital assets across US metropolitan areas, 1980–2000," *Economic Geography*, vol. 86, no. 3, pp. 233–249.

Scott, Allen J., 2012, *A World in Emergence*, Cheltenham: Edward Elgar.

Servillo, Loris, Rob Atkinson, Ian Smith, Antonio Russo, Ludek Sýkora, Christophe Demazière, and Abdelillah Hamdouch, 2014, *TOWN: Small and Medium Sized Towns in Their Functional Territorial Context*, Luxembourg: ESPON.

Shapiro, Scott, 2015, "New species of city discovered: The university city," *Next City Network*, September 16. nextcity.org/daily/entry/what-is-a-university-city-new-definition-urban-typology.

Shreveport Coordinating and Development Corporation, 2014, *Northwest Louisiana Comprehensive Economic Development Strategy, 2013–2017*, Shreveport, LA: Coordinating and Development Corporation.

Shreveport Metropolitan Planning Commission, 2010, *Great Expectations Shreveport–Caddo 2030 Master Plan*, Shreveport, LA: Metropolitan Planning Commission.

Smith, Robert L., 2013, "Youngstown's improbable comeback attracting attention and creating jobs," *Plain Dealer* (Cleveland), March 2.

Sobrino, Jaime, 2003, *Competitividad de las ciudades en México*, Mexico City: El Colegio de México.

Social, Economic and Humanities Research Institute of Vidzeme University of Applied Sciences (HESPI) and the European Urban Knowledge Network (EUKN), 2015, *Challenges of Small and Medium-Sized Urban Areas (SMUAs), Their Economic Growth Potential and Impact on Territorial Development in the European Union and Latvia*, research report to support the Latvian EU presidency 2015. www.eu2015.lv.

Stanford, Eleanor, 2014, "How Youngstown, Ohio, became a poster child for post-industrial America," CNBC/*GlobalPost*, August 12. www.cnbc.com/2014/08/12/how-youngstown-ohio-became-a-poster-child-for-post-industrial-america.html.

Story, Louise, and Stephanie Saul, 2015, "Hidden wealth flows to elite New York condos," *New York Times*, February 8, p. 1:2.

Sutcliffe, Anthony, 1993, "Capital cities: Does form follow values?" in John Taylor, Jean G. Lengellé, and Caroline Andrew, *Capital Cities/Les Capitales*, Ottawa: Carleton University Press, pp. 195–212.

Taylor, Peter, 2009, "Urban economics in thrall to Christaller: A misguided search for city hierarchies in external urban relations," *Environment and Planning A*, vol. 41, pp. 2550–2555.

Taylor, Peter, 2013, *Extraordinary Cities*, Cheltenham: Edward Elgar Publishers.

Thatchenkery, Tojo, and Jessica Heineman-Pieper, 2011, "Diversity and endogeny in regional development: applying appreciative intelligence," in Robert Stimson, Roger R. Stough, and Peter Nijkamp (eds), *Endogenous Regional Development*, Cheltenham: Edward Elgar Publishers, pp. 83–110.

Thissen, Mark, Frank van Oort, Dario Diodato, and Adjan Ruijs, 2013, *Regional Competitiveness and Smart Specialization in Europe*, Cheltenham: Edward Elgar Publishers.

Tomaney, John, 2010, "Commentary: Local and regional development in times of crisis," *Environment and Planning A*, vol. 42, pp. 771–779.

UNC School of Government, 2008, *Small Town, Big Ideas: Case Studies in Small Town Community Economic Development*, Chapel Hill: University of North Carolina, School of Government.

United Nations Department of Economic and Social Affairs, 2014, *World Urbanization Prospects: the 2014 Revision*, New York: United Nations.

United Nations-Habitat, 2003, *The Challenge of Slums: Global Report on Human Settlements 2003*, London: Earthscan.

United Nations-Habitat, 2012, *Small Town Development Approaches*, Nairobi: UN-Habitat.

US Census Bureau, 2006, *Dramatic Changes in US Aging Highlighted in New Census, HIH Report*, Washington, DC: Department of Commerce, US Census Bureau.

Vermont Department of Education, 2011, *Vermont's Education Funding System*, Montpelier: Vermont Department of Education, June 3.

Ville de Lausanne, 2014, "Plan Directeur Communal – Cahier 1," Lausanne: Ville de Lausanne.

Waitt, Gordon, and Chris Gibson, 2009, "Creative small cities: Rethinking the creative economy in place," *Urban Studies*, vol. 46, nos. 5 and 6, pp. 1223–1246.

Walters, Stephen J. K., 2014, *Boom Towns: Restoring the Urban American Dream*, Stanford: Stanford University Press.

Wang, Marian, 2013, "Breaking away: Top public universities push for 'autonomy' from states," *ProPublica*, October 7. www.propublica.org/article/breaking-away-top-public-universities-push-for-autonomy-from-states.

Weisman, Jonathan, 2015, "Republicans propose budget with deep Cuts," *New York Times*, March 28, p. A16:1.

Wiechmann, Torsten, and Karina M. Pallagst, 2012, "Urban shrinkage in Germany and the USA: A comparison of transformation patterns and local strategies," *International Journal of Urban and Regional Research*, vol. 36, no. 2, pp. 261–280.

Willon, Phil, and Abby Sewell, 2012, "Plenty of blame on long road to San Bernardino bankruptcy," *Los Angeles Times*, July 12. http://articles.latimes.com/2012/jul/12/local/la-me-san-bernardino-20120713.

Zimbalist, Andrew, 2015, *Circus Maximus: The Economic Gamble Behind Hosting the Olympics and the World Cup*, Washington, DC: Brookings Institution Press.

Index

Page numbers in *italics* denote tables.

Taylor & Francis eBooks

Helping you to choose the right eBooks for your Library

Add Routledge titles to your library's digital collection today. Taylor and Francis ebooks contains over 50,000 titles in the Humanities, Social Sciences, Behavioural Sciences, Built Environment and Law.

Choose from a range of subject packages or create your own!

Benefits for you

» Free MARC records
» COUNTER-compliant usage statistics
» Flexible purchase and pricing options
» All titles DRM-free.

REQUEST YOUR FREE INSTITUTIONAL TRIAL TODAY

Free Trials Available
We offer free trials to qualifying academic, corporate and government customers.

Benefits for your user

» Off-site, anytime access via Athens or referring URL
» Print or copy pages or chapters
» Full content search
» Bookmark, highlight and annotate text
» Access to thousands of pages of quality research at the click of a button.

eCollections – Choose from over 30 subject eCollections, including:

Archaeology	Language Learning
Architecture	Law
Asian Studies	Literature
Business & Management	Media & Communication
Classical Studies	Middle East Studies
Construction	Music
Creative & Media Arts	Philosophy
Criminology & Criminal Justice	Planning
Economics	Politics
Education	Psychology & Mental Health
Energy	Religion
Engineering	Security
English Language & Linguistics	Social Work
Environment & Sustainability	Sociology
Geography	Sport
Health Studies	Theatre & Performance
History	Tourism, Hospitality & Events

For more information, pricing enquiries or to order a free trial, please contact your local sales team: www.tandfebooks.com/page/sales

---

Routledge
Taylor & Francis Group

The home of
Routledge books

www.tandfebooks.com

For Product Safety Concerns and Information please contact our EU
representative GPSR@taylorandfrancis.com Taylor & Francis Verlag GmbH,
Kaufingerstraße 24, 80331 München, Germany

Printed and bound by CPI Group (UK) Ltd, Croydon, CR0 4YY
01/05/2025
01858355-0002